A Beginner's Guide to Urban Design and Development

This book provides invaluable guidance to all those with an interest in placemaking and the built environment, from those with no experience to those who have worked for many years in industry, illustrating key principles that will secure higher quality, more sustainable design in accessible, jargon-free language.

The author explains the design process in a straightforward way, exploring the different roles and highlighting the opportunities and limitations different agencies have to influence design over the various stages of the process. Examples from the UK and worldwide look at how the system operates and how best practice can make a real difference on the ground. Case studies examine situations where quality or sustainability fell short – and how this could have been avoided. This book also showcases a variety of evaluation tools, explaining how they operate, and giving guidance on how to create project-specific tools to drive schemes forward. With community empowerment at its core, the book explains technical language and shares bountiful knowledge to broaden place democracy and make influencing design accessible to many, not just a few.

This is a book that brings together all the various parties involved in shaping the built environment, demonstrating that collaboration and mutual understanding are key to achieving better quality, more sustainable design.

Laura B. Alvarez is a writer, critic, and commentator, with more than 20 years in international urban and architectural practice, in which she has designed award-winning schemes and written ground-breaking planning guidance that has placed democracy at its core.

Laura's research on socially sustainable neighbourhoods led to the development of applicable theory and has been widely praised for its innovative approach. She lectures at various universities and collaborates with acclaimed institutions, publications, and broadcast media.

A Beginner's Guide to Urban Design and Development

The ABC of Quality, Sustainable Design

Laura B. Alvarez

Routledge
Taylor & Francis Group
NEW YORK AND LONDON

Designed cover image: Laura B. Alvarez.

First published 2023
by Routledge
605 Third Avenue, New York, NY 10158

and by Routledge
4 Park Square, Milton Park, Abingdon, Oxon, OX14 4RN

Routledge is an imprint of the Taylor & Francis Group, an informa business

© 2023 Laura B. Alvarez

The right of Laura B. Alvarez to be identified as author of this work has been asserted in accordance with sections 77 and 78 of the Copyright, Designs and Patents Act 1988.

All rights reserved. No part of this book may be reprinted or reproduced or utilised in any form or by any electronic, mechanical, or other means, now known or hereafter invented, including photocopying and recording, or in any information storage or retrieval system, without permission in writing from the publishers.

Trademark notice: Product or corporate names may be trademarks or registered trademarks, and are used only for identification and explanation without intent to infringe.

Library of Congress Cataloging-in-Publication Data
Names: Alvarez, Laura B., author.
Title: A beginner's guide to urban design and development: the ABC of quality, sustainable design / Laura B. Alvarez.
Description: Abingdon, Oxon; New York, NY: Routledge, 2023. | Includes bibliographical references and index. |
Identifiers: LCCN 2022049695 (print) | LCCN 2022049696 (ebook) | ISBN 9781032154145 (hardback) | ISBN 9781032154152 (paperback) | ISBN 9781003244059 (ebook)
Subjects: LCSH: Sustainable design. | City planning—Environmental aspects. | Sustainable architecture. | Sustainable urban development.
Classification: LCC NA9053.E58 A48 2023 (print) | LCC NA9053.E58 (ebook) | DDC 307.1/416—dc23/eng/20221026
LC record available at https://lccn.loc.gov/2022049695
LC ebook record available at https://lccn.loc.gov/2022049696

ISBN: 9781032154145 (hbk)
ISBN: 9781032154152 (pbk)
ISBN: 9781003244059 (ebk)

DOI: 10.4324/9781003244059

Typeset in Helvetica
by codeMantra

Contents

List of figures	viii
List of tables	xiv
Foreword	xvi
Preface	xviii
Acknowledgements	xx
Acronyms and abbreviations	xxi

Introduction   1

1 Understanding good, sustainable design   6

    What 'makes place' and the need for placemaking
    Good design in simple words
    The beauty debate
    The design quality debate
    The sustainable design debate
    Design quality and sustainability
    Lessons learnt
    TOOL 1: Sustainable design priorities checklist

2 The design process   43

    Knowing where to begin
    Case studies
        Case Study 2.1: A school designed with the support of social sciences
        Case Study 2.2: Securing land value
    Lessons learnt
    Tool 2: Urban design plan of work
    Stage 1: Context

Stage 2: Networks
Stage 3: Agents and influencers
Stage 4: Place vision
Stage 5: Accountability tools
Stage 6: Site analysis
Stage 7: Data gathering
Stage 8: SWOT or CO
Stage 9: Development framework
Stage 10: Supplementary documents
Stage 11: Concept design
Stage 12: Development brief
Stage 13: Developed design
Stage 14: Detailed design
Stage 15: Post-occupancy

3 Design agents 100

The design team
Case studies
    Case Study 3.1: A project with 60 clients
    Case Study 3.2: Urban supermarket
    Case Study 3.3: Social housing
    Case Study 3.4: Office building
Lessons learnt
Tool 3: Design agents' map

4 Influencing design 132

Transparency and trust
Why do we like the familiar?
From coercing to empowering
Closing the influence loop
Case studies
    Case Study 4.1: Neighbourhood plan engagement
    Case Study 4.2: Social housing engagement
    Case Study 4.3: Two towns engagement
Lessons learnt
Tool 4: Influence programme

5 Design form — 170

   An issue of skills
   Case studies
      Case Study 5.1: Housing in context
      Case Study 5.2: Village extension in context
   Lessons learnt
   Tool 5: Critical form parameters

6 Evaluating design — 230

   Objectivity of design appraisals
   Case studies
      Case Study 6.1: Edification code
      Case Study 6.2: Code compliance appraisals
      Case Study 6.3: Design quality system
      Case Study 6.4: Design code
   Lessons learnt
   Tool 6: Design evaluation

Conclusions: The ABC of quality, sustainable design — 257

   Accountability
   Balance
   Collaboration

Glossary — 262
Bibliography — 265
Further reading — 268
Index — 271

List of figures

1.1	Ramification of built environment specialisms.	8
1.2	Human perception and interpretation of space.	12
1.3	Fraction of the ceiling of the Roman Pantheon dome, Rome, Italy.	15
1.4	Friends resting after a bike ride at Attenborough Nature Reserve in Nottingham, UK.	15
1.5	Notre Dame, Paris, France. Footprint in context.	17
1.6	York Minster, York, UK. Footprint in context.	17
1.7	Notre Dame, Paris, France.	18
1.8	York Minster, York, UK.	19
1.9	Human perception and interpretation of beauty.	21
1.10	The three spheres of sustainability. Adapted from Passet, 1996 by the author.	26
1.11	Loch Lomond, Trossachs, Scotland.	27
2.1	Layout of the neighbourhood arrangement and the proposal compared.	52
2.2	Familiar environment recreated through design:1. the neighbourhood arrangement, 2. the proposal from bird's eye view, 3. the proposed basins area, 4. The proposed dining area.	53
2.3	Comparative areas of the existing town in the North and the proposed extension in the South.	55
2.4	Garden sizes as proposed by the authors of Responsive Environments (1886).	57
2.5	Three types of urban pattern cul-de-sacs (or dead-end roads), curved streets, and straight streets (or cadastral pattern).	58

List of figures

2.6	Traditional plotting process versus an efficient plotting process.	59
2.7	Some of the plot design parameters set by legislation or convention in the UK.	60
2.8	Residential street in The Malings, Newcastle, UK.	70
2.9	Residential street in Trent Basin, Nottingham, UK.	70
2.10	Residential street in Houlton, Rugby, UK.	71
2.11	Service strip in residential development in Nottingham, UK.	71
2.12	Mural in the Catholic area of Belfast City, Northern Ireland, UK.	77
2.13	Mural in the Protestant area of Belfast City, Northern Ireland, UK.	77
2.14	Engagement groups according to communication tools and workshop strategies required during events.	81
2.15	Example of poor integration between the proposal and the setting.	85
2.16	Concept masterplan example.	89
2.17	Comparison between layouts with equal streets and layouts with street hierarchy.	92
3.1	Examples of a crossing and junction designed with an urban design approach and a crossing designed with a highway engineer approach.	106
3.2	Existing project layout.	109
3.3	Proposed project layout.	110
3.4	Supermarket as proposed following the food-store model and supermarket proposal adapting to the context.	116
3.5	Supermarket proposal in 3D.	117
3.6	Roles of the different teams involved in the project.	119
3.7	Office building location plan and layout analysis.	125
4.1	The change trilogy.	133
4.2	Primary school children working on a city centre masterplan.	135
4.3	Members of the community working on design guidance for a city in the UK.	136
4.4	Concept design in plan, showing the main road as a tree-lined avenue.	140

List of figures

4.5	Detailed plan of the solution to delivering a tree-lined avenue that works for all the design agents involved.	141
4.6	Contemporary Nottingham City Homes dwelling where chimneystack-like light wells above the stairwells and corridors were introduced.	145
4.7	Data collection during community event.	147
4.8	Participants contributing towards improving the planning process during a community event.	148
4.9	School pupils contributing towards the design of a new façade during a community event.	149
4.10	School pupil contributing by making a physical 3D model of a co-designed façade during an engagement event.	150
4.11	Community event with no participants.	161
5.1	Typical homes built in the Victorian and Edwardian eras, Sherwood, Nottingham, UK.	173
5.2	Typical homes built after the Victorian and Edwardian eras, Sherwood, Nottingham, UK.	173
5.3	Typical semi-detached homes built in the Victorian and Edwardian eras, Sherwood, Nottingham, UK.	173
5.4	Typical terrace homes built in the Victorian era, Sherwood, Nottingham, UK.	174
5.5	Diagrammatic layout of the project.	175
5.6	Development as proposed by the applicant.	177
5.7	Development as amended by the local authority.	178
5.8	Connected green infrastructure.	182
5.9	Gestalt theory of recognition.	188
5.10	Internal courtyard of a palace in Alhambra, Granada, Spain.	189
5.11	Church of St. Domenico in Ancona, Italy.	190
5.12	Alte Oper building in Frankfurt, Germany.	191
5.13	Victorian home in Nottingham, UK, where the window hierarchy is clearly defined.	191
5.14	Façade of a building in Alhambra, Granada, Spain.	192
5.15	Neo-classical building in Nottingham, UK.	193
5.16	Modern building in Nottingham, UK.	194
5.17	World Maritime University, Malmö, Sweden.	194

List of figures   xi

5.18	Kevin Lynch's mental mapping components.	196
5.19	Chinese Bell Tower landmark in the Nottingham Arboretum, UK.	197
5.20	A church spire in Riga, Latvia.	198
5.21	The front facade of the Adams building in Nottingham, UK.	199
5.22	Cityscape of Oxford, UK.	200
5.23	A church in Riga, Latvia.	201
5.24	Urban pocket square in Stockholm, Sweden.	202
5.25	Residential area of Nottingham Business Park, in the UK.	202
5.26	Author's illustration of architectural rhythm.	203
5.27	Hanseatic building on Bremen Market Square, Germany.	203
5.28	Corner building in London UK.	204
5.29	Building with intense rhythm in King's Cross, London, UK.	205
5.30	Diagram demonstrating how geometrical mathematical ratios work in practice.	206
5.31	Stortorget, Stockholm, Sweden.	206
5.32	San Ciriaco cathedral, Ancona, Italy.	207
5.33	Example of how to break up urban massing through façade treatment.	209
5.34	Three storey historic buildings in Nottingham, separated by a very narrow gap.	210
5.35	Contemporary three storey building in Nottingham that was built over three original plots of land, where a gap was re-created by design.	210
5.36	Diagram comparing a facade with a small grid against one with a large grid.	212
5.37	A child (the author's son) next to a plant with giant leaves in Cornwall, UK.	213
5.38	A man (the author's father) walking towards the Doll's Palace at Children's Republic theme park in La Plata, Argentina.	213
5.39	Public square in Birmingham City Centre, UK.	214
5.40	Roofs with distinctive form in the Peak District, UK.	215
5.41	Roofs with distinctive form in the Riga, Latvia.	215
5.42	Photograph of buildings with distinctive form in Bergen, Norway	216
5.43	Bullring shopping centre in Birmingham, UK.	217

5.44	Buildings in Flåm, Norway, painted to integrate with the natural environment.	218
5.45	Brick colours in Trent Basin, Nottingham, UK.	219
5.46	Service installations in Trent Basin, Nottingham, UK.	219
5.47	View of the Library of Birmingham, UK.	220
5.48	Stone wall in Rimini, Italy.	222
5.49	Gothic window frame with deep reveals and sculptures surrounding the opening.	223
5.50	Typical street façade in Amsterdam, Netherlands.	224
5.51	A modern street façade in the Java Island development in Amsterdam, Netherlands.	225
5.52	Sketch plan of a fragment of Marrakesh, Morocco.	226
5.53	Sketch plan of a fragment of Rome, Italy.	226
5.54	Sketch plan of a fragment of Orlando, USA.	227
6.1	Children's demarcation of their play zone in a public beach in Cornwall, UK.	232
6.2	Demarcation of territorial occupation in a public beach in Cornwall, UK, during the Coronavirus pandemic.	233
6.3	Example of building restrictions in La Plata, Argentina.	237
6.4	Plaza Moreno, La Plata, Argentina, where high buildings were built in close proximity to key heritage buildings, as permitted by the edification code.	238
6.5	The potential result of an edification code for a block of 100m by 100m, assuming different designers would develop different plots, but with a restriction to build in the centre and a demand to building to front line in order to form a block that gives consistent enclosure to the street.	238
6.6	The potential result of an edification code for a block of 100m by 100m, assuming different designers would develop different plots, but with a restriction to build in the centre, a demand to build to the front line, and with building heights limits.	239

List of figures

6.7 The potential result of an edification code for a block of 100m by 100m, assuming different designers would develop different plots, but with a restriction to build in the centre, a demand to build to the front line, and a building restriction zone fronting one of the streets, to allow for wider pavement and front gardens. 239
6.8 Home with a blank corner facade, Nottingham, UK. 243
6.9 Corner building in Trent Basin, Nottingham, UK. 244

List of tables

1.1	Definition of good design, as proposed by Roman architect Vitruvius and as interpreted by the author for contemporary application.	11
1.2	Definition of design quality based on the quality assurance system.	23
1.3	Forms of participation: consultation versus engagement.	34
1.4	Examples of sustainable development tools.	36
1.5	Lifespan of buildings or places.	38
1.6	Key definitions.	39
1.7	TOOL 1: Sustainable Design Priorities Checklist.	40
2.1	Traditional and alternative approaches to housing site layout compared.	61
2.2	Example of how to meassure the public realm.	64
2.3	Land optimization example.	72
2.4	Case study analysis summary.	76
2.5	Escential urban design skills.	96
2.6	TOOL 2: The Urban Design Plan of Work.	96
3.1	Roles of the key design agents involved in Case Study 3.1.	112
3.2	Roles of the key design agents involved in Case Study 3.2.	117
3.3	Layout efficiency comparison between the Design team and the Urban Design team proposals.	121
3.4	Roles of the key design agents involved in Case Study 3.3.	122
3.5	Roles of the key design agents involved in Case Study 3.4.	126

3.6	Case study analysis summary.	128
3.7	TOOL 3: Design Agents' Map.	130
4.1	Case study analysis summary.	163
4.2	TOOL 4: Influence Programme.	165
5.1	Case study analysis summary.	185
5.2	Basic rules of composition.	187
5.3	TOOL 5: Critical Form Parameters.	228
6.1	Example of a design code that addresses place character variables.	247
6.2	Case study analysis summary.	249
6.3	TOOL 6: Qualities of a Good Design Evaluation Tool.	255
7.1	Summary of tools for urban practice.	260
7.2	TOOL 7: The ABC of Quality Sustainable Design.	260

Foreword

"Nothing is more revealing of how some architects don't grasp how people use spaces than to be invited as a journalist to report on a new civic structure, such as an airport terminal. Firsthand, you hear the architect complain how their 21st-century cathedral will soon be 'spoilt by all those disgusting McDonald's and Boots' concessions'. Did they imagine the terminal owners wanted people to move from landside to airside in neat file, like goons on a North Korean parade ground, or could they need rents from those 'disgusting concessions' to pay for the gloriously arching roof? Or did they believe their building was so beautiful it would suspend holidaymakers' need for a breakfast bap and sun-tan lotion?

This is the gap between architecture and urbanism. Beauty is two-dimensional, photogenic, fragile, a concept that the users and owners of places quickly reshape to their prosaic needs. Urbanism is three-dimensional, gritty and anticipates how humans use places and what will make them durable. When an urbanist takes a photograph, it is often to show the gap between the design intention and the outcome, recording what could be done better next time. Their approach is of learning and capturing how to get it right more often. The architect would expect their fawning published to Photoshop any blemish.

Many people who know Laura recognise her great skill in mitigating the theories and aspirations of design guidance to the practicality of their application in real situations. She wants the same as the authors of design toolkits want, better outcomes. But she recognises that structures, such as design codes, only work where there are techniques to ensure compliance and ways of updating their strictures when competing guidance, such as local plan parking standards change, as people and their behaviours change.

Foreword

The value of reading this book is to discover her simple process-structure to ensure sustainable urban design, her 'ABC' in the last chapter. To avoid spoiling the pay-off from reading this short book, I shan't explain her formula. But it is simple to understand, easy to memorise and is exactly what any urban design shepherd needs confronted by aesthetes looking up at the stars and too many wolves happy to drag it down to the gutter. This book is wholly worth your time."

David Birkbeck
– Chief executive at Design for Homes, Housing Design Awards director 2005 to date, Honorary Fellow RIBA 2008

David Birkbeck helped set up Design for Homes as a social enterprise. He wrote *Building for Life* in 2002 and co-wrote a revised edition in 2012, endorsed by the National Planning Policy Framework and by Homes England which uses it to their principle design test to screen all bids for land or grant. A new version of this was launched in July, updated to reflect the Putting Health into Place principles published by NHS England focussing on active travel and greater use of the public realm for exercise and leisure. David contributed to the 2009 HAPPI report which showed how homes designed for seniors can be at least as appealing as general needs homes.

Preface

This book has been in the making for at least 30 years, along with a broad collection of draft urban practice manuscripts and case study analysis that still lingers in my portable drive.

Those who know me well might claim I am someone with a huge instinct to have things said, good and bad. In my mind, progress tends to raise from honest, reflective examination and a strong desire to push boundaries. Yet I work in the built environment field, one that still operates whithin a culture of blame and egocentrism, and the pursue of status quo. Perhaps this contadiction explains why I write so much, it is my escape route, a form of therapy that keeps me positively focused.

I have been interested in applicable theory and feasible long-term change for as long as I can remember. In all aspects of life, I have a passion for doing my very best to make everything a little bit better than the norm. I am always keen to dwell on experiences, to think about projects for a long time after I have completed them and yes, I keep a project diary with all the quarky details. Inevitably, the time comes when I eventually see those traumas in a positive light. After all, it is from pain we learn the most!

Probably this is why I chose to write this book as an examination of a lifetime in practice. I included real life case studies; some of which are more than 20 years old, some of which I had just completed. I analyse these case studies openly and truthfuly here, to illustrate recurrent errors, most of which I also saw in many other schemes. Issues that, repeatedly, diminished the quality and sustainable credentials of buildings and places. By sharing these examples I hope I can help other practitioners benefit from - or relate to - my experiences, and that future generations can learn from the mistakes and successes of our time.

Preface

Besides my natural interest in philosophical reflexion, I am also an advocate of inclusion and democracy. I truly believe the solution depends on everybody working together. That is why I wrote this book in a non-technical way, to make my thinking and work experiences open to everyone interested in exercising their civic right and becoming involved in placemaking.

Sadly, restricted by a tight wordcount, I was only able to mention the examples that are most relevant to the topics discussed. I hope one day I have the opportunity to write about other schemes and the wonderful, talented people I met along the way.

Acknowledgements

I dedicate this volume to the memory of my mother, Maria de los Angeles Lardelli, who taught me to empathise with others, to pursue social justice and equity, and to care for our environments. And to the memory of my father, Oscar Emilio Alvarez, a quality assurance engineer who taught me about self-discipline, commitment, and work ethic. Both supported me unconditionally in my studies under strained financial circumstances. I will be eternally grateful for their belief in me.

This book would not have been possible without the help of many people. Firstly I would like to thank my family, for their patience and support, and for the time I missed with them whilst I was writing this book; mainly my children Sebastian and Marina. Especially I would like to thank my husband Jared, for inspiring me with his confidence in my work and for understanding this boisterous passion for design that I carry wherever I go.

I would also like to extend my gratitude to those overseas who actively collaborated to make this happen: my sisters Cecilia and Lorena, for their advice and encouragement, and architect Juan Cristino for his help with some of the illustrations.

My thanks also extend to the Urban Design Group, an organisation that was instrumental in my professional growth; especially to Director Robert Huxford. Also, thanks to my urban design tutor at the University of Nottingham, Dr Katharina Borsi, who guided me and supported me to explore new fields of knowledge during my PhD course; those who reviewed the book proposal and offered their comments, which undoubtedly improved the quality of this work. Finally, my dear colleagues, fellow practitioners, and academics, who support me and accompany throughout my career.

Acronyms and abbreviations

AONB	Area of Outstanding Natural Beauty
ARUDO	Association of Regional Urban Design Officers (UK)
BREEAM	Building Research Establishment Environmental Assessment Method
CO	Constraints and opportunities
DQF	Design Quality Framework (Nottingham, UK)
NPPF	National Planning Policy
SDG	Sustainable Development Goals
SWOT	Strengths, weaknesses, opportunities, threats

Introduction

Modern lifestyles and constant population growth are putting pressure on a planet that is already struggling to sustain life. Societies that revolve around mass consumption have exacerbated social inequalities and the impact we, as a species, impose on the natural world. But what can we do from wherever we stand to make things a little bit better?

Aiming to bring back a degree of balance after the global recession of 2008, some experts have been exploring a re-calibrated system that many call 'inclusive capitalism': an approach with a keener eye on sustainability. In 2020, Legal & General explained this model as "…using money and investment as a force for good, to create real jobs and better infrastructure to transform the UK's cities and towns and tackle the biggest issues of our times such as housing, climate change, and ageing demographics".

In the UK, there has recently been a trend towards a radical reform of the planning system as a strategy to reactivate the construction industry. However, the plans to implement this level of change were dropped. The viewpoints are vast and varied, and the politics of sustainable development are extremely complicated. The issue for me is that in the built environment line of work, it is impossible to act without serious impact. Although the global environmental agenda seems to be moving in the right direction, I do not think policy change or on the ground action is fast enough. Back in 2015, the United Nations launched the Sustainable Development Goals (SDG), a framework to consider broader aspects of sustainability. The idea was that by meeting these goals, developers would be more likely to achieve a more equitable society, with a more balanced distribution of wealth, whilst inflicting less damage to the planet. But some countries did not embrace the scheme and others only did so superficially.

DOI: 10.4324/9781003244059-1

But the sustainability agenda began many decades ago. Initially, built environment activists tried to protect cultural assets and natural environments; later on in 1992, the notion of sustainable development was more accurately defined by the United Nations as development that could "meet the needs of the present without compromising the ability of future generations to meet their own needs."[1]

> "UNITED NATIONS DEFINITION OF SUSTAINABLE DEVELOPMENT: one that can meet the needs of the present without compromising the ability of future generations to meet their own needs."

Since then, innovative economic models have been constantly emerging. More recently, the acceptance of climate change and the need to prepare for what it might bring gradually changed the course of action. The idea of resilience, asset management, and adaptation began to dominate the scene. Steadily, the industry as a whole started to focus on different technologically driven strands, trying to understand the complexities of development and coming up with tools to put new thinking into practice.

In my view, although the built environment still needs to develop further on areas of expertise that are only just emerging, the next crucial step towards a more sustainable future depends on joining all the pieces: bringing all the knowledge together and combining the different tools and areas of expertise to achieve more balanced solutions. But this holistic approach would involve conglomerating different cultures, ways of working, goals, and ethos. The task is a huge challenge, more so since areas of expertise developed largely in isolation from each other, creating field-specific languages and focusing on very particular issues. Undoubtedly, the best way to co-ordinate it all would be through collaboration and mutual understanding; but this would require a vast amount of new skills and the development of groundbreaking integrative tools and software. Here are the most prominent, recurrent, and consequential downfalls I came across:

a. There is a strong fixation – amongst designers – with the physical aspects of place, also called the morphological dimension. This

Introduction

    puts the focus on the built product and tends to neglect the processes we go through to produce these outcomes.
- b. Lack of accountability on some of the determinants of sustainability tends to lead to an overview of some crucial aspects in favour of others; this tends to compromise the design quality and overall impact of development.
- c. Unbalanced design decisions carry long-term effects, which affect directly both the environment and its people.
- d. Lack of collaboration and communication amongst parties, often triggered by a fear to relinquish control, inevitably result in lower design quality.
- e. Attempts to automatise the built environment are leading to an increased complexity and over-reliance on field-specific software, which results in a gradual decay of the higher education curricula in favour of technology over critical knowledge.

My concern is that current built environment practices are inherently unsustainable, especially because these are still strongly pulled by economic gains in lieu of wider factors, which brings me to think that there are three possible ways for the industry to develop in the current climate:

1. Completely abandoning the sustainability agenda and embracing the natural evolution process, which may well take us a step closer to extinction.
2. Continuing to take tokenistic actions that will slow down, but not stop, the damage to the planet.
3. Accepting that the long-term risks are huge and so embracing a lesser degree of risk by committing to innovation.

Although it might be tempting to add a fourth solution, one that supports a radical reform, I am far too aware that our industry is slow in picking up and adopting new trends; so I decided to categorise the fourth option as a utopian one.

    I think it is probably safe to assume that, as it is the norm, the approach different administrations will take is largely dependent on particular socio-economic and political conditions. However, and perhaps naively, I would like to think that most governments will opt for the third way. Saying that, the outcomes of the 2021 United Nations Climate Change Conference in Glasgow showed a tendency to favour option (2). On that basis, I write this book as a practical aid for those working on the ground and for everyone with an ambition to become invested in innovative placemaking, acknowledging the realities of global legislative frameworks that lack ambition and are relegated by a tendency to sustain status quo.

In a nutshell, the most evident need for change comes from the lingering modern understanding of settlements as machines. We still analyse places as if they were formed by different layers that we deal with through different fields of expertise and which we administrate with different budgets and through different governance systems. As machines, these are parts that can work together, but they are part of a model where they retain their individual integrity. In our time, a much better way to think about places is to consider them as complex ecosystems. In other words, dynamic models that recognise that when one part of the system changes, it will potentially effect change to other components. In an ecosystem, understanding what links all the pieces together, how the components affect one another, and how things constantly change and move around is most critical. This is why, when it comes to design quality and sustainability, the design and delivery processes are as important as the built product: relations and exchanges matter as much as what we build. Therefore, the drive for quality and sustainability depends hugely on the systems we work with and the methods we use.

So, every time we implement change, we inflict consequences – good and bad – and we might trigger change that has additional benefits we can draw from. If we are going to be working with ever-changing variables, we will have to become more used to measuring what we do, embracing asset management far more than we do now. Here is exactly where the industry could begin to apply simpler cost-effective ways to achieve multiple gains without increasing investment: simply by exerting more thought. If artificial intelligence could develop to help us achieve more sustainable development, it would do so by linking together technical variables with all the targets we could impact on through development: public health, education, culture, inclusion, economic growth, and so on; this means modelling places as multifactor systems. The use of Building Modelling software gives us a preview of what might lie ahead,

Introduction

but social factors would need to be computed as well as economic ones and I am still to see a software that does this reliably.

If this view of the built environment develops, we will see the role of many agencies changing radically, and the distribution of power rebalancing organically. I am particularly interested in the role of design and planning as vehicles to seam the highly technical with the softer aspects of place; these are ideas I explore and exemplify in further chapters.

At present, my great worry is that I see new graduates lost in the demands of the real world and teaching becoming more preoccupied with visual impact over contextual understanding. On this point, I hope higher education curricula and literature is shaped to fill in some of the critical knowledge gaps of future professionals worldwide.

Readers not so familiar with the world of urban practice will embark on a journey that reviews examples from practice to remember old knowledge and rethink current methods, questioning their validity. They might then begin to grasp the complexity of the industry and why the process of designing places requires such careful consideration and a particular set of skills. Through the narrative, the need to collaborate and co-design becomes apparent, and with this comes a need for the multiple agents involved to acquire a certain level of accountability that could lead to more balanced design solutions arrived at through collaboration and mutual understanding.

Note

1   Rio Declaration on Environment and Development, 1992.

Chapter 1
Understanding good, sustainable design

This book is all about the quality and sustainable credentials of buildings and public places. Crucially, public places are understood as ecosystems: geographical settings occupied by humans – and other species – who interact with that space. Right from the start, I must stress the distinction between buildings and public places: buildings are shelters, public places are part of the geographical space. Both are component cells within the ecosystem.

Traditionally, architects focus on buildings and urbanists liaise with the larger scale: public places, villages, towns, cities, and so on. There are many commonalities between the world of architecture and urbanism; some skills, tools, and criteria can be transferable from one form of practice to another. However, there are also strong differences: the design processes and skill sets required to design at these two scales can be a whole world apart. After 20 years in both architectural and urban practice, I dare conclude that:

> One of the main factors leading to poor design quality and low sustainable outcomes is the lack of clear boundaries between the fields of architecture and urbanism, and the fact that so many professionals believe they can simply transfer their experience and knowledge from one field of expertise to the other.

I also discovered that finding good examples of quality, sustainable design on the ground is surprisingly difficult. In my view, it is indeed

DOI: 10.4324/9781003244059-2

Chapter 1: **Understanding good, sustainable design**

possible to design aiming for both goals simultaneously as design quality and sustainability are so intricately connected. I found a few tactics helpful: joining old and new techniques, listening to untrained and professional views, combining different fields of expertise, and pushing my own professional boundaries to try something new. Over the course of this book, I will share some of my thinking and my experiences from practice, and I will show how I tried to convert these tactics into useful tools for everyday use. But for now, let's begin with some basic concepts: how I understand place, good design, beauty, and sustainable development; these discussions will give us a solid foundation for the forthcoming chapters.

What 'makes place' and the need for placemaking

The components that make place are complex and deeply interconnected. At present, these are studied by different disciplines, but that was not always the case.

In ancient times, great architects faced serious issues with poor quality and utterly appalling design, just as we do now. Roman architect Vitruvius himself went on to explain his frustrations with what he called 'immoral' designers of low skills that could not reproduce the proportions of beauty the correct way, leaving seriously misshapen buildings that let whole cities down. I am sure wherever you live, you can relate to a building like this in your location!

It was this that prompted the architect to write to Emperor Caesar requesting permission to publish *The Ten Books on Architecture*, a compendium that one way or another influenced every future trend and which is still used in practice.[1] Vitruvius would be glad to know that the vast majority of those 'ugly' buildings did not survive – they were probably poorly built as well as badly designed.

If we place ourselves in the Renaissance Era, we will find that great thinkers like Leonardo da Vinci were capable of connecting and intertwining the knowledge from different fields into a comprehensive, holistic approach that informed design, quality, and beauty. Although these 'masters of everything' were only a handful, they demonstrated the

Chapter 1: **Understanding good, sustainable design**

potential of integrated thinking and how much this could help human development in science and arts if we prove capable of bringing things together. Neoclassical fellows in the field followed suit and learnt from the masters, more often than not copying old formulae but doing it very well.

Later on, in the modern world, the built environment became a less holistic and more technical discipline. Designers began to use mass produced components, and their main concern was to master the dimensions of the parts and to be able to join the different pieces in a durable way. It was at this point that architecture and urbanism gradually divorced themselves from the artistic world that tended to deal with human perception and emotions. This detachment from the softer factors of place went alongside an increased interest in form and function, which became the primary parameters to resolve when designing places (see Figure 1.1).

Criteria like form and function can be determined, measured, and evaluated mathematically, and are therefore more compatible with the use of machinery and software applications. Rapid changes in technology and computing sciences made this architectural trend more accentuated.

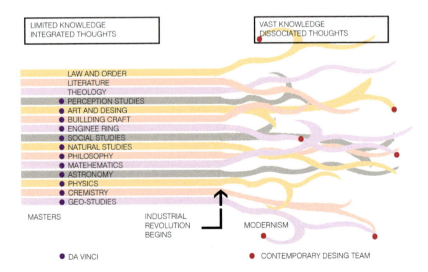

Figure 1.1 Illustration showing how different disciplines that historically were within the master architect's realm gradually became a specialism in its own right. Diagram by Juan Cristino for the author.

Chapter 1: **Understanding good, sustainable design**

Meanwhile, the softer criteria, which were more difficult to evaluate using machines, remained in the human science fields. New discoveries perhaps appeared to be of little application in the built environment, other than for attracting consumers and increasing sales. The problem with this approach is that humans never stopped being humans, and so the long-term consequences of neglecting crucial aspects of place started to become seriously visible, as we'll explore throughout this book.

Unfortunately, this detachment from social sciences evolved into the current form of design practice: one that is making both design quality and sustainability difficult to achieve. The main problem is that in order to be sustainable as a society, we must take into account all those human factors of place that play a huge role in driving our behaviours. This is important because how we act on a daily basis could be a meaningful route to protecting our planet from further erosion.

Now that we have entered a new communications era with highly developed artificial intelligence, perhaps it is time for us to focus on rejoining the various branches of 'place' that have become disconnected. But before we attempt too much so early in this book, let's debate the idea of good design a little further.

Good design in simple words

The concept of good design and the objectivity around determining what fits into this category have been discussed for thousands of years. If we go back to Roman architect Vitruvius, his highly successful definition of good design stated that there were three main criteria to meet in order to achieve it: (a) being useful, (b) being durable, and (c) bringing delight. I have taken the liberty to expand on this definition, updating it for practice in the 21st century:

> a. BEING USEFUL:
> A place is useful when it is fit for purpose, when it can readily accommodate the activity it was designed to host comfortably, and when its form is adequate to accommodate the operations that will occur there. But crucially, it also means that the

place needs to operate as a component of the context, and to do this, it needs to become just another fragment within a larger whole. For example, a railway station building can be designed to perfection, but if the infrastructure that connects it to the rest of the city is not there, or if the building is located out of reach from citizens, then the station is no longer so useful. The criterion here is that the place is functional in itself and as part of a larger whole, or in the words of design professionals: in context. This interpretation of 'purpose' is key to working within an ecosystem model.

b. BEING DURABLE:
For a place to be durable, not only does it have to be a space built to last, but it also has to be flexible to adapt, so it can continue to host different activities over time. As we will see in more detail later on, a place without activity is not a place; it is only a space. The criterion then is that the place is durable both in itself, to withstand weathering, for example, and durable as a host, to keep functioning as a part of the wider context.

c. BRINGING DELIGHT:
The issue of bringing delight is perhaps the most difficult one to define. There will be an element of beauty that comes from within the space itself as an object that has been crafted. This type of beauty can probably be defined through the use of rules or tools like proportional ratios, or by applying Leonardo da Vinci's concept of Vitruvian Man[2] or Le Corbusier's Modulor,[3] for example. Certain levels of compositional aesthetics can be formulated and prescribed. But there is also a type of beauty that comes not from the space itself, but from the place; a beauty created by humans inhabiting and activating that space and, critically, turning it into a place. This last type of beauty is the one that cannot be prescribed or formulated by a designer. What designers can do is understand it very well, to the point of being able to design a space that can eventually host a good place. The part when the space turns

Chapter 1: **Understanding good, sustainable design**

> into a place, also called the 'placemaking process', is made by people inhabiting that space. Over time, acting collectively, people 'placemake' when they give shape or meaning to the spaces they share, populating them, looking after them, and making them their own.

Table 1.1 Definition of good design, as proposed by Roman architect Vitruvius and as interpreted by the author for contemporary application.

Good Design		
Useful	Durable	Brings Delight
It can readily accommodate the activity it was designed to host comfortably. It operates as a component of the context.	It is built to last. It is also flexible to adapt for future uses.	It has an elegance that comes from within, as an object that has been crafted. It also has a vibrancy from the activities it hosts.

We humans evaluate place using our rational capacity, comparing it to previous knowledge – from the natural world, for example – or with a standard set of rules. We also interpret place cognitively, which, in turn, influences our behaviour. Therefore, people are not only capable of taking a space and transforming it into a place by behaving in certain ways or by generating activity there, but they could also apply some form of universal measure to appraise specific place qualities if they had adequate tools. We will come back to debate this topic further in Chapters 5 and 6, but for now, let us stay focused on defining good design.

If everyone can understand good design, then it should be relatively simple to achieve it, and yet badly designed buildings and poor-quality places are still abundant around the globe. I am sure you can think of plenty of examples in your locale, and this may even be the reason why you are reading this book!

Chapter 1: **Understanding good, sustainable design**

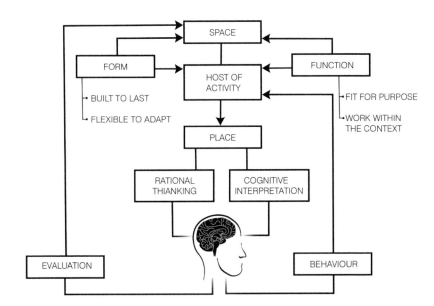

Figure 1.2 Illustration summarising the interpretation of place by humans: rational and cognitive. Diagram by Juan Cristino for the author.

People tend to fall in love with quirky streets and charming historic buildings, often travelling the world to see them. But most of what was built in the last century or so is no match for the beauty of historic places. Colleagues regularly ask me if I know what on Earth has gone wrong. My fellow urban designer Amy calls me "The rubbish planning Tweeter in disguise" (I think it is a compliment) since I send regular examples of international bad practice to the ARUDO[4] social network. We often debate how these places reached the handover stage without picking up these serious mistakes along the way.

People recognise good places when they see them: they might not be able to explain exactly why a place is better than the norm, but they know it is; they can feel it. Understanding what makes good places or good architecture is not as complicated as it might seem. Producing good designs can be difficult without adequate technical expertise and training, but by knowing some simple rules, anyone should be able to not only recognise but also explain good design.

Chapter 1: **Understanding good, sustainable design**

In very simple terms, like good food, good design requires quality ingredients to begin with, in this case building materials; a good recipe or step-by-step process to follow; and an experienced, knowledgeable cook to prepare it, or in our case, skilful designers and builders. Now, I will ask the reader to imagine how this cooking analogy could apply to the construction industry:

- Without quality ingredients, a good recipe, and an experienced cook, it will be more likely that the quality of the food will suffer.

- Every professional has their own style. Two cooks with exactly the same ingredients following the same recipe are unlikely to produce exactly the same result.

- Those tasting the dish might like it or dislike it based on their own personal preferences.

- Personal preferences might influence opinions but they never define whether the dish is of good technical quality or not, because quality is assessed by looking at specific technical factors. For example, if the medium steak was cooked to point, rather than if critics like meat or not.

- Some classic combinations, like strawberries and cream, are commonly accepted and do not need questioning beyond the quality of the ingredients and how these are used.

- Experimental combinations or recipes that have not been widely tested and accepted before, like Blumenthal's cauliflower with white chocolate,[5] will be subjected to further scrutiny and will probably generate some doubt to begin with, taking a little longer to become accepted by the public. In this case, not only the quality of the ingredients will matter, the combination itself and the techniques applied will need to be proven to work.

- Locally resourced ingredients and seasonal cooking are always a positive way to respond to the identity of a place. When in Whitby, one might want to eat fish and chips; in Bakewell, it would be a pity to leave without a traditional tart!

- Restaurant critics can understand food quality, although they might not be able to reproduce it. Likewise, those reviewing schemes should be trained to identify the rules of design and they should find it easy to spot design talent or lack of skills when they review a scheme, although they should not be expected to know how to design.

So, in simple words, good design is not too different from good cookery. It all comes down to three main factors: good materials to begin with, skilled designers, and sound design processes. And just as with food, we do not have to like everything we taste, no matter how well prepared and cooked the meal was. I have yet to sample Blumenthal's cauliflower with white chocolate; architecture and urbanism is not necessarily as financially rewarding as one might assume.

The beauty debate

In the UK, the concern with beauty has recently made its way to national policy, featuring strongly in the design debate once more, even suggesting that beautiful proposals should be fast-tracked to obtain permission to build much faster than ugly designs. This has opened a series of discussions in the field: some practitioners have expressed concern with the validity of certain universal truths as determinants of beauty and with the claim that beauty can be seen as a determinant of design quality. Many worry that beauty standards cannot withstand in a court of law. The examination of this topic merits exploring the key conceptual differences between design quality and beauty, to understand why the former can be assessed with a certain degree of objectivity, whilst the latter one shall remain subjective.

Sometimes people agree in designating an object, building, or place as beautiful; sometimes they don't. Some places and buildings seem to be more widely considered intrinsically beautiful than others. Take a natural landscape: it is difficult to find anyone who would deem a place of natural beauty as ugly. Human-made structures are more likely to evoke debate, but I am still trying to find someone who finds the Roman Pantheon ugly. This means that there can be instances when everyone

Chapter 1: **Understanding good, sustainable design** 15

Figure 1.3 Photo showing a fragment of the Roman Pantheon dome ceiling, where perfect geometry appears as an abstract form.

Figure 1.4 Photo showing two boys in a park sitting on a large rock after a bike ride looking at a lake.

asked agrees a place – or a view – is beautiful. But what makes people agree sometimes and disagree other times?

Let's assume a group of people is presented with a sound appraisal system to evaluate design quality, a way to ensure everyone can measure the design equally. There is no reason to believe the individual results should vary so significantly that the overall outcome would become affected by personal perceptions. If the appraisal criteria are quantifiable, then every assessor should arrive at the same result. An easy way to explain this is to look at a simple, practical example:

> I was always fascinated with medieval buildings, especially the forms of construction and the collective processes that brought some of them to life. Back in 2005, I had the fortune to first visit York Minster, a 12th-century cathedral that is circa 160 metres long and which has a 72-metre high tower. Only a couple of months later, I visited Notre Dame in Paris, a cathedral of a similar age that is 128 metres long with a tower height of 35 metres. My first instinct when standing in front of Notre Dame was one of deep disappointment. I remember thinking: "This must be a quarter of the size of York Minster".
>
> Curious, I went to research this further. How I would have liked to be proven right! But dimensions do not lie: they are relatively accurate comparisons against a set parameter – the metre. I could then work out that in length, York Minster was only one and a quarter times the length of Notre Dame, and that the tower was twice the height. I thought about this error of judgement and soon I realised how different the contexts were. The buildings surrounding the York structure were smaller in size and scale, and the place was more compact. Paris gives this overall impression of large scale and grandeur that makes Notre Dame seem relatively smaller and somehow dwarfed amongst the open spaces surrounding it and the many large competitor buildings craving visitor's attention. The metre judges the dimension parameter consistently, whilst my human eye did not; not even with 12 years of training and substantial time in professional practice.

Chapter 1: **Understanding good, sustainable design** 17

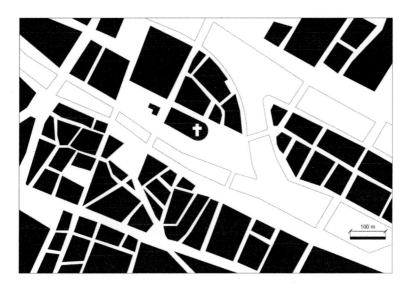

Figure 1.5 Sketch showing the figure-ground map of the area of Notre Dame, Paris, France. The large area without buildings around the cathedral becomes apparent.

Figure 1.6 Sketch showing the figure-ground map of the area of York Minster, York, UK. Smaller buildings surrounding the cathedral become apparent.

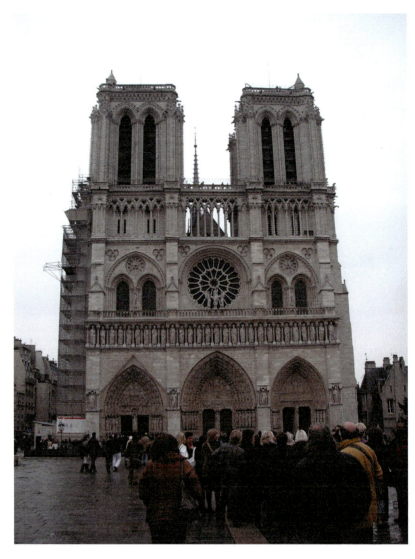

Figure 1.7 Image shows a photograph of Notre Dame, Paris, France.

Chapter 1: **Understanding good, sustainable design**

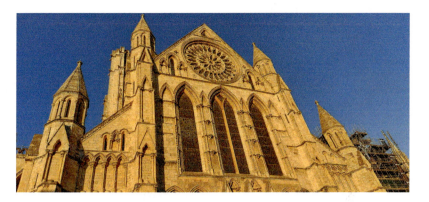

Figure 1.8 Image shows a photograph of York Minster, York, UK.

The example shows how the human eye can make judgements based purely on perception, how our understanding can be affected by many different factors, and how our judgements can be unintentionally inaccurate.

We will debate some measurable variables of design quality in Chapter 5, when we will see how design can be rationalised into mathematical rules and patterns. What concerns me now is to ascertain whether or not every single human being could have the same emotional reaction when observing a design. In line with national UK policy and guidance, I refer to the work of Roman architect Vitruvius once more, this time looking at his idea that something beautiful brings delight, great pleasure, and ultimately happiness.[6] But can we build in such a way that we make every single human being that ever existed happy?

Philosophers have ruminated on this matter since antiquity and there is still no consensus. Ever since I was a student, I was curious to know what others have concluded on the topic. Back then, I found myself immerse in a universe of definitions, hypotheses, and contested arguments, noticing that over the years of research, I was never any wiser than before. So, in the last couple of decades, I decided to tackle the problem a different way: I began enquiring about the place factors that trigger an emotional response and how we could understand the emotional impact places have on us, bringing a sense of happiness.

Very early in my research, I realised that what we design are spaces, not places. Built environment professionals set up a space in a specific manner, with certain form and made of particular materials. The design solution normally emerges from a series of practical considerations and creative ideas. But it is people's perceptions and behaviours in a space that make it a 'place'. Places exist only when there are relational forces associating the observers with the geography. Without humans, buildings and spaces are nothing but sterile objects. This means that the emotional response we might have in a place is intrinsically linked to those relations and, therefore, already charged with human factors. This would mean that we can only understand how a place might bring us delight and happiness when we understand the relations between us and the space around us and between us and other people around us behaving as a result of being in that space.

With this model, I concluded that even when a space might be rationally of high quality, if the relations established between the observer and the space are not also of high quality, the place cannot deliver delight. For example, a space can be designed in a way that is mathematically impeccable but being there reminds us of a childhood trauma. A dentist's surgery, however well designed, could be a prime example of this for many. If we had created a negative relation with a place of similar characteristics, we might not be able to withdraw a sense of happiness from that place.

On the basis that observer-geography relations sustain a place, it is unlikely that a place is beautiful to each and every one of us. It is 'our' relationship with that place at an individual and societal level that rounds up the notion of beauty; a beauty only 'we' can feel and therefore understand (see Figure 1.9). This hypothesis also explains the counterpart: why low-quality spaces can sometimes be perceived as beautiful places by some.

The question is: if the cognitive process is so relevant to the interpretation of place and the assignation of beauty, why is the built environment not so interested in these factors?

The design quality debate

If we accept that design quality does not necessarily equate to beauty, I would like to leave the issue of beauty to one side to begin the quality

Chapter 1: **Understanding good, sustainable design** 21

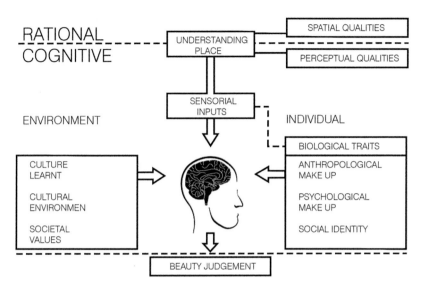

Figure 1.9 Illustration summarising the process of place beauty judgement by humans using both rational and cognitive faculties. Diagram by Juan Cristino for the author.

debate by exploring why we are having poor design so often and so broadly across the globe. The first two things that come to mind are the role of knowledge and the professional accreditations of those who design. Anyone can make an attempt to design and construct buildings and places worldwide; in fact, not many administrations expect qualified architects to be the only people to put forward proposals. Not everyone involved in transforming our built environment has the qualifications to do so, yet they might have the entitlement. But a University degree, or many years of training, does not always guarantee design excellence. Many professionals have the qualifications but are not sufficiently skilled to practise certain specialisms; some might lack experience; some might be more inclined to different aspects of the work; some might take shortcuts to deliver on budget. Deciding whether a practitioner can deliver a project or not is a matter of professional ethics; there is always the case of those who do not know what they do not know. Fields of expertise are evolving at a huge pace, and although academia is increasingly deploying action research, most designers are very busy in a hugely competitive industry and fall behind, continuing old practices that are now seen as outdated. This is a huge problem because accrediting bodies and professional associations can no longer guarantee or police good practice from their members when the huge new knowledge volume cannot be absorbed by registered practitioners. I often wonder whether the role of such organisations needs to be radically reviewed, but that is a discussion for another time.

This thinking might lead us to conclude that a lack of adequate skills could be one of the main reasons for poor design. However, there is also the issue of schemes changing significantly from their paper version to construction. Sometimes the materials specified are not available on the market; sometimes contractors cannot find skilled labour; sometimes people misinterpret drawings. So, what happens during the whole process is also important.

Planning is, in most countries, the mechanism to assess schemes against certain criteria that discerns them as lawful developments and sanctions permissions to build. Some authorities – in Argentina, for example – evaluate design against a set of prescribed criteria, such as design codes or regulations. Some design criteria are more prescriptive than others, but generally speaking, planners know what to look for when appraising schemes. Other authorities – such as in England – look at schemes on an individual basis. This is a good way to ensure design flexibility and response to local character through design, especially in historically rich areas. The difficulty with this method is that when designers are not clear of what the design criteria are, the process can be very long, frustrating, and resource-consuming. Sadly, most planning authorities often lack the power to revert poor design once the building is underway or completed. I have seen cases where the approved proposal was very different to what was actually built, yet no remedial action was possible. Not long ago, I had an email from my colleague James, an excellent case officer. He wanted me to confirm an error he had picked up during inspection and to work with him on a solution to the problem. A block of flats recently built had the ground floor windows set back, forming a reveal that produced nice shadows onto the window frames, but the top floors had the windows installed flush with the external brick wall, in contrast to the drawings approved at planning stage. This was a discrepancy that we felt made the whole building look cheap and unrefined. We both looked at the drawings submitted for planning and yes, all

Chapter 1: **Understanding good, sustainable design**

windows should have been set back, like the windows of all other buildings in the area. James organised a site meeting with the contractor who soon confirmed to us that by changing this detail, they could save the cost of cavity closers and they would give tenants a little window shelf where they could put ornaments.[7] With this reasoning, they went ahead and changed the design thinking nobody would notice. During the site visit, all three of us agreed to a solution that would not be so expensive but that could achieve the expected and agreed effect. James instructed the removal and reinstatement of all top floor windows, and the building looked much better as a result.

What this case tells us is that design quality might look different to those involved. Whilst planners were worried about the external appearance of the building and its impact on the street scene, the contractor was worried about saving costs and adding internal space. So, besides the issues of knowledge, experience, and skill, there is also the very important question of how we define quality and what type of quality each one of the parties involved is trying to achieve. Also, without a sound quality assurance process, quality can change along the way.

After all these years in practice, I found that the best way to understand the concept of design quality in any field or application is to begin from the quality assurance premise that quality has to be present in the characteristics of the product or outcome, in our case a building or a place, and that it also has to be present in the process we apply to arrive to that result, in our case the design process. This takes us back to the example of cookery and the importance of good ingredients, a good recipe, and adequate skills.

Table 1.2 Definition of design quality based on the quality assurance system.

Process Evaluation				Design Evaluation
Strategy Values Policies	Sound Process	Design Quality	Good Product	Functional Durable Delightful
Regular audits will lead to persistent revisions and improvements				

To ensure quality is consistent, the process followed to deliver the design needs to be sound, clear, and prescriptive. Evaluations against set criteria can then take place on both the object produced and the process itself. After said regular evaluations or audits, the process can be revised as necessary to improve the quality of the next product.

The key to quality control is an open, cyclical, continuous process of appraisals and updates. If this way of working is not within the culture of those involved, design quality can be hugely compromised.

Let's see, for example, how this idea of using the quality assurance ethos applies to the design of buildings. Suppose I want to design a house in the Peak District, a national park designated as an Area of Outstanding Natural Beauty in the centre of England:

> A quality appraisal on the product, in this case the house, will be an analysis of how successful the form, function, and beauty of the proposed building are. I will probably have a way to evaluate the impact my design has on the local setting, which is very sensitive. A way to appraise the process might look at the steps I took, evaluating how fast I was, how many staff or how much time it took to deliver the final result, how many times I had to alter the design to achieve planning consent, why I had to change it, and how can I avoid delays in the future. If I find that having opted for a different approach could save me time and resources, I would probably do it differently next time I have a similar project. Also, the quality system would set up ways to audit adherence to the vision and concept at different stages, making sure changes do not depart the scheme from the proposal that was signed off. This is what design quality looks like in practice. Of course, the larger the project, the more complex the evaluations.

So, for the time being, it is important to note that good designs alone are not sufficient to deliver quality. There is also the design process to think about. The reality is that, in practice, many designers pay little attention to the process, which is mainly dictated by the systems and requirements set by clients and authorities. There is often a tendency in industry to assume that urban planners, who sign schemes off, are

Chapter 1: **Understanding good, sustainable design**

ultimately responsible for the quality of what is built, but even when planners and designers might appraise design thoroughly, they often have little power to influence what happens after the proposal is signed off. This clearly demonstrates that achieving quality development with high sustainability credentials is the responsibility of everyone involved.

I often feel that as an industry, we would progress much faster if we took the time to humbly and honestly contemplate what has not worked. The case studies I included in this book evidence that achieving good quality is a complex, collective process, and everybody taking part is responsible for the outcome. I have seen excellent designers producing poor results at no fault of their own. Similarly, I struggle to understand why single individuals or design firms can ever take full credit for good design. It is my hope that readers will find that once they have finished this book, they might begin to think differently about their roles and the parts others take in delivering design quality, and about the systemic faults that prevent us from achieving high quality development. Perhaps design awards can become more comprehensive and praise teams, systems, the resources invested, the power distribution, the handiwork, and the overall sustainability credentials at different stages rather than specific individuals or firms. That said, I would be grateful to receive an award for this book...

The sustainable design debate

It is difficult to begin this section without feeling daunted by the shear enormity of the subject, so I will begin with one of the most widely applied definitions of sustainability in the built environment: René Passet's Spheres of Sustainable Development (1979). Globally accepted and broadly applied in the industry for decades,[8] Passet's idea of sustainability is formed by three Spheres: Economy, Environment, and Society (see Figure 1.10). According to this model, if we consider all three spheres in equal measure, we can arrive at balanced decisions that minimise the negative impact on the planet.

The issue is that as we tend to trade in monetary terms, the only sphere we can measure with some degree of accuracy is the Economy sphere. We can put a price on things and add it all up on a spreadsheet. We can

Chapter 1: **Understanding good, sustainable design**

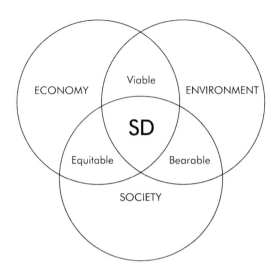

Figure 1.10 The three Spheres of sustainability: Economy, Environment, and Society. SD stands for Sustainable Development. Adapted from Passet, 1996, by the author.

decide how to make that cost smaller or higher by adding and removing items from the list. We can establish maximum budgets based on our affordability and financial resources. Everything we do – and do not do – can be measured by its economic cost, but there are not many well-known ways to put a price on the other spheres. For example, let's see how this works if I were to book a holiday to Scotland (which I often do):

> I might think about visiting the Trossachs, an area very close to my heart. I would start by setting the maximum I could spend, and I would look for a type of accommodation that meets my needs: something quiet, ideally surrounded by nature, a short walk from a good pub, and so on. Whilst I book my accommodation, I might be making many decisions that will impact on how much I will enjoy the break, but I can only price those by looking at my economic budget. It is likely that the larger the space, the closer to incredible views and amenities, and the higher the

Chapter 1: **Understanding good, sustainable design** 27

> standard of the service, the more expensive my holiday will be. But I have no way of knowing if the amount of money I spend is proportionate to other gains such as life experience, happiness, and contact with nature. There are no 'culture value currencies' or 'natural value currencies' to put a number on these other aspects of the holiday. If we had those as well as money, I might find myself with a more complex but probably more balanced costing, and might even want to spend more because it will be clearer to me that some options might give me far higher cultural or natural value for money. Alternatively, I might decide to stop at a Travel Inn on the M8...

Figure 1.11 Photo of Loch Lomond in the Trossachs area of Scotland showing a small boat on the shore and the water and vegetation in the background.

When we design schemes, we only have the economic currency to quantify things. This puts any negotiators seeking other values in a very difficult position, because they are comparing quantifiable monetary currency to something intangible. This issue is further discussed in the book, and some case studies show how this lack of multiple currencies impacts on the sustainable credentials of developments. Additionally, whilst there are many tools to aid the consideration of relevant aspects of all three spheres, we are not enforced – often not even inclined – to apply them in the built environment industry.

Everybody talks about sustainable design. Climate change is now a fact of life and it has been accepted that we must all do our best to protect our planet. In this time and age, everyone needs to know what sustainable design means, but even good designers struggle sometimes. The reality is that sustainable development is very difficult to achieve in practice, often almost impossible. During the design process, professionals have to make many tough decisions regarding costs, available technologies, and building time frames. These decisions often force the team to compromise the sustainable credentials of schemes. By this, I do not mean that savings made by removing solar panels are necessarily unsustainable. Contrary to common beliefs, some energy-efficient buildings might become less sustainable with the introduction of certain technologies. But this industry tends to focus greatly on the amount of carbon dioxide a building consumes for its operation, which relates to the energy it needs for heating or cooling, for example. Experts call this 'operational carbon'. The use of low-consumption or renewable technologies can help achieve lower operational carbon, but green energy is not always carbon-neutral. There are carbon emissions invested in producing, transporting, and disposing building parts and materials. The addition of all those factors is called 'lifetime embodied carbon' and is not always taken into account when designing. The tendency is to use technology to reduce energy consumption or to achieve operational carbon neutrality, simply because these goals can be measured mathematically.[9] However, in order to be truly sustainable, developments must perform on three key aspects of sustainability: economy, society, and environment. All three aspects need to be well considered and taken into account in equal measure. Fundamentally, this must take place whilst addressing present needs in a lawful and future-proofed way. So, an energy-efficient building can be unsustainable by damaging cohesive communities or by depriving

Chapter 1: **Understanding good, sustainable design**

neighbours from healthy lifestyles, for example, blocking light and ventilation. The United Nations Sustainable Development Goals clearly define the many aspects of sustainability that designers need to consider, and anyone familiar with those would know that the complexity is such that knowing when a development is truly sustainable is very difficult. When designers refer to a development as 'sustainable', it is normally because:

1. They have categorised it by measuring against a sustainability rating tool.
2. They have compared it with other similar buildings.
3. They have judged it against what could have been delivered instead.

In order to understand how sustainable a development is, it is very important to know how its sustainability credentials were assessed and what the scoring rate really means. This is a fast-growing field of expertise that is beginning to puzzle designers and planning authorities. So, rather than aiming for Net Zero to achieve what some believe to be the highest levels of sustainability, which is very difficult to determine or justify in practice, designers tend to try to achieve developments that are 'as sustainable as is reasonably possible'.[10]

What urban practice should aim to do is to look at the three aspects of sustainability and explore how they can be addressed in every step of the design process and throughout the lifespan of the design. But here is where the first hurdle appears: all three aspects of sustainable development are deeply interconnected (in fact, it has been impossible for me to write about these separately). Yet, that is how we study them, is how we analyse them, how we legislate for them, how we administrate them, how we budget, and how we think about them most of the time in education and industry. Sadly, economy, society, and environment are actually three independent realms dealt with by different professions with distinctive, exclusive goals. But let's see how deeply they can interrelate.

Take the economic benefits of development, for example; these are most usually labelled as job numbers, commercial activity, and consumption rates. If more people move into an area, local shops will prosper, contributing to localised economic growth and increased tax revenues. Equally, economic gains could counterbalance other facets of place, particularly to do with social and environmental conditions. Economic growth can force the less affluent in society to move to more affordable areas, losing their community support networks and having to adapt to a new norm. This phenomenon, commonly known as 'gentrification', which alludes to making the area more 'gentile', continues to be a contested consequence of economic growth in residential areas and a big fear amongst communities over decades. As places change and the shape of neighbourhoods is modified, residents can be directly affected by this change. In deprived areas, this can leave vulnerable people in greater risk, as regenerating neighbourhoods not only means demolishing or refurbishing the urban structure, but also destroying social systems, which are essential to many people's survival, often causing grief symptoms and damage to their psychological and physiological health. For example, researchers conducted a study in Boston's West End and showed that 73% of residents from a relocated group showed extreme grief symptoms including vomiting, intestinal disorders, nausea, crying spells, and clinical depression; 20% were depressed for two years after moving.[11] The study also showed that the stronger the social ties, the greater the grief people experienced.

During my doctoral studies, I looked at the social impact of changes to urban morphology in residential areas, amongst other placemaking correlations. I found that in The Meadows, Nottingham, there were strong social identities and self-segregation behaviours amongst community networks that went hand in hand with strong physical boundaries, like main roads or the character of their area. Participants tended to define themselves as coming from 'The New', 'The East', or 'The Old Meadows', and referred to each other as being 'from the other side', claiming that the new tramline running along a former boulevard had divided the community further. They also commented on how radical structural change and gentrification in some zones had caused population replacement with impact on social outputs. For example, the impact on people's health and wellbeing as well as children's school performance was evidenced during a community meeting with the researcher attending incognito, where there were several cases reported:

i. A teenage girl whose school had reported on her gradually poorer performance due to the stress caused at home regarding moving home.
ii. A woman who had suffered a stroke as a result of having to leave a former council home she bought.
iii. A single mum with an 11-year-old boy who was awarded 'Community Boy of the Year' by the local Scouts group. The woman had her

disabled/ill father living across the road and she cared for him on a daily basis, taking food to him, bathing him in the night, caring for his home, and so on. The mother and the boy were being relocated to another neighbourhood, which meant she would have to either stop caring for her father or stop working, and the boy would lose all the community ties he created.

iv. A single father with a daughter who had to be relocated to a one bedroom flat in another community. The father's name was not in the child's birth certificate. Her mother had left them after suffering mental health problems and he was asked to demonstrate by a privately taken DNA test that he was the biological father of the girl in order to qualify for a two-bedroom property, but he could not afford the test. This caused him anxiety and depression.

In the other three of the thesis case studies, I found that residents shared a common understanding of spatial boundaries through mental mapping, which was independent of their socio-economic backgrounds and lifestyles. The residents' mental map of the four neighbourhoods, and their sense of belonging, lined up with the urban fragments or zones created by road morphology. Neighbours and community groups adopted this division and related geographically and operationally to either one area or the other. Participants in all case studies were fully aware this was the case and commented about this:

> People who live at the top [of the hill] know each other, we live here on the other side at the bottom [of the hill] and do not know who lives next door to us, but my brother in law lives just round the corner.
> (S Participant 2015)

> There is the people that live here at the old village [1880s], and newcomers that live on the other side in the new estates [1970–1980s]. They ruined everything when they built them houses on the hills. We knew everyone here, now is like they're strangers.
> (K Participant 2015)

> We all know that the village has two sides; the village [the 1880s part of town near the railway station] and the top [the modern and

1970s extensions to the north of the railway]. We often refer to people as coming from the other side of the rail.

(D Participant 2015)

My thesis concluded that road hierarchy was a fundamental parameter that determined fragmentation in neighbourhoods, especially when there were zones with different plot patterns (square block or curvilinear roads). Road hierarchy led to the formation of social groups and a sense of place belonging. These strong place identities produced both positive place care and negative tribal attitudes. Interestingly, urban patterns where building blocks were square or rectangular, with well-formed streets, afforded more casual, informal contact at a street level and more place care attitudes (especially stewardship – or looking after the place) than modern streets with unusual geometries or suburban curved roads with cul-de-sacs; indeed, the latter showed the lowest rates of casual, informal contact. This suggested that when people were living physically closer together, they were also closer in terms of community bonding. Public buildings, and associated public open spaces around them, were crucial in neighbourhoods, as they made it easier for people to form social networks, which, in turn, led to more social cohesion and social support between neighbours. When these public buildings were accessible, open, and neutral and were strategically located, they helped different community groups coming together, and they fostered social integration amongst the different groups. In short, community links were far easier to build when living in closer proximity and sharing a communal space.

But urban growth does not need to bring social division, nor does economic growth has to result in gentrification. Well-managed processes that consider social aspects of place can deliver a type of growth that also benefits the most vulnerable and those in greater need. There are many tested ways to re-balance or level up areas by measuring economic gains against social or environmental outputs. When tracing or altering neighbourhoods, knowing the social impact of urban form – and how to mitigate potential issues – is crucial to delivering sustainability and balanced, resilient communities. All the findings of my doctoral studies suggested that zones divided by road hierarchy can indeed be stitched together by applying strategies such as activity, strong links, and continuity of urban forms and street shapes; the strategic location of open, accessible, neutral public buildings and spaces that act as magnets across zones; or, ideally, by a combination of both approaches.

Ethical developers conduct design evaluations considering these aspects of place. Good, diligent local authorities scrutinise the process before granting planning permission. However, these types of comprehensive studies do not always take place because they are rarely compulsory. These are not factors normally covered in legislation, and skills in these fields are not usually applied to built environment practices. In my view, there is a whole world to be discovered in this line of work.

A good way to balance all three aspects of sustainable development already available is applying the principles of 'Social Value in Construction'. In the built environment, Social Value is often associated with the capacity places have to be sustainable from a social point of view. A socially sustainable settlement not only meets the basic needs of its residents, but, crucially, it has a community with an ability to maintain and build its own resources and with the resilience to prevent and address problems in the future. The response to the Covid-19 pandemic could be seen as a strong indicator of social sustainability. In some locations, people quickly found each other, they organised themselves, and they found the resources to help those in need and to support one another. That is social resilience, and it was different in each village, town, city, and country around the globe; some places showed more resilience than others. The construction industry offers countless opportunities to increase social resilience, yet these are rarely acted upon.

The design and building process can do wonders to prepare communities for adversity; for example, by creating neighbourhoods where people have the chance to meet, work, and play together to get to know one another over time. This type of impact on communities can only be possible if designers begin the process by understanding existing local assets and resources and if the design process brings local people on board. That is what designers call Placemaking Engagement: design made with people, for people, and ideally by people; at least to a certain extent.

Conversely, current practice remains interested in participation, a tokenistic form of consultation still mainly focused on site-specific events designed to discuss particular proposals in a specific moment in time. Good participation happens when the community can give information and opinions to designers, who can use that input to inform schemes. By contrast, placemaking engagement is a continuous, collaborative, multidirectional approach that focuses on the benefits of the process itself. Participatory consultation is about the information local people can give to designers. Placemaking engagement is about what the design, planning, building, and maintenance processes can offer to communities

Table 1.3 Forms of participation: consultation versus engagement.

	Participation	
	Consultation	Engagement
Input	Participants have the opportunity to express an opinion regarding a proposed design solution	Participants are given the opportunity to be part of the design process and shape that design solution in collaboration with professionals and other agents
Influence	Participants' input might inform the scheme or it might not	Documentation is produced to demonstrate how participants' input informed the scheme
Time frame	It happens at specific times during the process; often it happens only once	Normally happens very early in the design process, from feasibility stage and ideally even before, and continues during the design process
Communication	Events are normally advertised through public forums and there are no information sharing platforms in place	A participants' network is created to inform on progress and share information throughout the design process, as well as using public forums

Chapter 1: **Understanding good, sustainable design**

to help them build social resilience. The latter, combined with Social Value in Construction principles, can begin to deliver the social aspect of sustainability. But this shift from participation to continuous engagement is still not part of built environment professional training, and many practitioners either lack the skills to understand these processes or mistakenly perceive additional risks and power loss in the adoption of broad collaboration methods. We will come back to these points in Chapter 4.

Based on the above, it would make sense to think designers should become familiar with the social dynamics and the lifestyles of the site, but this is rarely the case. Designers tend to focus on the technical aspects of the scheme because that is how they are trained. In recent decades, with industrial pollution and climate change, nature became more relevant as a topic, and designers began to take an interest in how to create more environmentally friendly buildings and how to apply energy-saving technologies, partially incorporating the environmental dimension of sustainability. The economic dimension is monitored by quantity surveyors, who are part of the team. Looking after social issues has always been the responsibility of local authorities, who measure social needs, legislate accordingly, and set goals for improvement, so designers do not feel they need to address the social aspect of their design. Sadly, the impact of planning authorities on design is limited and often comes too late in the process.

However, the impact of design on society started to become more relevant in recent years when the need to adapt for climate change grew. Increasing numbers of academic publications became interested in the impact of design on health, wellbeing, and communities. Nowadays, it is well known that the ways in which we design places can make or break communities and people's health and wellbeing, as well as being a determinant to trigger certain behaviours. But it is still early days, and there are not many tools for the built environment practice, at least none that has been broadly adopted to assess the social impact of development.

The fight against climate change and its more recent 'climate adaptation' facet have become very popular in leading economies. Thankfully, some people have started to realise (if a little too late) the damage this consumption frenzy is doing to our planet and what that means to us who inhabit it. Local groups and communities have increasingly demanded the protection of green areas and have campaigned against polluting practices. Unfortunately, this passion led to further confrontation in many cases. Some communities began to demand technologies and levels of commitment that are still unaffordable and which cannot be sustained in the long term.

For greenery to be feasible – and more importantly 'sustainable' – it must be designed in a way that is future-proof, it should last and be maintained, and it should not hinder the achievement of goals in the other two strands (Economy and Society). One could argue that more green can only be beneficial to people, but that is not strictly true. There could be too much green or green in the wrong place. Some proposals are very built-up, dense, and compact, and yet they have an overall positive impact environmentally. Other proposals look very green on paper, with lots of grass, but they offer very little to local species and the natural world. A very good tool to measure the implications of proposals is the Environmental Impact Assessment. If a scheme is evaluated with this tool and achieves an overall net positive environmental gain, this means that it is better for the natural environment to have the development than not to have it and leave things as they are. It does not mean

Table 1.4 Examples of sustainable development tools.

Economy	Environment	Society
Budget control	Ecological surveys	Health and wellbeing
Value engineering	Biodiversity analysis	net gain
Business models	Historic analysis	Social network
Funding mechanisms	Flood risk	mapping
Margin evaluations	Contamination	Community cohesion
Contribution	Geology	analysis
considerations	Archaeological surveys	Social support system appraisals
		Health indicators mapping
		Placemaking proposal

that the scheme is fully sustainable or that it is as good as it can be for nature, but it means that it is environmentally feasible and better than what is there presently. This is why promoting brownfield development is very positive, although protecting green field is often – but not always – the best solution. We will see a case study later on where opposition to green field development prevented environmental positive gains.

Environmental Impact Assessment net positive gains have just been made compulsory in the UK at the time of writing this book, but some developers, designers, and authorities were already making a commitment to deliver schemes that score positive results.

Design quality and sustainability

The word 'sustainability' has dominated the built environment discourse for decades, although many are still unsure what it really means and why it is so relevant to our industry. The fact is that our planet has finite resources, and although we have the capability to sustain life without causing excessive damage, we don't always exercise it. This is what sustainability is all about: doing the very best with the tools and resources one has at hand; nothing less, nothing more. It certainly does not mean that we need to achieve the impossible, but it surely means we need to try our very best to minimise impact when we make an intervention.

Most of us learnt about natural cycles and ecosystems in primary school (even I did growing up in a military junta in Argentina). We studied the water cycle, for example, and how climate affects what happens to water. We also learnt about the food chain by looking at the rainforest, savannah, or lagoon ecosystems. All places where humans inhabit work in a similar way to those wildlife ecosystems we studied when younger, yet, when we design, plan, and build, we tend to pay little attention to how we are altering those habitats. We are more focused on calculating budgets and illustrating the form, colour, and overall appearance of developments, and we tend to leave out the most important part of all: how it will sustain life.

If we developed in a more considered way, we would understand the ecosystem first, and we would contemplate how our interventions could affect life in the long-term future. If we could be certain that we had done our very best to achieve balanced design solutions with minimal negative impact across all aspects of sustainability, we could then be satisfied that we have achieved a high-quality result. In fact, I believe that design quality and sustainability are so intimately related that I often find it difficult to separate the two, yet we tend to think about them as two separate concepts in urban practice.

Another point to make here is that design quality should consider the whole lifespan of buildings and places, instead of remaining fixated with the granting of planning or handover stages. There is a lot to be said about how buildings are run, maintained, and disposed of. These aspects of design quality are also deeply related to the sustainable credentials of schemes. Let's explore this concept a little further.

Table 1.5 Lifespan of buildings or places.

Design	Construction	Use	Disposal
From the initial idea of creating or adapting a place down to the moment when the contractor is ready to build	From the moment the site is made available for clearance down to the moment when the key is handed over to the owners	From the moment the key is handed over until the building is vacant and declared out of use	From the moment the building is vacant until the site is cleared and materials are disposed of
These four stages often overlap			
Sometimes the detailed design is done at the same time or after the site is cleared and made ready for construction	Sometimes building works continue, for example, if there are some details to finish or minor repairs to be done, a process referred to as 'snagging'	Sometimes the building is not completely vacated or tenants and owners leave the site at different times. Disposal might occur with occupants still on the site	

Chapter 1: **Understanding good, sustainable design**

Table 1.6 Key definitions.

Sustainable design	Design that meets the needs of the present without compromising the ability of future generations to meet their own needs in the Economic, Environmental, and Social Spheres
Good design	Design that is fit for purpose, durable, and brings delight
Design quality	How well conceived or achieved design ideas are when compared against a set standard
Quality assurance	Evaluating the outcomes and the processes regularly to implement improvements
Beauty	The result of a process of perception and cognitive interpretation by a human being
Place or building lifespan	All stages from concept design down to demolition and disposal

Lessons learnt

I sincerely hope this chapter offered a good introduction to what I regard as built environment foundation knowledge. Design quality and sustainability can never be achieved without setting the basis of what really matters or without identifying the core reasons that drive us to create or adapt places and buildings. Table 1.6 shows a compact summary of key definitions that set the foundations of the debate and prepare the reader for what we will discuss in forthcoming chapters.

TOOL 1: Sustainable design priorities checklist

There are times when professionals, authority agents, and communities need a simple way to identify unsustainable design at a glance or to see if there are any gaps in the design itself or its process that could be better addressed. These exercises often take place in short time frames, at a single meeting, or with a shortage of resources. To aid these tasks, I created a tool: a table that shows a simple Sustainable Design Checklist;

whilst it is not a comprehensive appraisal system, it is a good starting point.

Critical thinking is becoming rare in the built environment, perhaps because designers feel trapped in a world of tough competition with long working hours and little room to be truly influential; but I think we must all give it a good go. Although the priorities on my tool are

Table 1.7 TOOL 1: sustainable design priorities checklist.

Resources	What is being used and where it comes from
Lifetime	The building, its technologies and its materials' durability, and the embodied energy involved in producing and disposing of those
Passive design	The skin of the building is designed for the site conditions and its local microclimates with adaptability in mind
Energy efficiency	How much energy is consumed in running, cleaning, and maintaining the building
Social impact	If the design itself and its process address the social issues in the area
Physiopsychological impact	If the design itself and its process address the health and wellbeing of users
Community impact	If the design itself and its process strengthen local communities and their cohesion and resilience
Economic impact	If the design itself and its process address local economy issues using circular economy models
Natural impact	If the design itself and its process have a net positive environmental gain
Climate change	If the masterplan itself and its process address water management and respond to the climate of the area and the long-term climate change prognosis
Cultural impact	If the design itself and its process acknowledge, address, and strengthen local character and culture

Chapter 1: **Understanding good, sustainable design**

fundamental to me, I would encourage designers to give this some thought to attempt to come up with a sustainability checklist of their own, and to go back and edit it every once in a while as new knowledge and experiences are incorporated and as new tools become available.

Notes

1 Morgan, *Vitruvius: The Ten Books on Architecture* (New York: Dover Publications, 1960).
2 The Vitruvian Man is a drawing by Leonardo da Vinci (circa 1487), which shows a male figure in two superimposed positions with his arms and legs apart and simultaneously inscribed in a circle and square. It is accompanied by notes based on the work of the Roman architect Vitruvius Pollio. The intention of this work is to demonstrate human proportions.
3 Modulor is a scale of harmonic measures that set the dimensions of architectural elements in proportion to human dimensions. Renowned modern designer Le Corbusier published Le Modulor in 1948.
4 ARUDO is an informal group of British local authority urban design officers working outside London who share experience and best practice examples and support each other in their efforts to achieve better design quality.
5 Heston Marc Blumenthal, OBE, HonFRSC, is a renowned British chef and food writer. He is considered as a pioneer of multi-sensory cooking and a flavour specialist. He introduces scientific methods and technologies to create innovative recipes.
6 Marcus Vitruvious Pollio, *The Ten Books on Architecture*, 2nd ed. (Morris Hicky, Morgan trans.; Ipswich: Deez Books, 2004).
7 External walls normally have a gap between the outside and the inside face of the building; this is normally where thermal insulation is installed. A cavity closer sits around the gap where windows and doors are fitted to act as a seal, preventing external water vapour and damp from entering the cavity wall and the building, whilst also preventing heat from being lost through the gap.
8 Susan Baker, *Sustainable Development*, 2nd ed. (New York: Timothy Doyle, Routledge, 2015).
9 Being Carbon Neutral means having no net release of carbon dioxide into the atmosphere, in other words, to take out or absorb as much as is released. There are two main types of carbon measures for buildings: (1) Operational Carbon, which refers to the carbon dioxide emitted during the 'running' of the building such as heating and cooling; and (2) Embodied Carbon, which

refers to the carbon dioxide emitted during the whole lifecycle of the building, for example, as a result of producing, transporting and disposing the materials.
10 Net Zero refers to having no net release of carbon dioxide (CO_2) into the atmosphere, in other words, we take out as much CO_2 as we put in.
11 Paul Bell et al., *Environmental Psychology* (Boston, MA: Cengage Learning, Inc., 1990) 349.

Chapter 2
The design process

In Chapter 1, we looked at how critical design quality can be to achieving sustainability, as both concepts are intimately related. We saw how design quality requires focus on the quality of both the product and the process.

Now we will explore the design process in more detail, especially looking at how a development becomes part of a greater whole: a city, town, village, or place. We will see how a simple urban design process model could be used and adapted in practice to encompass complex, continuous collaboration frameworks that, with simple measures, could secure more sustainable outputs.

Let's begin this chapter with an example that illustrates my thinking. Probably most of us can intuitively assert that designing and building a garden shed is not the same as designing and building a school. Both projects require different types of skills, different materials, different timings, and different processes; they involve very different mechanical and electrical installations and have different health and safety regulation requirements. To state the obvious, without devaluing the merit of garden sheds, the school seems like a more complex type of building, which probably requires more varied specialist skills. A lay person would probably venture to design or build a shed very successfully, but they would soon realise that does not mean they can go and design or build a school. Besides which, we all know that children are the toughest critics!

Now let's compare the complexity of a school building to the complexity of a whole city. Well, they are almost impossible to compare. A school and a city are different in nature and they involve diverse skill sets and very different processes. Building designers, also known as architects

DOI: 10.4324/9781003244059-3

or architectural designers, should have the training and expertise that enable them to successfully design a school with the support of specialist technical expertise, but they could not build it all by themselves. Equally, they should realise that unless they are fully trained (such as tough postgraduate studies), they are probably not equipped with the knowledge or experience to design whole areas involving multiple buildings, streets, and public spaces. This is the expertise of urban designers, who train to acquire a whole range of different skills. It is not rare, however, to see architects aiming to design masterplans for large, complex developments. Knowing how to draw plans, façades, and perspective views is not sufficient to engage in the design of large developments with places between buildings, though not all architects are aware of or will accept this.

Accrediting bodies such as the Architects' College in Argentina or the Royal Institute of British Architects (RIBA) in the UK set up guidelines and standards of practice for professionals to follow. These are very useful and normally result in a consistent approach to contractual arrangements and fee structures. Understandably, these types of guidance only cover the scope of work that concerns the profession and do not go beyond the realm of expertise their members trained for.

Town planners, also called city planners or simply planners, are capable of understanding citywide, and even regional and national, place systems. They can prepare strategic plans and write legislation to forecast and sometimes steer the patterns of growth and change in large areas. Their focus, however, is the legislative aspects of the built environment; in other words, the law of the land. By allowing conditioning or forbidding certain uses or the size of developments, they can ensure that the sum of all those interventions will result in the expected overall outcome. Planners do not receive design training to the extent architects do. In the UK, when officers have to appraise schemes for their individual merits and with the central government's push for beautiful buildings, planners have recently been under pressure to acquire enough design skills to be able to evaluate schemes on the basis of their designs. They could not design buildings though. Architects can design buildings, urban designers can design cities, and planners can regulate and control growth and change.

To assist UK architects with guidelines about the process they need to follow to design buildings and the relationships and contracts they

Chapter 2: **The design process**

should establish and maintain during that process, RIBA has produced a summary called The Plan of Work.[1] This is very useful indeed. I have used it myself and I have seen architects and assistants consulting it to plan their work ahead, to check they have not missed any critical steps, and to produce the schedule of work for other members of the design team and contractors to follow. Professional bodies in other countries have developed similar tools. Therefore, if we had to know about the process involved in designing a building, we would probably know where to find the information. At the very least, this would be an excellent starting point.

Failing to find equivalent guidance for large-scale projects like sizable master plans, neighbourhoods, village extensions, or new towns, designers often apply the RIBA process model, adding and subtracting fragments to try to make it fit their large-scale project requirements. The problem is that buildings and large areas are not the same at all; they require entirely different processes as much as they require a different set of skills, just like the shed and the school or the school and the city. As we stand, the industry as a whole does not have a uniform, clear process model to follow for urban design, leaving those involved to reinvent or translate tools across fields of expertise, which leads to serious inconsistencies, delays, and errors of judgement along the way in turn, this leads to poor design. Now, based on the discussions of Chapter 1, this gap in industry is a real problem, given that the design process is a key factor in securing the quality of development and its sustainability credentials.

Knowing where to begin

Returning to the cookery analogy I used in Chapter 1, if I had to prepare a new dish, something I had never prepared before, I would probably start by finding a good recipe, whether I consider myself a good cook or not. A step-by-step guide that listed the tools and ingredients I am going to need would certainly be most helpful. If I learnt the basic process of how to bake a sponge cake, for example, I could later on adapt it to my individual needs. I might want to change the colour, add nuts for texture, or introduce a new flavour. This basic recipe is exactly what urban designers lack. Even when every project is different, a basic process one can follow, adapt, or expand would help. To make matters worse, the emphasis of higher education seems to be consistently on the design aspects of the profession; the more critical procedural complexities that are difficult to recreate in a studio often remain under-addressed.

We now begin to understand the importance of a good process to secure design quality, yet many practitioners still pay little attention to this, and instead of planning a sound process to help them arrive at better results, they jump immediately to the blank piece of paper and start by thinking about shapes, often without even visiting the site. In doing so, they consider a huge number of form-led criteria: the geometry of the site, the position of windows, colours, and materials, the client's aesthetic preferences, building volumes, heights, and so forth. But, in my experience, the best designs always emerge from a good understanding of the context and with a level of understanding that cannot be achieved virtually from the desk. A responsible designer always visits the site and explores it in depth at least a couple of times. This sensitive approach to design is especially important in a time of climate emergency. I arrived at this conclusion from my own personal experience despite the fact that at university, I was told how heroically Le Corbusier designed Casa Curuchet in La Plata, Argentina, without visiting the site back in 1948. From site plans and photographs, he managed to create a sculptural building that wraps around a tree and frames a view towards a great palm tree in the park across the road. However, he did not design the building from scratch: La Plata city has a strong Edification Code that sets key design parameters the modernist designer used as a design framework, and he had the help of local architect Amanico Williams, who run the project on the ground. We will explore the use of design parameters in some detail in Chapters 5 and 6. For what it is worth, Casa Curuchet is visually interesting, but it has proven something of a white elephant as a place to live.

In our century, the more designers prepare, the higher their chances to succeed. Designing by looking at the environment first, making everything else work afterwards, is a strategy I call designing *outside-in*: shaping a new place or building for the context and the location where it will sit. This does not mean sacrificing function over form: it is rather the opposite – looking at function in a broader, more holistic manner;

Chapter 2: **The design process** 47

understanding the terrain before you settle, as if you were going wild camping in a place you have never been before. You would take the time to assess where it would be best to place the tent, what is the best spot for the open fire, away from the wind, how can you be sheltered from the wild, and so on.

Looking at the constraints and opportunities of the site, good designers can find clues to come up with the initial concept, that first sketch that shows how the main characteristics of their proposals respond to the setting. The more designers understand the site, the more adequate the proposal will be, looking as if it had always been there. This study of the site conditions is called *site analysis*, and it is a fundamental part of the process, one that can make or break a scheme. Unfortunately, local authorities in many parts of the world, including the UK, tend to express concern about the weakness or total lack of contextual analysis. To be completely honest, I struggle to understand how anyone would work like this; I think it is much easier to find a solution to a problem when we know what the problem is. Designing is all about problem solving.

Once the site analysis has highlighted the constraints and opportunities for the area, designers tend to begin to shape their proposals, initially in the form of simple volumes and gradually adding more detail. They also begin to imagine how the place will function, how people will use the space, and what it will feel like being there when the new development has emerged. All of those ideas can be captured in simple words or in the form of images that illustrate a vision for the development. The design team, authorities appraising a scheme, and all the other agents will find that a clear, well-illustrated vision is a crucial tool, a point of reference, a direction of travel. Every time the proposal changes, whether it might be for technical, economic, or political reasons, the design team compares the revised design against that vision to ensure the final product still conveys what it was meant to achieve.

From my own experience, I know that it is possible to create a collective vision through collaboration, a picture of what the place will feel like in the eyes of those who might not have all the technical knowledge an architect or urban designer has. Most people understand instinctively when something looks right or wrong, and, more importantly, they know their area and are familiar with critical information like where to find nice views, the seasonal changes, and significant local building typologies.

I have been incredibly lucky to have the opportunity to work with communities to come up with different design options for various sites. Over the years, I have invested time and effort to co-design with other groups, and I arrived at the conclusion that what we often consider complex architectural principles can actually become familiar to anyone, including young children. I also discovered that if people understand those key principles, dialogue and collaboration are easier and much more enjoyable. In time, I found different ways to explain design to my students and the communities I work with, and I came up with some critical but basic design principles everyone could understand, which I explain in Chapter 5. Over time, I found that some design criteria were more relevant than others in achieving design in context. I conducted numerous experiments and analysis before I concluded that knowing how to manage these key design parameters is crucial to creating buildings, even landmark buildings, that sit well within their context. But before we go into exploring what those criteria are, let's look at some case studies from practice: where diverse, more collaborative processes lead to very different design outcomes than those usually achieved with standard forms of practice.

We'll see how the lack of site analysis is not the only issue. There are also errors rooted in the lack of adequate processes. In the absence of a model template for urban design processes, typically professionals would think that the first stage in creating a masterplan is to understand the site, to look at the area, and to do an analysis or evaluation of the surroundings. However, although this is often the most critical step towards achieving design quality, it is not the first step urban designers should take. The error of judgement comes from applying building design processes to large-scale design.

I can think of plenty of examples where things have gone wrong, very wrong indeed, when it comes to the design process. Over my years in practice, I have seen immense amounts of time and huge sums of money spent in trying to mitigate or correct the drastic outputs of a bad process. But in this case, I believe it would be more helpful to illustrate two best practice examples, something less common to see. Let's see how a different approach can result in much better outcomes; let's look at two successful case studies in different continents that exemplify this. In the cases discussed, the value of good design processes

Chapter 2: **The design process**

becomes clear and we will see how considering the views of different engagement groups helped enrich the sustainable credentials of these projects.

Case studies

> ### Case Study 2.1 A school designed with the support of social sciences
>
> This is the case of a new primary school in Argentina, in an area of deprivation with high percentage of minority groups. At the time, in 1997, I was an architecture student. This was a project that had enormous impact in shaping my career and the design ethics I would adopt for life. Our module leader at La Plata University was a visionary, an elderly man of great talent and incredible enthusiasm for designing places that worked for people. Our second year dissertation task was to design a school for an existing neighbourhood in a very underprivileged location. But there was a caveat: each one of us was going to work in teams formed by a student from the School of Anthropology, a student from Sociology, and a student from Psychology. To make things even harder for us, we had to co-design the school with the local community.
>
> The process was a huge revelation for me. Ever since this experience, I constantly wondered why the Built Environment is so detached from social sciences when it makes so much sense that designing places is all about people. The multidisciplinary teams got together and we began to plan our process. It was evident that so far, everything I had learnt at university was the wrong way round: how could I ever design for people if I do not understand them first?
>
> With anthropological and psychological expertise, we decided how to engage the community in a way that would be meaningful for participants; the *how* was sorted. In my role of designer, I knew the type of information I could incorporate without jeopardising

the integrity of the programme, so we had the *what* to ask. I also knew *when* I would need this to make sure it was not too late in the process. The Sociology student did a human geography analysis and found out *who* to ask and *where* to approach them for best results and further participation. The Psychology student worked on defining the optimum *environments* for the interviews and workshops. Together, we defined how to ask the questions so that we achieved unbiased answers that resulted in meaningful data that could be transferred to the design easily at the right time in the process.

With a clear plan of action and roles well defined, we set a schedule of work and we arranged the interviews and workshops. We went to a local school to work with children, we visited some homes, and even dined with local people to get a sense of their lifestyles and what mattered to them. Not only did we observe behaviours, movements, social encounters, and communication styles, but we also experienced them first hand. Now we had a strong bond with these lovely, welcoming people. We had opened a channel that would take the project to a different emotional level, one that made us care a lot more for the quality of what we designed. We did design together, social sciences students, local people, and me: the architect. My role was to translate the outcomes of the process into the shape of a space that could be built within budget, within the set time frames, responding to all legal requirements, and more importantly, open and flexible for its users to turn it into a place. Every detail in the design was informed by their home experience and the lifestyles they were used to. This was particularly relevant in this case, because at the interviews, teachers had expressed concerns regarding levels of attendance and poor nutrition amongst students. We had to create an environment that children wanted to be in, a place of safety and comfort. Again, children are the toughest critics.

The type of design information one can transfer from a social science piece of work to a building design is vast and varied. This is something we will discuss further in Chapter 6, but in this particular case, there were some strong clues about the use of space and the relevance of light in the lifestyle of the local community. For example, having very hot and compact homes meant that these large families would normally eat outdoors, in large tables under the shade of a vine or a tree, often a fig or a bay tree (see Figures 2.1 and 2.2). That table would be located in a small patio in the form of a courtyard surrounded by buildings. Natural light was always coming from the top, with sunrays reaching the table from the gap between the low buildings and the foliage. Most participants expressed that eating together was their most treasured moment in a day, when they were calm and felt loved. We decided to recreate that sensorial experience by designing with light, textures, and colours in the school dining room. The dining room is a very important part of the school day in these deprived communities as some children would only have access to a nutritious meal at school. The more comfortable, at peace, and happy they were at dinner time, the more positive the experience would be for them; which, according to our Psychology colleague, meant that they would be more likely to eat larger meals with a greater variety of food.

Children in these communities spent most of their lives outdoors, they played in large, cross-age groups, and they sat in circles when they wanted to talk. This type of information emerged from observation and from spending time with them and was as crucial for us as the responses we obtained from surveys and interviews. We designed every classroom with a fully equipped outdoor learning area of equal size to facilitate outdoor teaching and play. All these outdoor classrooms led to a larger patio area that different age groups shared, so that during breaks but also during classes, children could mix in a natural outdoors environment with other age groups as they did at home. This larger patio had a few circular seating areas that medium-sized groups could use to gather and integrate.

Chapter 2: **The design process**

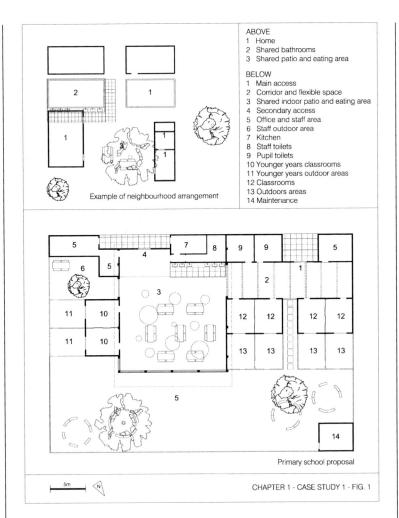

Figure 2.1 Layout showing how the neighbourhood arrangement and the proposal compare in term of spatial qualities. Illustrated by the author.

Chapter 2: **The design process**

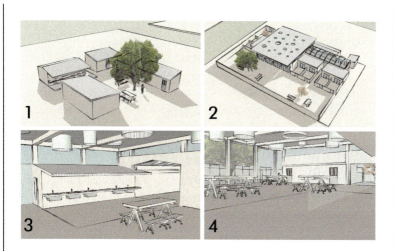

Figure 2.2 Three-dimensional sketches: (1) the neighbourhood arrangement, (2) the proposal from bird's-eye view, (3) the proposed basins area, and (4) the proposed dining area.

A relevant detail for us was that this community used toilets that were detached from the house and had a large, low sink on the outside that was used for a number of activities from hand washing to laundry and even to prepare vegetables for cooking. These sinks were often shared amongst a few families, almost functioning as the village fountains of medieval Europe – huge in anthropological meaning and encompassing a sense of collectiveness. That is exactly what we managed to re-create: communal sinks outside the bathroom, which could be used for hand wash, during art and craft projects, and to provide drinking water.

As the designer, I could have produced a proposal for a modern school that would have worked brilliantly for me as a child: a huge library, fully equipped indoor play areas, large classrooms leading to communal corridors, exhibition space to pin up posters, and small, intimate art rooms (and no gymnasium, PE would have been removed from the curriculum!). However, a proposal like that would have been alien to that particular community. We only know how to design when we know how to listen to those we design for or, ideally, *with*.

Our team won an award with this design and we handed over the proposals to the government, who approved the plans and went on to build not a school, due to their budget constraints, but a school extension, with the design principles of our proposals. I then transferred this experience as much as I could into my work, both abroad and in the UK. Crucially, it was this experience that inspired me to do a PhD later on in life on the subject of delivering social sustainability through the design process. I have a very inspirational Year Two tutor to thank for this.

Case Study 2.2 Securing land value

This is the case of a large proposal in England. The project involved a residential area of over 1,700 new homes, a new primary school, a main square, commercial areas, community facilities, touristic attractions, green spaces, and sports grounds. The significance of this proposal would be huge, given that it would increase the size of the existing settlement by 50%. Of course, the first consideration of the design team was the impact this could have on local people and their lifestyles. From day one, we were certain that we would have to engage the community very well every step of the way. The landowners, who proved to be very responsible clients, thankfully agreed.

Chapter 2: **The design process** 55

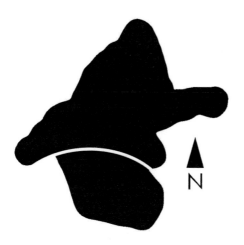

Figure 2.3 Diagram in plan showing the area of the development (South) in comparison to the area of the town (North).

The problem was that the delivery of housing schemes in the UK was becoming increasingly complicated at the time. There were many regulations to follow and long-winded approval processes involving many different authorities that did not always talk to each other. The pressure to provide affordable homes, large green areas with natural water management features, and improved highways and transport networks meant that for the clients, having certainty about the commercial viability of the scheme was crucial. In other words, they had carried out an economic feasibility study which suggested they could not afford to reduce the number of homes any further in order to accommodate additional infrastructure at a later stage. We wanted to co-design some aspects of the scheme, working alongside communities to create a place where they felt comfortable, but we could not afford to let any design input lower the size of the private market stock.

The most common thing to do in this type of project would be to define the boundaries that divide the private spaces from the public realm early on and fix them, so that the amount of private land available for sale would not be lost later on to serve the public realm. On this scheme, we did exactly the opposite: we shrank the private land and increased public land as much as possible from the outset, so that when design changes occurred during the engagement process, public land would pass onto private ownership and not the other way round. This meant that the financial liability risk would be reduced, as it is privately sold land that brings more profits in, whilst public land incurs long-term maintenance costs. In other words, we designed starting from the worst case scenario. Let's see how this works in more detail.

The design of building block (technically called land parcels) is a mathematical challenge. Finding the most efficient layout geometry is crucial to maximising returns on investment. Urban designers have to consider the amount of private front and rear garden that is acceptable for the development. This not only depends on the character of the area, but also on the amount of space a family of certain size needs outdoors. *Responsive Environments* is a book that illustrates this point very well.[2]

There is also a need to accommodate waste storage with good access for litter collection; considering this aspect at a later stage often results in the addition of alleyways for rear access gardens, which take up a lot of land. Additionally, the width of plots is sometimes dictated by the need to include integrated garages or side driveways, which, according to some highways engineers, should be at least 3.6 metres wide to allow the family to open the car doors once they have parked the car. On top of that, most local authorities set minimum back-to-back distances designers have to leave between neighbouring dwellings to ensure enough daylight and ventilation, and a degree of privacy in all homes. In the UK, this tends to be around 20–22 metres between two façades with windows, and 18–12 metres between a façade with a window and a blank wall (see Figure 2.7). There might be building heights constraints, views that need protecting, and so on. With all these considerations in mind, urban designers begin to resolve the geometrical puzzle, but there are different approaches they can take to do this.

Chapter 2: **The design process**

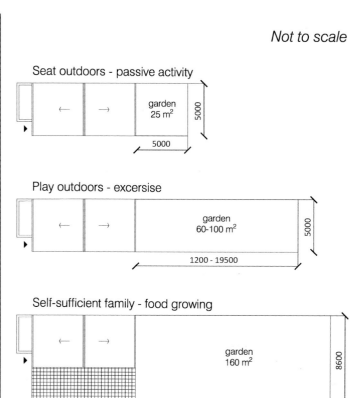

Figure 2.4 Illustration – by the author – of garden sizes as proposed by the authors of *Responsive Environments* (1986). All lengths are in millimeters.

With the UK standard masterplanning approach, parcels are defined to allocate the minimum necessary public space for the place to function and to comply with legal requirements, for example, regarding the amount of recreation space. We can see how a huge amount of land is taken by roads. Very often, after receiving highways authority comments, more land than was initially included in the housing plots needs to pass to public realm to allow for road widths and radii (the curvature of corners). This leaves the

Figure 2.5 Illustration – by the author – showing three types of urban layout pattern: a least land efficient one with cul-de-sacs (also known as dead end roads), one with curved streets and a most land efficient with straight streets and rectangular blocks.

Chapter 2: **The design process** 59

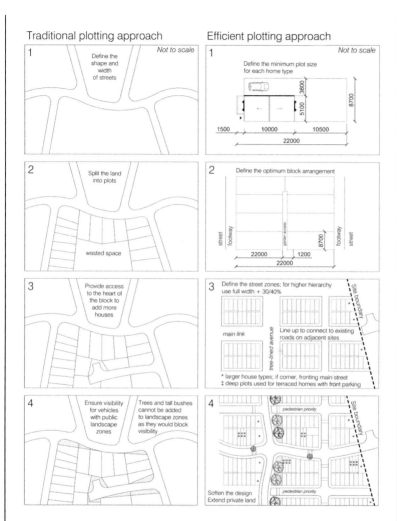

Figure 2.6 Diagram demonstrating the traditional plotting process versus the author's plotting process to minimise viability risks.

60 Chapter 2: **The design process**

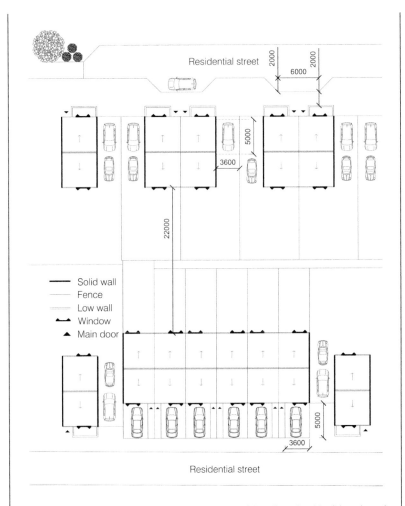

Figure 2.7 Layout illustrating an example of local authorities' legal and conventional requirements regarding residential arrangements to ensure amenity.

Chapter 2: **The design process**

public realm with lots of leftover patches that are no good for any use but that increase maintenance costs. This approach poses a commercial risk for developers as they cannot ascertain with certainty the amount of private land they will profit from. Inevitably, further down the line, some cost savings will have to be made, which often results in compromising the quality of the public realm.

With the alternative approach, private land begins from a bare minimum, starting from the footprint of the house and using the models the developer is going to build on the site. I normally apply a typology ratio that responds to the requirements of the local authority and to the commercial analysis, for example, 40% of four-bedroom family homes, 10% bungalows, and so on. This plotting approach leaves a lot of flexibility to design highways, to include planting, and to shape the public realm without compromising the commercial viability of the scheme. With this approach, it is likely that further down the line, as design progresses, land is taken from the public realm and allocated to private gardens, often even resulting in an increase in housing numbers and a far lower commercial risk for developers.

Table 2.1 Traditional and alternative approaches to housing site layout compared.

Design Stage	Traditional Approach	Alternative Approach
1		Find constraints and opportunities (levels, flood risk, etc.).
2	Site analysis	Protect assets and place character determinants (views, landscape, etc.).
3		Understand site conditions and microclimate (wind, soil quality, etc.).
4	Access and movement	Resolve access and main route and green spaces and water networks.

(Continued)

(Continued)

Design Stage		Traditional Approach	Alternative Approach
5		Add secondary and tertiary routes splitting the land into similar size parcels.	Add secondary routes and work out the position and dimensions of street landscape, sustainable drainage, cycling, and transport infrastructure, maintenance, waste collection, lighting, services, and natural speed control, as shown in the example on Table 2.2.
6	Plotting	Position as many houses as possible according to the parcel geometry.	Work out the optimum land split mathematically, allowing for tertiary routes and using ideal plot dimensions (including parking), as shown in the example on Table 2.2.
7	Detailed design	Resolve parking and waste collection.	Add tertiary routes and additional pedestrian links.
8		Design speed control and adjust to maintenance and service requirements.	Position houses to resolve surveillance and frontages.

(*Continued*)

Chapter 2: **The design process**

(Continued)

Design Stage	Traditional Approach	Alternative Approach
9	Incorporate drainage solutions to the layout already designed.	Determine how landscape (including water) and building character will work together to create place hierarchy and legibility, forming a green space network.
10 Placemaking	Incorporate landscape and open spaces design to the layout.	Work on a placemaking map assigning function and meaning to the public realm, equipping as necessary with a community-building focus.
Overall result tendency	Public realm compromised by design changes along the process. Lower number of houses and inefficient land use with awkward leftover spaces.	Commercial viability and good quality public realm secured. Higher number of houses and more efficient land use.

NOTE: Both approaches can be carried out by designers or through collaborative process, like participatory design and co-design.

Table 2.2 Example of how to measure the public realm.

Item	Reasoning	Example (Nottingham, UK, in 2022)
Carriageway	Different authorities have different requirements regarding the width of roads that serve specific uses and quantum of development. The best way to design is to confirm with the authorities the carriageway dimensions for each street type prior to designing the layout.	Main road: 5.5–6.5 m wide. Residential street: 4.8–5.5 m wide. Private street: 3.6–4.8 m wide.
Footways	Like streets, the width requirements are set by the relevant authorities, as well as the need to provide footpaths that will become part of the highway network. Some authorities can often accept narrower or no footways in specific locations depending on their road safety standards. The best way to design is to confirm with the authorities the need for footways and their dimensions for each street type prior to designing the layout.	Main road: 2 m wide minimum on both sides. Residential street: 2 m wide minimum on one or both sides. Private street: 1.2–2 m wide or no footway depending on street design, connection needs, and whether the street will be private or part of a network. For example, level footway demarcated with insets.

(*Continued*)

Chapter 2: **The design process**

(Continued)

Item	Reasoning	Example (Nottingham, UK, in 2022)
Sustainable drainage	Management of surface/rainfall water and potential flood mitigations need to be considered ahead of any feasibility study. Best place design with highest biodiversity impact can be achieved when water and greenery are designed together. Redesigning layouts to incorporate sustainable forms of drainage can have significant impact on site capacity and often decreases development potential.	It is difficult to regulate drainage because the type and size of design solutions depends highly on site conditions. Minimum standards for sustainable drainage are publicly available in Nottingham and design support is available during pre-application and planning stages.
Street landscape	Deciding where street trees will go is hugely important. Trees are linked to air quality, health and wellbeing, biodiversity, and other benefits. Trees planted in front gardens must not be considered street trees because home owners are at liberty to remove them.	Charge per tree on adopted highway: from £1,500 (2023). Trees planted in public land under a maintenance contract are best issued with a Tree Protection Order that prevents maintenance companies or residents from removing them.

(Continued)

(Continued)

Item	Reasoning	Example (Nottingham, UK, in 2022)
Cycling routes	Safe, easy-to-use cycling routes must be integral to the design. Thinking about these later in the design process can not only impact on the efficiency of the scheme, but can also lead to places being poorly connected. Residential streets do not need dedicated cycling lanes; it is assumed vehicles and bikes can share the carriageway, especially when speed is designed to 20 miles per hour or less.	Dedicated cycling lanes: 2.4 m wide. Combined cycling and walking lanes are not favoured but can be designed when there is no other option. Footways of 3–5 m in width can serve pedestrians and children cycling or scooting to school.
Transport infrastructure	It is common to see developers struggling to adapt their designs for new bus routes, often due to tight pavement widths or highways restrictions that make it difficult to add bus stops. Future-proofing the development by providing adequate space for future transport infrastructure must also happen prior to any feasibility study taking place.	Bus route carriageway: 6.5 m wide. Minimum standards for transport infrastructure are publicly available in Nottingham and design support is available during pre-application and planning stages.

(*Continued*)

Chapter 2: **The design process** 67

(Continued)

Item	Reasoning	Example (Nottingham, UK, in 2022)
Waste collection	Designers tend to assume waste collection will be resolved after a layout is designed, but this is a common mistake that causes developers serious headaches along the way. Local authorities will have guidance regarding their individual waste collection methods, the size of vehicles they use, and the specification of roads for service vehicles. It is highly advisable to contact the highways authority at the outset to establish their requirements.	Individual residential bins must be kept away from the public realm, with easy front access to bins rather than via alleyways in rear gardens. Terrace houses require front bin storage to be integral to the building design. Home owners are expected to walk a maximum of 23 metres to deposit their waste in their bins. Communal bins are favoured in large developments. Waste collection vehicles will not enter a private road or space for collection.

(Continued)

(Continued)

Item	Reasoning	Example (Nottingham, UK, in 2022)
Maintenance	Highways road maintenance teams have a wealth of knowledge regarding the types of materials that work well in their local areas, and contacting them early in the design stages can save developers a huge amount of time. Experts are in tune with how the authorities and service providers manage their repair budgets and can help deliver a more resilient and durable public realm.	The maintenance team in Nottingham worked in collaboration with urban and highways designers to create a guide for developers and applicants. For example, Nottingham will not accept block pavers in corners and around bends because vehicles turning tend to move them, damaging the surface; instead, they recommend tarmac in bends.
Services	Unfortunately, it is not rare to see developments suffering during construction stages when service strips carrying cabling, for example, for lighting, cannot be delivered or conflict with tree pits, urban furniture, or large tree canopies.	Standards for the inclusion of services (e.g. lighting) are publicly available in Nottingham and design support is available during pre-application and planning stages.

(*Continued*)

Chapter 2: **The design process**　　　　　　　　　　　　　　　69

(Continued)

Item	Reasoning	Example (Nottingham, UK, in 2022)
Natural speed control	Designing speed down is much better achieved if it is conceived from the outset and not as an afterthought.	On-street allocated parking: 2.4 m × 6 m Straight roads are favoured because they tend to be more efficient in terms of use of land and quantum of development, but natural speed measures must be included from the outset: horizontal methods (such as chicanes) are preferred and speed bumps are discouraged. Design guides showing how these can be achieved are publicly available.

NOTE: Managing all this information in advance tends to result in more efficient use of land and better quality places.

70 Chapter 2: **The design process**

Figure 2.8 Photo showing The Malings in Newcastle, UK, a residential area where the carriageway adopted by the highways authority is relatively narrow (under 5 metres wide).

Figure 2.9 Photo showing Trent Basin in Nottingham, UK, a residential area where the carriageway adopted by the highways authority is relatively narrow (under 5 metres wide).

Chapter 2: **The design process**

Figure 2.10 Photo showing Houlton in Rugby, UK, a residential area where the carriageway adopted by the highways authority is relatively wide (over 5 metres wide), making the area feel car-dominated.

Figure 2.11 Photo showing a residential area in Nottingham, UK, with a floor arrangement that looks like a very narrow footway and kerb (approximately 400 centimetres wide), but which is simply a service strip containing lighting cables, not an area for walking.

Table 2.3 Land optimisation example.

Item	Reasoning	Example (Nottingham, UK)
House dimensions	If developers have their own house types, plots can be designed to suit those layouts. However, the most land efficient way to work is to determine the house type and layout responding to the proportions and characteristics of the site. If parcels are deep, terrace houses will be a better choice; if there is a very shallow plot, wide frontage layouts such as English cottage style would be more beneficial in that location.	Terrace: 4.5 m wide × 9 m deep. Cottage: 9 m wide × 4.5 m deep. Box: 6 m wide × 8 m deep. *All based on two-storey homes*
On-plot parking	Draw up an option for side parking and one for front parking for house types with no garage. Consider that many people would not park the car in their garage and therefore the authorities might not accept it as a form of parking provision.	Side: 3.6 m wide × 5 m long. Front: 3.6 m wide × 5.5 m long. Garage internal dimensions: 3.6 m wide × 6 m deep.

(*Continued*)

(Continued)

Item	Reasoning	Example (Nottingham, UK)
Front garden	Front gardens are a huge determinant of character and their dimensions are as important as the materials selected for the boundary and surface treatments. A little space at the front of the house is enough for residents to make their own mark with plants and ornaments. In larger spaces, people can plant trees, add furniture, bird feeders, and other items that activate the street scene and make it unique.	Minimum: 0.9 m deep (plants, ornaments, bird feeders). Small: 1.2 m (trees, fountains, chairs). Medium: 2.4 m (small table, bikes, toys). Large: 3.6 m (table set, planters, barbeques). Maximum: 5 m deep (careful to avoid people converting the garden into a parking space). The provision of hard boundaries is a conditioning design criterion.
Rear garden	According to *Responsive Environments*,[10] the average size of a rear garden depends on the types of activities it is designed for: 1–2 people seating: 25 m^2 Children playing/family meals: 60–100 m^2 Growing vegetables: 160 m^2	Nottingham follows the *Responsive Environments* parameters.

(*Continued*)

(Continued)

Item	Reasoning	Example (Nottingham, UK)
Access to rear garden	Some authorities require bins to be stored in rear gardens, which leads to very long, intricate alleyways to avoid going through the house with the bins. A better option would be to provide purpose-built front bin storage as an integral part of the design, which will save lots of land whilst providing a neat, convenient solution. Access to rear gardens does not justify small corridors between houses. This not only wastes space but also creates more external walls, which are more expensive to build and require much more insulation.	Small corridors between dwellings are strongly discouraged. Integrated bin storage solutions are required, mostly in the front aspect of dwellings. Shared rear garden access corridors: 1.2 m wide and to be minimised in length, with locked gate and fully paved, level surface.

(*Continued*)

(Continued)

Item	Reasoning	Example (Nottingham, UK)
Waste storage	Waste collection is a very important factor, as bins left on footways and litter spillage can completely ruin the appearance of a place and can lead to movement issues for some people (e.g. wheelchair users). Bin collection points should not be too far from the house and must be in a location that is fully accessible by the service providers.	Individual bins: 1 m deep × 2 m wide × 1.3 m high. Communal bins (approximately every six homes): 3 m × 4.5 m × 1.5 m high. Bin collection points must be no more than 23 m away from the dwelling they serve. *Size and type determined by local authority*
Utility storage	Designers must always consider a range of lifestyles and needs, from where residents will leave their coats and muddy shoes as they enter the house to where they will safely store equipment they might use on a daily basis, such as prams or mobility scooters.	Mobility aid: 1 m deep × 1.5 m wide × 1.6 m high. Pram: 0.6 m × 1.2 m × 1.5 m. Bicycle: 0.6 m × 1.2 m × 2 m per bike. Scooters: 0.5 m deep × 1 m wide × 1.2 m high.

NOTE: Managing all this information in advance tends to result in more efficient use of land and better quality places because plots are no bigger than necessary but not too small to compromise function; they are just right.

Lessons learnt

Perhaps the main conclusion I can draw from Case Studies 2.1 and 2.2 is the absolute imperative to understand the site inside out before beginning to make design decisions. It is true that humans have the faculty to reason and make logic decisions when confronted with problems; we can also understand data, process it, and come up with answers and ideas. However, designers must never forget that the first thing humans do when they arrive at a place is feel it. We are, above all, emotional beings. People tend to refer to places by saying things like "I love New York", "Buenos Aires is an exciting place", "There is something about Amsterdam; I cannot put my finger on it but the place feels cool."

We are designing places for people. The more detached we become from the way people 'feel' places, the more detached our designs will be from achieving that quality and sustainability we aim for, and the best way to understand how people feel is to work alongside them. Case Study 2.1 showed that when professionals move towards more inclusive

Table 2.4 Case study analysis summary.

Case Study	Topic	What Was Different?	Outcome
2.1 School	Support of social sciences	Collaboration between different fields of expertise during the design stage	Positive
	Community engagement	End users had the time and appropriate environment to explain what places meant to them	Positive
2.2 Housing	Exhaustive understanding of local regulations	Bringing detailed design information to the beginning of the design process	Positive
	Securing land value	Designing for the specific public space and service requirements: *outside-in* urban design	Positive

Chapter 2: **The design process**

Figure 2.12 Photograph of a mural in a Catholic area of Belfast, Northern Ireland, UK. The image depicts an armed militia soildier and a sign saying: "You are now entering loyalist Sandy Row, heart of South Belfast Ulster Freedom Fighters".

Figure 2.13 Photograph of a mural in a Protestant area of Belfast, Northern Ireland, UK. The mural portraits the Queen Mother, a poem, and the royal coats of arms.

forms of practice, where placemaking is everyone's job, this will not jeopardise the role of professionals; rather, it will strengthen it.

I will raise a simple thought: doctors can give you a diagnosis and often offer you alternative solutions, perhaps a prescription or other form of treatment, such as suggesting lifestyle changes. But ultimately, it is your decision to accept their advice or not; it is your body. I see place professionals in a similar way: we can offer technical support to people on how they can inhabit their places. I believe people and places are so intimately related that one could not exist without the other. People give places meaning over time, they pack it with cultural references and a singular identity that develops over time. I could never imagine designing a public place for Belfast, for example, without a deep understanding of how people feel about their socio-political context, a level of understanding that literature could never reach.

Tool 2: Urban design plan of work

The role of urban designers is to offer and co-ordinate the technical and social sciences knowledge to serve the end user. This is a task of such complexity that planning the optimum way to work for each case is an absolutely critical step to take. So, based on my experience in practice, I will share an Urban Design Plan of Work for those in urban practice to adapt as they see convenient. Of course, as is the case with the RIBA Stages of Design, the relevance and length of each stage will depend on the type and scale of the development.

Stage 1: Context

Before attempting to learn anything about a site, one should always understand the regional context covering the three strands: Economic, Social, and Environmental. This should be done in a longitudinal way, which means studying the topics over time. The first stage in any urban study is understanding the role of the site as part of the larger whole through its history, finding patterns of change and evolution. This involves, as a bare minimum, looking at key historic events, political powers surrounding the area, the meaning of the place to local people across time, its role as part of a productive or economic landscape, its role as part of the larger natural ecosystem, and the visual impact of the site in the area and vice versa. This information will be useful to shape the content and characteristics of the rest of the process. It will be particularly helpful to find those key groups, people, and organisations that can help designers achieve a proposal that is truly in context. It is also a key stage in the design process to ensure proposals can offer the best to local people, including any strategies to erode the segregation and disadvantage of specific groups. Given the impact large-scale developments have in our social, economic, and natural landscapes, approaching a design process without completing this essential part of the job is not only irresponsible but also unethical: it could potentially lead to seriously unsustainable results.

> For example, a surgeon is highly unlikely to attempt a serious operation without prior information regarding the patient. Yet, designers go ahead building neighbourhoods without adequate social impact analysis. The damage designers can cause with large-scale developments could potentially be enormous.

Stage 2: Networks

The second stage in the process is mapping the collaboration networks that will make the process effective, efficient, and rich in content. With a decent amount of information and gained knowledge about the region and local area, the urban designer can begin to establish working partnerships and plan collaboration strategies populating a schedule of work. Knowing who to talk to and where to go for information and networking is a critical part of the process, which can make or break the success of the scheme. This social network analysis is no different to mapping environmental or historic assets. Urban designers can colour historic buildings on a map by age or significance, and we often do just that. We could also mark green spaces and classify them by rating their biodiversity or recreational worth, and we often do that, too. However, I have never encountered a social network map in practice. It is not difficult to do, especially since many community groups are very active on social media. It is as simple as collating a contact list of potential key contributors, classifying them by looking at their potential input by theme or area of interest, and finding out where they are based. So, if designers crave map colouring, they could always produce a map showing the areas, places, and buildings where people meet, classifying them by frequency of activity or by interest. These areas are crucial magnets that generate movement flow, and mapping them could help visualise the social assets of an area, also establishing if there is lack of spaces that foster activity. Urban designers could also explore how long these groups have been operating in the area, if they are formally organised like a sports club or if they operate informally like a walking group. Often, members belong to more than one network, so connecting these groups in the shape of a web. This is a very significant piece of information, crucial to ensure a meaningful engagement strategy and securing high levels of participation in events and workshops that can help shape the scheme. Finding out the group leaders or administrators is a very speedy way to reach out to numerous people and groups within communities, a brilliant channel to distribute information and to collect feedback. Planners and urban designers very often complain that not enough people participate in consultations, yet this crucial step that can prevent poor engagement is consistently missing from the process. This issue is explored further in Chapter 3.

Stage 3: Agents and influencers

The third stage is to plan the schedule of work and co-ordinate collaboration between all the different parties that will become involved in the process: authorities and organisations, industries and academia, and communities. At this point, it would be good to remember that authorities and organisations regulate, legislate, and control what happens in the land: they averse in all the different legal clauses that

Chapter 2: **The design process**　　　　　　　　　　　　　　　　　　　　81

Figure 2.14 Diagram showing the author's classification of engagement groups according to communication tools and workshop strategies required during events: authorities and organisations, industries and academia, and communities.

will apply to the project. Industries will eventually make things happen, and they have a wealth of knowledge about what could or could not work in practice, what is feasible and what is not. Communities will turn the space into a place, they will live it and give life to it, they will make it either a success or a failure, and they will transform it over time. No urban designer can do their job effectively without the input of those three groups; in fact, the job of the urban designer is actually to co-ordinate all thinking and to bring parties together in the best possible way for the best possible outcome – not to think on behalf of others.

Stage 4: Place vision

The fourth stage is to initiate an idea of a vision for what the place will be and the role it will have as a component of a larger whole in the short, medium, and long term. When I am doing design reviews as an expert panel member in England, I often ask the question: how many years in the future have you designed for? The answers I have had so far ranged from 5 to 20 years.[3] But I would like to think that we are designing cities and neighbourhoods that will live longer than that. Future-proofing developments implies thinking at least 100 years ahead, which is a very difficult concept to grasp but one that is fundamental for achieving greater sustainability. Many of the roads we drive through in Europe were planned and first built by the Romans – not hundreds, but thousands of years ago! Granted, in the UK, many of them look as if they had not been resurfaced since!

Sometimes it is landowners that have a dream about what the place will be like in the future, other times the first glimpse of a vision comes from designers, landscapers, or other members of the design team. At times, it is politicians that inspire the future of a place or planners with their development framework documents for the region or the local area. With the launch of the UK National Planning Policy Framework,[4] the agenda to decentralise power by the British government initiated a period of increased neighbourhood engagement and governance through the introduction of Neighbourhood Plans[5] and other planning mechanisms like Local Development Orders[6] and Local Listing.[7] All of these tools were designed to encourage local communities to create visions for their localities. Although this was a positive first step in encouraging place democracy, these tools were optional, and underprivileged communities often found themselves lacking resources and skills to deliver the strategies. Additionally, the technical complexity of the British planning system became a barrier in many urban areas. With these tools, community empowerment was heavily reliant on existing social capital.[8] The reform proposed by the Ministry of Housing Communities and Local Government (2020) afterwards went a step further, bringing community engagement to the early stages of the design process. With this approach, communities could engage in processes led by local authorities, developers, or landowners prior to any design

Chapter 2: **The design process** 83

taking place. In a nutshell, communities have been given the right to participate by informing that place vision. This is an internationally growing trend, the product of a social media-focused lifestyle where people feel they can express their voice in all matters with immediate effect. Some see this perception of rights over places as dangerous, as a way of losing power or control, whilst I see it as refreshing, and although it is challenging, I cannot wait to see how people feel more empowered in the future.

Stage 5: Accountability tools

Ideally, the urban designer would lead the process of creating a place vision shared by all, where everyone understands the limitations and constraints of the site and where everyone appreciates the social, economic, and environmental assets that need to be identified and built upon to create more successful places. It is at this point that the critical task of setting tools to appraise design quality and sustainable credentials needs to take place. This is the time for all the parties involved to agree to the level of accountability and how and when evaluations are going to take place. A simple way to achieve this is adopting a combination of already available and well-tested tools compatible with the project location. UK-based design teams I am part of normally adopt schemes like the RIBA Sustainable Goals[9] for buildings, the Manual for Streets[10] guidance for roads, and British Building for a Healthy Life[11] for the design of neighbourhoods as a bare minimum. It is the role of everyone involved to stay up to date and informed about new tools and software applications for use in practice.

Stage 6: Site analysis

Assuming landowners, developers, and other specialist agencies progress with their land agreements and other legal documents, it is now time for urban designers to commence the in-depth site analysis. Although designers need a huge sense of commercial awareness and understanding of land optimisation techniques in order to make the most of the land, the details regarding costs, budgets, and commercial agreements are not in their hands. Often, commercial decisions taken later on in the process force design changes that diminish the strength of the original place vision. It is the job of the urban designer to ensure this type of negative impact is minimal. The site analysis we are referring to here involves the more technical evaluation of physical and sensorial aspects of the site (how we feel about the place); sadly, the latter is still rare to see in practice.

Technical investigations depend on the nature of the site, but the first aspect to cover is the legislative framework, or in other words, the laws and regulations that apply to the land. These are normally a combination of national, regional, and local policies and planning guidance. Urban designers should review these legal documents to ensure that their future designs are in compliance with statutory requirements and that designs respond to the aspirations of the region or area. For example, an archaeological survey might be required by law if there is the suspicion of ancient settlements on the site; a flood risk analysis is always required in the UK to mitigate any impact of climate change; a biodiversity study would highlight the need to protect or enhance specific natural assets; site levels might be necessary to estimate how steep roads will be or if rainwater can drain naturally towards the lowest point. Every country, province, or region will have some specific technical appraisal requirements. Every site is different and some might merit further in-depth analysis in certain area of expertise. The urban designer would be the person who recommends which studies are relevant for the site and which are necessary to inform the design on the basis of potential technical or legislative constraints.

A good urban designer will also conduct sensorial investigations. This involves going to the site to systematically walk through and around it, capturing and mapping information like noise, smells, microclimatic conditions like sun and shade or wind, and looking for key views from and towards the site. A walk around the perimeter would be crucial to identify potential boundary issues and opportunities: perhaps there is a neighbouring property in close proximity with overviewing challenges; maybe there is a pedestrian path that could connect directly with a new street in the development. Ideally, this evaluation would be carried out at different times of the day, in different seasons and weathers, but it is

Chapter 2: **The design process** 85

usually impossible to extend the design process for such long periods of time. This is when the local community could come to the rescue. Nobody understands the place like those who live there and experience it regularly. This is why doing a site walkabout with the local community is such an important step in the process, because it is a simple and

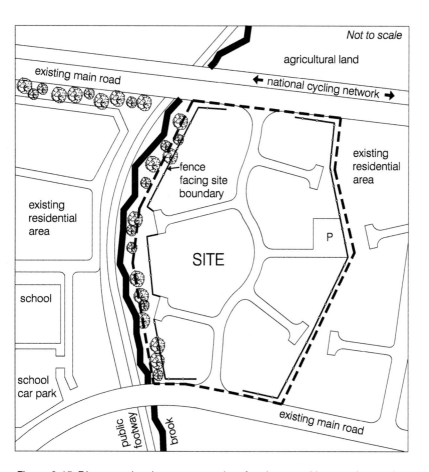

Figure 2.15 Diagram showing an example of a layout with poor integration between the existing area and the proposed development, where pedestrian and cycling links are not provided, the rear garden fence faces public spaces, and new roads do not connect with existing streets.

effective way to gather critical information, whilst strengthening the relationship with neighbours.

A critical point to make is that far too often, master planners are driven by the red boundary that delineates the extent of their client's land ownership. This is particularly problematic and frequently results in poor integration of the scheme with its immediate environment. I have witnessed the construction of streets and paths with dead ends that do not connect new areas to the existing neighbourhood, blank walls facing gorgeous views, and inaccessible water streams and green zones. The red site boundary should not be included in drafts or working plans; it should first appear in the plan after the relevant design stage has been completed. One thing is the legal boundary of the land transfer, in other words, the bit of land that will be sold; a very different thing is the design zone boundary: this is further away from the legal edge of the land because the new design needs to be stitched to the existing environment. Clients, developers, and landowners need to be educated in the issue of boundaries to mitigate poor integration.

Stage 7: Data gathering

This stage involves gathering all the regional and local information and forming a catalogue of data, which could be classified by theme or chronologically as the urban designer finds most appropriate for the project. This data should be formatted in a way and medium that facilitates transparent information sharing, as it will be needed by multiple parties along the design process. A combination of digital platforms is often a good way to manage information, but at the time of writing, there are still those who have no or limited access to technology, so provision should be made for printed versions of the regional and site analysis findings. It might also be appropriate to produce a presentation or some form of video that can be shared with the public to explain the key characteristics of the place and the core assets that might be significant in informing the design solutions. The most common error developers make is to hide information from the public. What I find in practice is that people see information sharing as a sign of transparency that results in a build up of trust and a higher likelihood to establish a more honest and open debate. Reluctancy to share information is mainly seen as a sign of having something to hide or a lot to hide, sometimes.

Stage 8: SWOT or CO

Stage 8 is all about understanding the strengths, weaknesses, opportunities, and threats of the site, a process often referred to as SWOT. Some designers combine these into opportunities (strengths and opportunities) and constraints (weaknesses and threats) to produce a simpler version of the analysis. Both are equally valid and their use largely depends on the type and complexity of the project. The crucial point here is to either determine these working alongside all relevant *engagement groups*, including authorities, industries, and communities, or to make sure the urban designers' classification is corroborated and agreed with by all engagement groups. This is extremely important because it is the main strategy urban designers have to help others make sense of the design decisions that will follow. Without a shared information platform, a common understanding, and consensual agreement about the key site assets and issues, negotiations during the design process become virtually impossible. If everyone knows what the problem is, everyone will appreciate ideas for solutions, they will debate them, and, together, they will agree the best way forward. Without knowing the problem, any suggestion might be perceived as capricious, threatening, or deliberately beneficial to some, even when that is far from the truth.

Stage 9: Development framework

With all the site investigation information from the previous stage, plus the initial vision, urban designers can move on to gathering all relevant parties to collaborate in producing a development framework that everyone agrees with. This document will determine the design approach and principles, critical design criteria to deliver the place vision, relevant processes and procedures, participation and engagement methods, delivery phasing, minimum environmental credentials, expected social outputs, appraisal tools adopted, and so on. Ideally, this is a process that happens through combined workshops and joint action. Bringing people from different backgrounds together to understand and shape a place that will affect their lives is a powerful way to help form alliances, trigger community projects, build up skills, increase social cohesion, and ultimately raise the levels of social resilience. However, there are times when there is historic conflict or tension between groups or agencies and when it is better to begin with individual groups, gradually eroding those frictions through the process to bring people together for a joined goal. This is why it is so important that urban designers complete STAGE 2, so as to understand social structures, local powers, and potential clashes or conflicts.

Stage 10: Supplementary documents

Documenting the process and its outcomes up to this point is now a critical part of the job. A new brief will contain information about how the networking and engagement took place. Another document will deal with the summary of the outcomes agreed by all parties. With a shared, consensual vision, a list of opportunities and constraints, and a wealth of information about the site, the urban designer can begin to think about setting a schedule of work to start shaping the proposals.

Stage 11: Concept design

Perhaps it is time to notice that we still have not got a design and yet we are already entering Stage 11. Fear not, this level of preparation is what will make the scheme a successful one. However, it is not rare to see master planners jumping straight into the design stage simply because it is the one they are most familiar with or because it is what clients are prepared to pay for. At this point, the urban designer can proceed in two different ways: they can produce a concept design based on their knowledge and experience to then work alongside the engagement groups in perfecting those ideas or they can go to the engagement groups with a blank piece of paper and go through the process alongside them, co-designing the concept scheme. The first approach allows the urban designer to test

Chapter 2: **The design process** 89

various options and corroborate commercial viability with their expert team members prior to committing to any idea the public might like. This is positive, in that it is faster as a process and might remove some of the risk of disappointment in those community members that put time and effort into trying to influence the design. The second option is more open and transparent, but it requires longer time frames and more resources.

Figure 2.16 Diagram showing an example of a concept masterplan, where zones are indicated in different colours and lines and arrows are used to summarise the thinking behind the proposal rather than a finished design.

We will come back to explore this topic further in Chapter 6. The important point to make is that from this step, the urban designer will leave with a set of concept design principles that will help them start shaping the scheme. These might include the location of access points, the position of the main road, clues about necessary enhancements to public transport provision (such as new bus routes or cycling lane connections), the protection of nice views or heritage and natural assets, and so on. These agreed principles can now be marked in an indicative plan, which normally takes the name of *concept design diagram*.

Stage 12: Development brief

Now it is time for a desktop task: the production of the development brief, a summary that tells the story of the whole process and its outcomes. This brief should address all the issues described above and all the research evidence and technical aspects of the site as well as the shaping of the place vision, the summary of constraints and opportunities, and the concept design diagram. This is the brief that tells everyone how the design principles were informed by the site investigations and how collaboration took place with all key parties. As nature is a little slower than builders, if areas of tree planting have been highlighted, now is the time to get this done ahead of schedule, to ensure trees achieve some growth, giving time for the ecosystem to develop before people occupy the space.

It is also a good time to begin the process for the provision of new infrastructure or enhancements to existing networks, if this has not already taken place. Crucially, if there are any pending legal agreements regarding land ownership transference, commercial agreements, phase development commitments, or potential contributions (moneys the developer must hand over to the authority to upgrade services or infrastructure) between parties, now is a good time to put those in place.

Stage 13: Developed design

Now that there is a clear guide to follow, urban designers can move towards the developed design stage, repeating the process, but this time adding more detail to the concept design. In Chapters 3 and 4, we will explore how the different agencies have different levels of involvement at each stage in the design process. This developed design stage is all about beginning to look at the different layers of the design, zooming in with information and specification. For example, thinking how domestic waste will be collected, establishing the location and hierarchy of streets, defining the use of green or public areas, assigning protected view zones that cannot be built on, locating zones of rainwater storage, and so on.

Urban designers can also begin to plot the land. The optimum way to do this would be to establish the depth and width of plots according to the shape and conditions of the site, to make the place work harder to accommodate the different uses more efficiently. In some countries – the UK, for example – large areas of land are released for housing, so, instead of building in individual plots as happens more commonly elsewhere – for example, in South America – house building developers and contractors build whole neighbourhoods in one go. To make this process more manageable, less risky, and more profitable, house builders have model houses that they repeat across the land. This process means that the plot sizes have to be tailored to those models, as we saw in Case Study 2.2. It is not rare to see unused strips of land or plots that are larger than necessary in a housing masterplan. This is an inefficient way to partition sites, which ultimately results in lower housing numbers than the land could accommodate, and very often creates less interesting places.

A critical task that can be completed at this stage is the definition of roads. Everyone knows that there are some roads that need to be wider than others, some that are lined up with trees, some are narrower. This step gives urban designers an opportunity to start thinking about that essential place structure that will give the neighbourhoods their own character and identity. In the English language, there are several names for roads: streets, lanes, avenues, boulevards, crescents, walks, and so on. All these names have different meanings and suggest different types of environments. This road characterisation is one of the design resources that can make one zone different from another, and it helps people find their way around the neighbourhood and orientate themselves. Now imagine a place where all houses and all roads look the

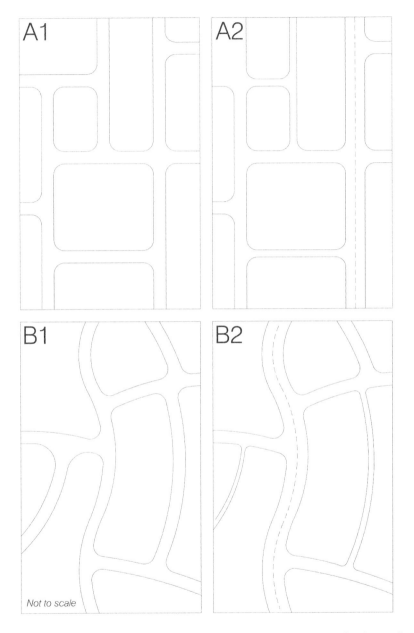

Figure 2.17 The figure shows two example layouts (A1 and B1) where all streets look exactly the same, and two layouts (A2 and B2) with street hierarchy.

same; it would be something like an urban maze. Unfortunately, a lot of that has been built in the UK in recent years.

Having followed the whole developed design stage process, the urban designer now has a *developed design plan* that they can confidently submit for approval or sign off by all relevant parties, such as clients, authorities, and communities. In the UK, the project would now be ready for Outline Planning submission, which means that the principles of design are agreed and approved by the authorities, whilst a lot of the details are pending further approval. This process is useful, as it can give developers greater certainty about their investment.

Stage 14: Detailed design

Once everyone agrees on the idea and potentially the design achieves permission from the authorities to go ahead, the urban designer can begin the next step: to start defining the details of the design. At this stage, they would be looking at surface materials, colours, planting species, urban furniture, lighting, bin storage, and so on. If there is any opportunity for the community to co-design or co-build parts of the development, this is a good time for the urban designer to organise people into groups and plan the engagement strategy. Also, this is a good time to begin to define how the building stage will be carried out, such as the logistics of deliveries, which plots will be built first, and where the showroom will be.

After the detailed design stage is completed and agreed with all parties, the project will be ready for submission to obtain all necessary legal approvals. In the UK, this would be the Full Planning submission stage, when most of the details are agreed. If some remain pending, these are items that can be decided at a later stage through a process called Planning Conditioning. For example, it might be difficult to be explicit about the colour and type of bricks if they are likely to become unavailable due to production shortages; planners know that this detail can be agreed later on in the process, and in the UK, they *condition* the planning approval, which will only be fully validated upon submission of all necessary information later on. This is helpful for developers because it means they can commence groundworks avoiding major delays.

Many administrations across the world use documents called 'design codes'. These are similar to the development brief mentioned above, but they tend to focus on the physical and aesthetic aspects of the design, specifying the key components and the 'dos and don'ts' of the development. Design codes can be produced at the concept stage, at the developed design stage, and/or at the detailed design stage. Of course, the level of detail will vary according to the stage in the process the project is at. These codes should be developed in collaboration with all the engagement groups for the design to work for everyone. At the very least, the engagement groups should be given an opportunity to comment on its contents, and the final result must be agreed by all parties. This is an essential part of the process, because it secures place democracy, which helps make communities more resilient, as we will see in Chapter 6. Engaging broadly is also the best way to address, Passet's Social Sphere (see Chapter 1) and the social sustainability credentials of the development are at lower risk of becoming compromised (see Figure 1.10).

Stage 15: Post-occupancy

What happens after the project is handed over to its occupants or owners has been an area of neglect in the field. Designs that are not fit for purpose in the long term are highly unsustainable. How the project is run, and how the proposal is built, maintained, and disposed of, can make a huge impact on its sustainability credentials. Designers must try to imagine all possible scenarios, testing their proposals are capable to adapt and withstand future demands. Of course, predicting the future is very hard – think of the unexpected impact of Covid-19, for example, but we must use reliable information available to us to make our best estimations.

Traditionally, public realm design is concerned with the safety and security of users. For example, safeguarding the public from potential attacks, vehicular collisions onto pedestrians, ventilation – in case of a global pandemic – and so on. In some locations, public place design is so strongly dictated by the need to keep people safe that public safety becomes the priority, often compromising aesthetics, mobility, and access. This is a way to future-proof the development based on contemporary tendencies.

Post-occupancy design is also about understanding how the design performs functionally and if it is practical for all. Understanding what works and what does not is a crucial aspect of sustainability, one that should be an integral part of the design process from day one. Designers aiming to deliver sustainable developments must advise their clients that a thorough open evaluation of the project has to happen after occupancy. Ideally, developers would welcome an opportunity to correct serious errors and publish best practice guidance based on the evidence gathered. Wishful thinking perhaps, because, sadly, neither developers nor designers tend to put themselves in a position where they might become publicly criticised, often for fear of reputational damage. This is partly why post-occupancy reports are rare. However, this can help developers to learn and progress for future developments, to make them even more successful.

One under-explored aspect of post-occupancy is the capacity of projects to create communities, to build up social resilience, and to deliver social value. This is generally the case because the design process is not considered a placemaking continuum or a geographical ecosystem. In the current form of practice, the design process finishes when the building is handed over to its occupants or owners. The reality is that places change constantly; in fact, the best places are developed over time and with input from a wide range of agencies. If the industry understood the meaning of place, there would be a far more flexible path to long-term delivery, one that accepts that a number of transformations must happen before the agreed place vision begins to emerge. Instead, we work with a format that assumes the project begins at construction and concludes at handover.

As we might begin to gather, urban designers need diverse and specific skills to tackle all the complexities of their work. I sincerely hope this chapter begins to show now that the difference between designing a building and a whole area or neighbourhood is immense. It is a different job, both in content and process.

Now the specialist skills an urban designer needs are probably becoming apparent, not only they should be able to design, but also to moderate, co-ordinate, organise, and act as diplomats.

Table 2.5 Essential urban design skills.

Good Urban Designers Can Do These Things:		
Work	Think About	Understand
Within political frameworks Negotiating to add value Based on evidence Bridging theory and practice Joining disciplines and communities	Human needs first Systems and processes Space between buildings Long-term changes Context and culture	Society and behaviour Policy and land ownership Design and form Economy and value Natural environments

Table 2.6 Tool 2: The urban design plan of work.

Stage 1	Context	Understanding the region covering the three strands: economic, social and environmental, and how they change over time.
Stage 2	Networks	Mapping the collaboration networks that will make the process effective, efficient, and rich in content.
Stage 3	Agents and influencers	Co-ordinating collaboration between all the different parties that will become involved in the process: authorities and organisations, industries, and communities.
Stage 4	Place vision	Initiating an idea of a vision for what the place will be and the role it will have as a component of a larger whole in the short, medium, and long term.

(*Continued*)

(Continued)

Stage		
Stage 5	Accountability tools	Setting, adapting, or adopting tools to appraise design quality and sustainable credentials at different stages during the design process.
Stage 6	Site analysis	Conducting legislative, technical, and sensorial site investigations.
Stage 7	Data gathering	Gathering all the regional and local information to form a catalogue of data, which could be classified by theme or chronologically.
Stage 8	SWOT/CO	Understanding and summarising the strengths, weaknesses, opportunities, and threats of the site.
Stage 9	Development framework	Agreeing design approach and principles, critical design criteria to deliver the place vision, relevant processes and procedures, participation and engagement methods, delivery phasing, minimum environmental credentials, expected social outputs, appraisal tools adopted, and so on.
Stage 10	Supplementary documents	Documenting how the networking, engagement, and agreement took place and setting up a schedule of work.
Stage 11	Concept design	Producing or co-producing a concept design based on the work produced and evidence gathered to date.
Stage 12	Development brief	Producing a summary that tells the story of the whole process and its outcomes and how the technical information led to various design ideas and the chosen design solution.
Stage 13	Developed design	Producing or co-producing a more developed proposal based on the work produced and evidence gathered to date.

(Continued)

(Continued)

| Stage 14 | Detailed design | Defining or co-defining the details of the design once the proposal obtained consensus or outline permission to build. |
| Stage 15 | Placemaking and post-occupancy | Returning to the place regularly to evaluate the outcomes of the design, summarising successes, and lessons learnt. |

The main focus of this chapter was to illustrate a typical urban design process with the understanding that, as happens in architecture, every project is different and will require process adaptations and modifications according to the political, social, economic, and environmental nature of the development. However, as architects use and adapt their model Plan of Work, urban designers could use the template suggested in this chapter to begin planning their own urban design processes.

Perhaps the one thing that has become apparent in this chapter is how the many different agents involved in the process have a role to play and how they might have very important information or knowledge to input at different stages of the process. In further chapters, we will see who all those different agents are, what their roles and powers are in shaping the design of developments, and what impact their actions could have in the sustainable credentials of a project.

I would now like to ask those studying or practising urban design – or masterplanning – to reflect what design stages they tend to prioritise and the reasons why they do so, and to consider if they might have omitted some of the stages we discussed, and why this is the case. Could your project have been more successful had you followed all suggested stages?

Notes

1 RIBA, *Plan of Work* (London: RIBA, 2020). Accessed on 09.18.21 at www.ribaplanofwork.com.
2 Sue McGlynn, Graham Smith, Alan Alcock, Paul Murrain, and Ian Bentley, *Responsive Environments: A Manual for Designers*, 1st ed. (London: Routledge, 1985).

Chapter 2: **The design process**

3 A design review is a process where an independent panel evaluates a design during the planning process and makes recommendations for improvement.
4 Ministry of Housing, Communities and Local Government, *National Planning Policy Framework* (2014). "Communities were allowed to form working groups to produce evidence-based legislation and recommendations for development in their area. Neighbourhood planning gives communities direct power to develop a shared vision for their neighbourhood and shape the development and growth of their local area. They are able to choose where they want new homes, shops and offices to be built, have their say on what those new buildings should look like and what infrastructure should be provided, and grant planning permission for the new buildings they want to see go ahead. Neighbourhood planning provides a powerful set of tools for local people to plan for the types of development to meet their community's needs and where the ambition of the neighbourhood is aligned with the strategic needs and priorities of the wider local area." Paragraph: 001 Reference ID: 41-001-20190509; Revision date: 09.05.2019. Accessed on 07.12.21 at www.gov.uk/guidance/neighbourhood-planning--2.
5 See endnote 4.
6 A planning tool to grant planning permission within set boundaries without the need to go through a planning application process.
7 Communities could justify the need to protect historic or community assets they found valuable by demonstrating public support. After a scrutiny process, the asset could enter a Local List to be considered of special community value.
8 Social Capital: concept in social science that involves the potential of individuals to secure benefits and invent solutions to problems through membership in social networks. Social capital revolves around three dimensions: interconnected networks of relationships between individuals and groups (social ties or social participation), levels of trust that characterise these ties, and resources or benefits that are both gained and transferred by virtue of social ties and social participation (*Encyclopedia Britannica*, 2022).
9 Royal Institute of British Architects, *RIBA Sustainable Goals* (London: RIBA, 2019).
10 Department for Transport, *Manual for Streets* (London: Thomas Telford Ltd, 2007).
11 David Birkbeck and Stefan Kruczkowski, *Building for a Healthy Life* (London: Design for Homes, 2020).

Chapter 3
Design agents

Chapter 2 looked at how critical the design process is to achieve design quality and sustainability. It suggested starting projects by planning very carefully what to do at each stage and it gave a model Urban Design Plan of Work to follow and adapt. During the chapter, the collaboration potential and the critical input of various groups and agencies at different stages began to become apparent.

This chapter will explore those design agents in more detail, especially focusing on how non-designers can – and sometimes must – contribute to the design process effectively to make the scheme fit for purpose and to secure a smooth transition during handover and beyond. Those who are just beginning to immerse themselves in the world of the built environment will find this a practical aid to clarify the different roles and responsibilities in the field. The examples I have chosen will help decision-makers appreciate the consequences that lack of delegated power, accountability, and specialist skills can have on the end result and how it can increase the amount of time and resources needed to complete the project tasks.

In an architectural design process, there is normally a client or a group of clients who commission the architect to produce a design – or various options – for them, or simply to test what can be built on their land, or how their existing buildings can be converted, updated, or repurposed. These tests are concept designs that will probably never be built but that demonstrate the potential of the client's assets; these types of exercises are called *feasibility studies*. They are very useful documents to sell assets or to borrow money against those assets as well as to plan their future. In fact, the vast majority of what an architect designs will remain on paper. Preparing feasibility studies is a huge proportion of an architect's job. A similar thing happens with masterplans and large-scale projects. In the UK, it is rather usual to see landowners prepare planning applications simply to demonstrate the value of their land, which they often aim to sell. Many clients commission urban designers to produce these plans for this purpose; then they sit and wait to see that commercial value rise, as housing – or other uses – become more urgently needed in the area.

As also happens with the design of buildings, any proposed masterplan will change many times, often vastly, as different agencies comment on how to make the design work for their requirements and legal frameworks. For example, it is not unusual to see the highways authority asking designers to alter the shape and size of streets and crossings to meet their own regional criteria. I would consider it miraculous if the initial masterplan goes to construction stage. In fact, just as in architecture, probably most of the work urban designers produce will never materialise. Some people have asked me whether I find this frustrating, but the truth is that a new blank piece of paper is a new challenge, a new puzzle to resolve. The excitement of having to visualise how a new place could work soon overrules any frustrations from the previous project.

The input clients have during the design process can vary immensely, from simply letting designers get on with the job to becoming very involved and co-designing the scheme. The power of clients is also variable: I have worked with clients who think they have just found themselves a design machine; they would call me at four in the morning to ask for an additional drawing for their meeting; they would set deadlines from a Friday to a Monday, subsuming my weekend, and some made me work like Sisyphus.[1] I worked for a very well-known supermarket chain that did just that, but other clients are more relaxed: they follow professional advice and value their design team's expertise, which makes the job a lot more enjoyable.

There are projects that have more than one client, and this is not rare to see. Often, buildings will be shared or the land will be split between various owners. I had a large job where two landowners had joined their plots to build a larger area together. This was better than producing two small, different-looking neighbourhoods. Both had different ideas of what they wanted to build but an equal stake in the project; it was my job as an urban designer to harness their views and produce something that worked for both. But clients are not the only agents who will have a significant say on the shape of a development. It often happens that design changes need to take place for legal reasons or in order to obtain permission to build from the authorities. In cases like this, clients are rather powerless and can do little to influence the design. This shift of power happens many times during an urban design process, mainly because the complexity of the large-scale jobs means that different expertise fields will need to make an input to make the place work. In that sense, it is the design team rather than the urban designer that comes up with design solutions that are adequate for the place. We will talk about how different agencies can influence design in Chapter 6; let us look at the lead design agents in more detail now.

The design team

The size and skills of a leading design team will vary depending on the nature of the project. For example, for a typical project of 200 new homes, the team would normally involve, as a minimum: the clients, a planner, a landscape architect, a highways engineer, and an urban designer. The client will provide the brief for the scheme, stating what is it that the team needs to achieve in order to make the project work commercially (how it will sell) and financially (how much it will cost). They will also provide all the necessary information to enable the design team to complete their job. They will commission any necessary further investigations such as soil studies, flooding and drainage reports, heritage assets investigations, and so on. The planner will look at the legality of the scheme and will appraise how the proposals respond to policy. The landscape architect will appraise and manage the impact of the scheme in its context, looking at views, the type of planting species that will work in the area, and so on. The highways engineer will be in charge of roads, streets, bridges, and access points. They will verify if the proposal complies with the highways regulations of the area and they will confirm that the new network will have enough capacity, avoiding major impact, further traffic, and congestion on existing road

Chapter 3: **Design agents**

networks. They will also make sure road safety standards are met. The urban designer brings everyone together and joins all the pieces of the puzzle in a coherent way. It is the urban designer who will look at the functionality of the scheme as a whole, how it links with the existing context, how the place achieves its unique character and identity, how it functions, and what it will look and feel like. Now we can see how some of the different parts that form this team have critical roles, which explains how those powers to influence the design will shift at different stages in the design process. This power shift is something an urban designer needs to understand and manage well, sometimes negotiating trade-offs and using diplomacy to come to suitable agreements. The role of an urban designer goes far beyond the technical and design-led realms, and their training should always involve project management, organising, and leadership skills. This is why:

> Now let us imagine a group of five people holding a fire safety net, ready to receive a person jumping from the third floor of an apartment block that is ablaze. All five people need to pull the net tightly for it to work properly; if one of them lets go, the shape or tension of the net will change and the person jumping might get hurt. The urban designer is the team leader, making decisions such as how hard to pull the net and where exactly to be standing in order for the device to work. This is how a good design team works: everyone does their bit and each one of the members is as crucial as the other.

Too often, design teams work in a dissociated manner, with some team members only commenting on the drawings urban designers produce and sending those drawings back for amendments, as if their job were only to review the work. This way of working not only puts an absurd amount of pressure on the urban designer, but also results in highly inefficient forms of practice that are time-consuming and that misuse valuable resources, also leading to compromised design results. Clients must invest in the necessary skills and must always be prepared to direct, or even replace, those agents who are not good team players, as they can seriously compromise the quality and sustainable credentials of the project.

This core team will then engage other specialisms that will join them or advise on significant matters as and when necessary. For example, it might be necessary to bring an ecologist on board as part of the main design team if the scheme involves large or significant green spaces. The expert will assess the ecological value of the land before and after the development takes place, also advising on ways to generate higher ecological value for the scheme; in other words, make it work harder as an ecosystem and as part of a larger whole. A conservationist might advise on the preservation of a historic asset. An archaeologist might carry out a survey to avoid damaging anything of significance during the works. A flood specialist might calculate the volume of rainwater that will have to be discharged or temporarily stored on the site.

Comments from any of the specialisms that need to be part of the process can seriously impact on the scheme, often causing drastic changes to layouts and making the team rethink their proposals; sometimes it is literally going back to the drawing board, and the process begins again. This is why it is so important to remain open-minded and flexible during the design process. It is often clients or communities that find it difficult to cope with a constantly changing proposal. Clients need commercially sound studies that guarantee a good return on their investments, but ironically, they are often reluctant to invest in these, even when it is those changes that can jeopardise their budgets and affect value calculations. Communities tend to assume a masterplan will happen once it has been shared with the public, but that is rarely the case. As the design team progresses with further levels of detail, new information appears that can trigger changes to the scheme. It is rarely the case that what they have seen during an engagement or consultation event is what gets built. This is why it is so important that those with an interest in a development become involved in the long term, following updates and being prepared to make further comments. A responsible design team will provide a continuous information channel, updating news about the project and the progress made regularly. Those who invested time and effort in engaging at different stages need to be able to follow and comment on the evolution of the scheme and the decision-making process that leads to the end result. We will explore the different levels of engagement in more detail in Chapter 6.

Other than the core design team and the technical support they may have, authorities and other legislative agencies might also have a strong voice on how the design evolves. Ultimately, if the authorities do not sanction the development, then it simply cannot happen. The problem arises for urban designers when different authorities or different departments do not achieve consensus between them, having different views on how to develop. A recurrent example of this type of constraint is the case of local planning authorities and the highways authorities in the UK. Some municipalities have a joint administration where one authority manages both highways and the public realm; this is the case in Nottingham, for example. The majority, however, have both administrations running independently, in separate buildings in most cases. The problem with this is that an urban designer, for example, might submit a proposal to the local planning authority and receive comments from their own urban designer regarding the need to provide more pedestrian-friendly environments, with softer highways treatments and good, straight, fully connected paths. These types of requests might be based on vast research evidence that shows that easy to walk environments have a high impact on health and wellbeing and can help reduce social issues like obesity or loneliness. The urban designer amends the drawing and sends it back; they are told that is a much better design solution. The drawing is then sent to the highways authority, who responds with comments requesting the removal of straight pedestrian crossings, as these are less safe because drivers tend to speed up and can cause accidents; designers are referred back to the highways guide that requests crossing to be stacked by a minimum distance. A similar type of discrepancy is often found in relation to pedestrian crossings near corners. Now the urban designer is stuck between a rock and a hard place: is it going to be a safe crossing or a healthy one? How could it be both?

These types of inconsistency are typical in the UK and not alien to practice in other countries; they cause a huge amount of delays and they consume valuable resources in both authorities and design teams. I have been known as one of those urban designers that pushes authorities for a joint meeting, with coloured pens and tracing paper to

Chapter 3: **Design agents**

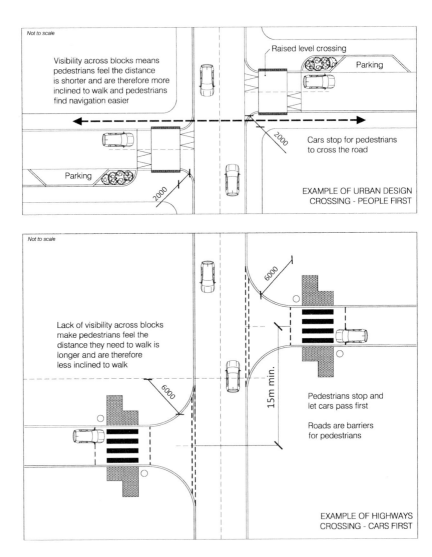

Figure 3.1 Layout showing a typical crossing designed with an urban design approach and a typical crossing with a highways engineering approach. The urban designer prioritises the pedestrian, making the car slow down and stop and giving the pedestrian a level surface demarcated with texture. The engineer prioritises the car, making pedestrians stop and look before crossing. Visually impaired people are likely to need traffic signalling with the second option.

Chapter 3: **Design agents**

agree on a solution that works for everyone. Sadly, there have been occasions where the lack of resources in local authorities have made this shortcut impossible to arrange. I know of many urban designers who would persevere when confronted with this process adversity, trying to find a sensible solution. Unfortunately, I have also come across many who lack the skills or the will to untangle problems of such magnitude, and who choose to please the authority with more power to secure planning approval and so avoid delays. Poor, irresponsible forms of practice are still abundant worldwide, with the added issue of corrupt administrations in some countries, which inevitably leads directly to an outcome of low quality and compromised sustainability credentials.

The lack of skills across fields and sectors of the built environment industry is a serious issue at present in the UK. Place design has led to enormous amounts of research and new evidence emerging in the past few decades, and it can be difficult for practitioners under pressure to keep up to date. Additionally, the rapid technological evolution has created further niche specialisms within the industry, as we discussed in Chapter 1. Regulations keep evolving and building standards become tougher. Designers work in a very competitive industry driven by profit targets, which means they are under pressure to deliver more, yet faster and cheaper than ever before. Understandably, this dangerous combination leaves professionals with little time to catch up with the vast advances in the field. Design practices can be left with two choices: (1) they employ junior, inexperienced, affordable staff to be able to compete commercially or (2) they specialise in a particular line of work and become leading experts in that area. The problem with the first choice is that junior staff do not have the experience to engage in large or complex projects and often lack confidence to work collaboratively across sectors. Frequently, a senior member of a design practice will attend key meetings – with the planner, for example – and then pass on the work to junior staff that were not part of the conversation and who might not have the skills to interpret the full message. This translates into revised drawings being submitted for planning that do not address the core of the issues discussed. The second choice is a very dangerous one because placemaking involves a degree of wholeness that encompasses a multiplicity of fields coming together. Even when designers cannot be experts in everything, they must have awareness about everything that might impact on – or become affected by – their designs. Someone who has no awareness of a field can never recognise when the time comes to seek specialist expertise. The solution to the problem is simple: *collaboration*. A culture of co-design and shared *accountability* could resolve many of the problems the industry is experiencing today. Local and regional authorities in the UK have seen their budgets shrink for some time, which results in reduced teams trying to cope with increasingly larger volumes of work. This lack of skills is not exclusive to design practice in the UK, but a couple of British case studies in this chapter illustrate the skills issue further; other examples show how different design agents can have a detrimental impact on the quality and sustainable credentials of schemes when the power of different agents is unbalanced.

These are huge issues because the impact of a building of poor quality, with low sustainability credentials, will last a few decades and will probably involve demolition and rebuilding, which is a highly unsustainable practice in itself. The real concern is that when we work at large scales, we are making the problem even bigger. Producing urban extensions and large masterplans means creating an infrastructure that will stand for hundreds of years. Once the highways and public land have been legally designated, it is very difficult to change them. For example, omitting the opportunity to connect places with pedestrian links or creating back walls or fences facing the public realm are huge errors of judgement. Large-scale development with compromised quality can have social, economic, and environmental consequences for centuries.

Now, let us have a look at some examples from practice in the UK. The first one showcases a simple but very successful case of collaboration in a project where such practices were not expected at all. The second and third case studies demonstrate how good, skilful local authorities can prevent poor outcomes when they have the power to do so, and how a lack of collaboration and skills can delay delivery and consume huge resources. The fourth case study illustrates how lack of accountability and balance can result in poor design with low sustainable credentials.

Chapter 3: **Design agents**

Case studies

Case Study 3.1 A project with 60 clients

This is the case of a leading supermarket in England with a large site redevelopment involving three buildings and a car park. A new superstore of 90,000 square feet would replace the existing smaller store and this, once converted, would be transferred to local authority ownership to function as the new indoor market. The old indoor market, in a state of disrepair, would then be demolished and new retail units would be built in its place (see Figures 3.2 and 3.3).

At the early stages of the process, the firm I worked for was commissioned by the supermarket chain to design and deliver the scheme. As I was in charge of the market conversion and the car park projects, the local authority, who would be the future landlord of the building and parking area, also wanted to have a say on how the place was developed so that it met their requirements, which

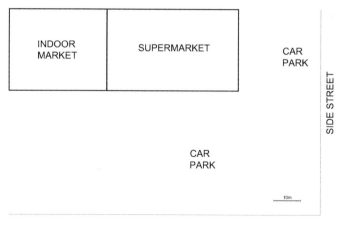

Figure 3.2 Drawing showing the existing project layout. Illustrated by Juan Cristino for the author.

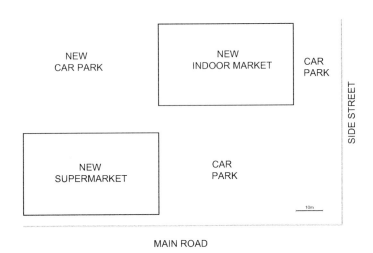

Figure 3.3 Drawing showing the proposed project layout. Illustrated by Juan Cristino for the author.

was totally understandable. So far, one client was paying for the work and the other client was influencing the design.

The problem began when the 58 market stallholders realised they could not plan their business future and became increasingly anxious because they knew nothing about the forthcoming layout, the size or shape of the installations, the lighting levels, the location of loading and offloading areas, and all the retail logistics a business owner needs to know to plan the premises move. Every time I visited the site, I was stopped by market stallholders with various queries and, every time, I was giving them short answers with limited information. Eventually, stall owners began to piece together the answers themselves. This was problematic because people were misinterpreting information and time frames, and tensions were rising. I then approached the local authority and explained the situation, proposing a phased but continuous engagement strategy to keep business owners in the loop. The local authority appreciated this immensely and assigned a very kind officer to work with me. Now there was an engagement team as well as a design team. We organised regular meetings to brief people, but the more questions arose, the more we realised that we did not understand their trade. There were serious issues with stock movement, specialist installations some people needed in order to operate, different illumination equipment, security concerns, and so on. I decided I had to spend time with them at the market to really grasp how things worked and what type of design features they might need. This time spent with people at their work was incredibly valuable and it made the process of finding the right products and design solutions much faster and enjoyable.

We arranged a workshop where, together with the authority and the stallholders, we managed to agree to the layout, defining where circulation and resting spaces would be located. It was as if I were working with 60 different clients at once. After doing a capacity study of the former store space, we realised that standard stalls were not compatible with the layout dimensions and that we could actually fit many extra stalls, which would also be larger in capacity, if we had something made to measure to the optimum proportions. We did a design workshop with the stallholders and we invited a local metalwork manufacturer to make sure the new structures could be built, installed, and maintained properly. Working with the end users, the local authority as a managing agent, and the industry who would produce and install the cubicles, we achieved an innovative product: a modular system that could deliver multiple stall sizes using a repetition of two components. This achieved a uniform look and total flexibility for expanding or contracting stalls in the future to suit potential new retail needs. The components also meant we could have totally enclosed stalls and open stalls and we could make these interchangeable by adding or removing parts.

The market traders became incredibly enthusiastic about the process. They felt heard and valued, they got to know one another better, and they began to prepare a huge launch party to show their passion for the scheme. The design won awards and appeared in the press at the time.

In this case, the collaboration between designers, clients, and industry was key to the success and smooth running of the project.

Some might think the process was resource consuming or slow, but that is far from the truth – hand over and reopening were very smooth operations, as everyone knew what to expect and they had exactly what they needed to reopen businesses fast.

Table 3.1 Roles of the key design agents involved in Case Study 3.1.

	Architect	Local Authority	Retail Store	Market Stallholders	Stall Manufacturer
Client		√	√	√	
Design team	√	√		√	√
Project management	√				
Supplier					√
Budget control		√	√		

Case Study 3.2 Urban supermarket

This case is about a scheme that I had to design whilst I was practising as an architectural designer in the UK, but that – thankfully, in my view – never materialised. A large supermarket client was aspiring to build a store in the centre of a former mining town in England. This project involved a young but very talented urban designer, who was determined to protect the built environment of the high street from inappropriate development.

As I mentioned before, I worked for an architectural firm that had an ongoing contract with a large supermarket chain, and this was their main source of income. I was already running projects on my own, and given my training and qualifications, I was the firms' champion in urban design, advising and supporting colleague architects in this line of work. A huge part of my work was

Chapter 3: **Design agents**

doing area and site analysis, putting together feasibility studies for a number of commercial firms, including the said supermarket chain. I would spend a long time arranging car park layouts to maximise capacity, always working to deliver standard design principles and models set by our client. Our job was to use these template buildings and fit them in a range of development sites across the country as if we were playing SimCity, placing them in the most efficient orientation to deliver large parking areas but ensuring good visibility of their signage and front entrance. There was a minimum size requirement for service access and a minimum number of parking spaces we had to deliver in correspondence with the size of the store. In this role, I was lucky enough to travel a lot, visiting empty parcels of land, walking the perimeters and the surrounding areas to assess whether the plot was suitable for a supermarket, and to test which store size we could use. I enjoyed these site visits. I would be in Aberdeen one day and in Bath the next. It was a great chance to see the British urban landscape and understand local character and typologies. Inevitably, there were times when my recommendation would be against developing in some areas. I found cases where the store would be in too close proximity to neighbouring homes, or where access was compromised, or where the impact on historic or conservation areas would mean the client would not be able to achieve planning consent for a store. On my travels, although I could not mention the client's name due to confidentiality, I had the opportunity to talk to people regularly, asking what they liked about their area and how they felt about their urban environment. I began to learn what worked and what did not for local people, what their fears and aspirations were, and what they would be prepared to fight for if the need arose.

    The time came when I had to recommend against building a particular store in the former mining town in question. The site did not seem suitable to me for the retail model we had to adhere to. I produced a full report with illustrations and feasibility analysis as usual for the client. Normally, after a recommendation against building on a plot, we would not hear any more about the site and we would move onto the next option. This time, however, that was not the case. Instructions came from the international headquarters putting pressure on the national supermarket management to build more stores fast. Quality and adequacy were not so much of a concern; the competitors' expansion was. But delivering buildings fast is not something that happens often in the UK; it is simply not the British way. Conscientious, responsibly built environment professionals know that a historically rich landscape in a compact, densely populated island ultimately dictates that whatever is built needs to be appropriate and suitable for the place. But senior management abroad insisted that the UK had to deliver new stores at speed, as if they were on the American continent. As this was very difficult to achieve indeed, several property managers lost their jobs in the course of only a few months; newcomers in the post began to feel scared of the prospect of their careers being cut short. Soon, instructions were given to buy land and tell architectural firms to press on with the job in hand. My recommendation against building in that particular site was ignored, and soon enough, I found myself arranging a meeting with the local authority to speed up things. I arrived at the County Hall. Officers from several departments were waiting for me: highways, town centre management, and planning, amongst others. Sitting right in front of me was a young, well-groomed, charming urban designer I will call S. I explained the scheme and the fact that the client had already bought the site to the listening cohort, waiting for a first reaction or some sort of body language signal to gauge their first thoughts. But, in the typical style of a British local authority, nobody blinked an eye. The first hurdle mentioned by an officer was that the huge plant room that was at the front of the site by the high street had to be relocated to the rear. This would delay the programme by two or three years, and it would cost a six- or seven-figure sum. This design item was picked up in my earlier report, but the clients had decided to clad the substation up and leave it in its original location; not a valid option for the local authority. From there onwards, things started to get really complicated. Not only the authority did pick up every single one of the points I included in my report, but I had to keep quiet as if I did not know how to do my job, as if I had not noticed these problems before. The urban designer spoke a great degree of sense. He was eloquent and spot on in his judgement; I could tell he understood design and human behaviour. He seemed to really care about achieving a good place. This made me feel truly awful, as if I were promoting poor quality design; I never felt so embarrassed in my life. After the meeting, as we were walking into the lift, S handed over a piece of paper with a phone number. It said: "We should talk about this scheme in more detail, let's go for a coffee."

That was my kind of thing, talking, trying to arrive at some form of consensus, and stopping the hard-nosed business approach. A couple of days later, I met for a coffee with S. As it turns out, we both knew exactly what was wrong with the scheme: it could not happen, not in that location. I had to make several iterations to the scheme, trying to make it work. S helped me through a very painful process, looking to find the impossible solution that would make it all work. We both agreed that a store with the front on the high street and the car park at the rear could potentially work, but that went against the store model so it could not happen (see Figures 3.4 and 3.5). The local authority did their job superbly, consistently opposing poor quality design without giving in. They knew how to protect the high street and they worked tirelessly to try to help me, the designer, come up with a formula that would probably get planning approval. However, the inflexibility of the client made the task an impossible one for a long three years, and the project never happened. After this experience, I began to wonder whether this was a career path that I wanted to stay on. Soon enough, I made a move to different practice, where I continued to develop my skills and knowledge with a broader range of clients. S and I became very dear friends and we both grew our careers with constant mutual support. Ten years after the project, we would be lecturing on the same university course, setting up a business together, and growing a lifetime friendship.

116 Chapter 3: **Design agents**

This demonstrates how lack of collaboration and flexibility to adapt can lead to delays and even put a stop to developments, causing great losses for all parties involved.

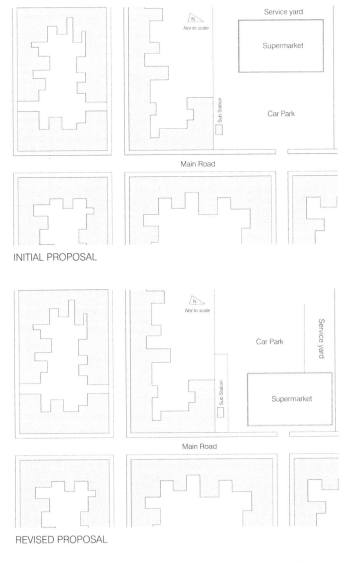

Figure 3.4 Layout showing the supermarket initial proposal (above) and the revised proposal (below).

Chapter 3: **Design agents** 117

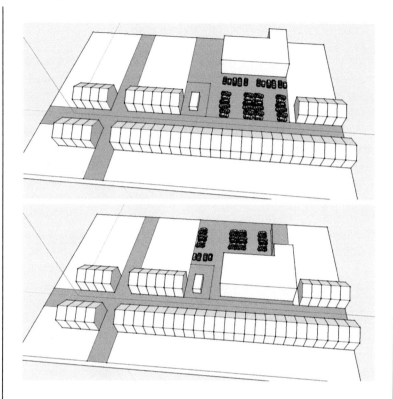

Figure 3.5 Supermarket proposal in 3D, following the food-store model (above) and as revised by the local authority (below).

Table 3.2 Roles of the key design agents involved in Case Study 3.2.

	Architect	Local Authority	Retail Store
Client			√
Design team	√		√
Project management			√
Urban design	√	√	
Budget control			√

Case Study 3.3 Social housing

Strap yourself in, this is the story of one of the most painful design processes I have ever experienced: a social housing residential block in England in the late 2010s. I chose to write about this project because it is a prime example of how the various agents involved are highly dependent on both skills and powers to deliver design quality, but, as I write, my eye starts to twitch.

This was a local authority that owned some land and made a decision to put together a planning application for a residential scheme on the site. At this point, it is relevant to mention that internal corporate procedures were put in place to avoid conflicts of interest and that the authority, acting as the developer, kept all the teams completely independent from each other, the same way as would happen with a privately commissioned design project. There were absolutely no gaps when it came to process and conflicts of interest; I was truly impressed with this. I am sure this is not always the case in all authorities.

So, back to the project. The Regeneration department were the client team, the Housing team did the project management, the Design team was the architects, and the Planning team retained its standard role as the authority body (see Figure 3.6). I was acting as the urban designer for the planning department. According to in-house regulations, the Regeneration team had no choice but to appoint the internal Design team for all social housing projects on their land; this was a corporate decision taken in order to reduce costs.

A pre-application submission landed on the planning desk. Also called pre-app, this is a draft set of drawings and briefs that is sent to planners in the UK for them to recommend any necessary changes or agree to work together with the design team to achieve a good quality planning submission, one that is more likely to reach planning consent and secure a fast, smooth process. As soon as we saw the drawings, the planner officers and I realised that there were serious errors in the design. Living rooms were dark and had little ventilation; site levels had not been accounted for; fire safety and access regulations had not been met; stairs did not

Chapter 3: **Design agents**

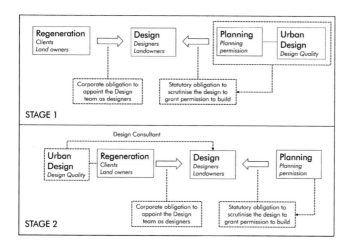

Figure 3.6 Diagram illustrating the roles of the different teams involved in the project.

work; windows and doors were disproportionate and in the wrong position; the list of problems was endless. These errors meant that the building would not only be ugly and poor in quality, but would also be unhealthy, dangerous, and impossible to build, at least in some parts. We produced a review brief for feedback and sent it back to the Design team for amendments. They undertook a site levels survey and changed the design. The planning department sent comments back and the design was altered once more. This process took place seven times and we were still nowhere near achieving an acceptable design. We organised training sessions, workshops, meetings, and co-design sessions to support the Design team along the way, but the knowledge gaps were such that could not be resolved in just a matter of weeks.

At some point, the Regeneration team grew concerned about the amount of time and resources that were being consumed to cover serious lack of design skills, but they were bound to retain the contract with those particular designers. Such was the worry that they were prepared to pay a fee to the planning team for us to redesign the scheme. To avoid conflict of interest, half of the planning team became a new design team working for Regeneration: the Planning-Design team. The planning drawings were completed satisfactorily, but due to contractual arrangements, these had to be submitted by the original Design team; now they only had to put the drawings produced by Planning-Design on a template with their label and submit them. When the new planning submission was received, the new Planning-Design team could not believe their eyes: the drawings were still wrong. A meeting was arranged and together, all parties realised that the Design team had altered the drawing issued by Planning-Design in the process of adding the labels, possibly simply to assert power but also possibly because of lack of care. We were back to square one.

We arranged another workshop to amend the errors once more. Then, the planning application was submitted again. The scheme was approved this time. Months later, we heard from the Housing team, who were once more in despair. As it turns out, the Design team had provided an incorrect site survey; the levels everyone had been working to did not exist, hence the whole design was faulty, and the scheme compromised. After an investigation, the Regeneration team was allowed to commission a local architectural firm that took over the job and successfully completed the project. The whole Design team left the local authority soon after.

This shows how, even with the best intentions, adequate tools, and appropriate systems in place, the lack of skills in one of the design agents can make things very difficult indeed, especially when the client does not have the power to replace underperforming staff. This local authority was fortunate to have a planning process in place that was effective in securing design quality, and they had the skills and capacity to appraise schemes properly, highlight design errors, and make relevant recommendations. But the fact remains that although poor design was prevented, the amount of time and resources invested in this scheme were enormous. My eye continues to twitch as I think back.

Table 3.3 Layout efficiency comparison between the Design team and the Urban Design team proposals.

*Denotes Improvement	Original (Design)	Revised (Planning-Design)	Savings (M2)
Number of units	48	48	
Area per unit (average) m²	51.16	50	*1.16
Total units' area m²	2,456	2,400	*56
Total plot coverage m²	1,186	1,102	*84
Total m² of development	3,559	3,306	*253
Communal circulation m²	460	441	*19
Circulation area percentage	13	13	Same amount per flat
Number of units with double aspect/cross-ventilation	12	42	*This provides a healthier environment allowing air to flow through the home. Different types of light (north/south, etc.) are good for mental health and wellbeing
Number of access points off street	4	5	*More activation on façades and rhythmical access points which makes the design easier to navigate

(*Continued*)

(Continued)

*Denotes Improvement	Original (Design)	Revised (Planning-Design)	Savings (M2)
Number of equal units (standardisation)	42 + 3 + 3	48	*Standarisation results in savings
Number of units on the ground floor	17	16	Ten fully accessible units needed
Number of bedroom windows facing street	36	21	*Fewer small windows
Number of living room windows facing street	30	36	*More daylight/ surveillance, better façade
Number of bedroom windows facing courtyard	12	27	*This is better for noise
Number of living room windows facing courtyard	18	12	*Fewer facing north

Table 3.4 Roles of the key design agents involved in Case Study 3.3.

	Regeneration Team	Housing Team	Design Team	Planning-Design Team
Landowner/ client	√			
Design team			√ (initial scheme)	√ (revised scheme)
Project management		√		
Urban design			√ (initial scheme)	√ (revised scheme)
Budget control	√	√		

Case Study 3.4 Office building

This is the case of a local authority that owned land parcels and was acting as a developer in an urban area in England before the Covid-19 pandemic. The first time I came across the site was a couple of years before as the local authority urban designer. I carried out feasibility studies on the land for a variety of different uses: residential, mixed use, and office space; so I was familiar with the site and its surrounding areas as I had completed the site analysis in depth.

The local authority had made a decision to build office space on the site. This might seem difficult to believe in a post-pandemic scenario where many people continue to work from home, but before Covid-19, there was a huge demand for large open plan office spaces in many parts of the UK. The Assets team, who were managing this project, hired a local architectural practice to design the building based on the feasibility studies I had done before. Soon enough, a pre-planning application was submitted for the scheme, ready for the planning team to make formal comments. The overall shape, height, and access to the building correlated completely with the previous feasibility study, so there were no concerns there. But, as the urban designer, I picked up on a series of issues with the scheme, so did the planning officers; we were in total agreement regarding the points of weakness in the proposed design. Most obviously, a back door and a blank façade at ground floor level faced onto the public square; this would create a dull, sterile urban environment of poor quality. Window proportions were incorrect and the ground floor glazing was too short and looked out of proportion with the rest of the building. Having trained as an architect myself, the main problems I found were to do with the sustainable credentials of the scheme. A south-facing façade was entirely made of standard curtain wall glass with no sun protection systems. This building would be not only reliant on mechanical cooling, but it would most probably reflect the heat onto the fully paved public square that was being proposed, which had no greenery at all.

Another fully glazed façade was facing, and very close to, a high concrete tram rail system that had regular services throughout the day. This could cause serious vibrations and could generate noise that would be reflected directly onto this huge wall of glass standing adjacent to it, projecting onto nearby houses (see Figure 3.7). On the south façade, the proposed office block was adjacent to a beautiful historic building: carved stone, three storeys in height, and detached from the proposal by a service driveway. This meant that the new building would act as a frame to the neighbouring historic building for pedestrians approaching from the busiest route: the link from the city centre. Despite this, the materials and colour palette proposed clashed with the historic building. Analysing this proposal, I came to realise that the building had been designed with little to no consideration of its relationship with the spaces around it. It had been designed with an approach I call *inside-out*,[2] a typical approach amongst architects these days. A far more sustainable approach would have looked at the design of the office block *outside-in*,[3] considering the impact this new building would have on the environment where it sits. Many other design concerns of that sort of nature were found. All of these were issues that could be corrected before a final planning submission was processed, so naturally, the planners sent the comments for designers to make the relevant amendments.

As the local authority urban designer, I made my comments, particularly regarding serious concerns I had about the sustainability credentials of the proposals. I explained all the points clearly and in detail, and made several different suggestions about how the scheme could be improved. The comments reached the architects and the Assets team that was acting as the client. A couple of weeks later, a planning application was submitted showing the previous scheme again, but this time with windows of different proportions and a glass door instead of a blank fire exit door leading to the square. No other significant changes were made. Comments on the sustainable credentials of the scheme and how its fabric could impact on the microclimate and feel of the environment around it were not taken on board. The planning officers and I challenged the applicants only to be told that budget constraints would not permit any further changes. There was no evidence to demonstrate that alternative, more sustainable options had been considered but could not be met financially. There was no mention of the environmental concerns raised about the

Chapter 3: **Design agents** 125

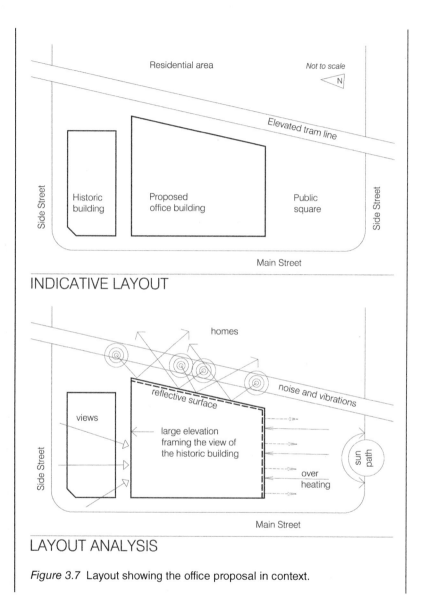

Figure 3.7 Layout showing the office proposal in context.

proposal. The architects were simply working for a client whose main concern was the economic aspects of the design. This lack of *balance* in the decision-making process, where the Economic Sphere of sustainable development dominates, is typical of pre-application submissions in the UK. The quality of design and the sustainable credentials of poor proposals are often contested during the planning process, but as there is a total lack of *accountability* across parties, officers have little powers to deliver better buildings without the back up of strong national legislation to lean on.

Fortunately, the pandemic put a stop to the office project and the building did not materialise.

Table 3.5 Roles of the key design agents involved in Case Study 3.4.

	Assets Team	Architects	Planning Authority
Landowner/client	√		
Design team		√ (initial scheme)	
Project management	√		
Urban design		√ (initial scheme)	√ (revised scheme)
Budget control	√		

Following this and other similar cases where sustainable credentials were compromised, the local authority brought on board a an independent review board, whose job is to evaluate and comment on proposals from an energy performance and overall sustainability perspective. The reports of this panel now form part of the material considerations to approve or refuse permission to build, which is a far more powerful tool than the judgement of the planning authority, who may have no field-specific expertise.

Lessons learnt

There are many lessons we could learn from this chapter, so let us have a quick recap. In the first case study, talking to people and bringing different roles together to amalgamate their needs into a coherent goal was what made the difference between success and failure. It avoided giant delays, additional costs, stress, broken relationships, lack of trust, and copious resources; in other words, collaboration avoided a slower, more expensive process.

In the second case study, the client's rigidity, lack of collaboration, and failure to understand their own power limitations cost them time and increased consultancy fees. Perhaps less arrogance from the client, more dialogue, and more flexibility could have been what was needed to make the project happen.

In the third case study, the lack of skills in one of the components of the human chain that delivered the project caused the issues to begin with. However, the real trouble here was the irrefutable decision made by the organisation regarding contractual arrangements. This left the process incapable of adapting. Huge amounts of time, monies and resources were dispensed.

The last case study in this chapter was about a client – or a designer, perhaps – that did not take into account the influence other critical agents in the process were trying to exert. If this project had reached the construction phase, it would have done so with a much lower design quality than was possible, and the sustainability credentials of the building would have been seriously compromised.

Overall, it seems that when different agents cannot understand their roles or the powers they hold, things can get pretty sticky. Many people have some form of input in large, complex schemes that run for long periods of time; it is often easy to lose track and see those key aspects that made the scheme a good quality one disappear. Word count prevents me from adding further examples in this chapter, but staff turnover is something else I identify as a serious issue. Staff can move to other jobs, they can retire, go on parental leave, and so on. Every new person to replace a previous member of staff might have a different vision or different values and priorities. Many

Table 3.6 Case study analysis summary.

Case Study	Topic	What Was Different?	Outcome
3.1 Indoor market	Co-design through engagement	Sixty clients, architects, and manufacturers involved in the design	Positive: better than expected
3.2 Urban food store	Client over-exerting their power	Client's inflexibility, reluctancy to negotiate, and adapt their model	Negative: project could not come to fruition
3.3 Social housing	Lack of design skills	Inflexible contractual arrangements reduced client's power	Negative: project could not come to fruition
3.4 Office building	Client over-exerting their power	The Economic Sphere was prioritised over the Social and Environmental Spheres	Negative: unsustainable design outcomes

organisations lack sound project procedures, especially for the final strands of the design or building stages. I have seen staff changes bringing serious inconsistencies and job duplication. Everyone is far too busy to keep a good record of why things change along the way or why some key decisions have to be made. I have even come across insecure members of staff that like keeping information to themselves so they become indispensable for the delivery of the scheme; a very poor behaviour that helps no one. In order to prevent these experiences, I used to create a contact list with names and details of everyone involved in each scheme. I would leave this in one of the data protected archives where relevant colleagues could find it. Evidently, this was still not enough to bring coherence, collaborative attitudes, and coordinated action to my projects, so over the years, I decided to explore how different agents can influence schemes a little more to see if I could devise a better way to work. We will discuss these in the next chapter.

Chapter 3: **Design agents**

Tool 3: Design agents' map

Everyone with the power or the opportunity to influence design is a design agent. Every design agent has the responsibility to deliver quality, sustainable design. The major issue at present is that although design agents might have a responsibility, they sometimes have limited or no accountability. The systems we work within do not force or persuade agents to demonstrate that they have done their best or explain why it was not possible for them to deliver better outcomes. So, when I say, "Everyone with the power or the opportunity to influence design is a design agent", I mean: you too, as a member of your community, you are a design agent.

As is to be expected, the extent to which communities are able to have a say and the ways in which they do depend heavily on the law of the land, the sensitivity and impact of the proposals, the good will of developers and landowners, the requirements of local authorities, and the design process adopted by the design team. Independent of the level of influence communities might have during a design process, they most certainly should fall into the design agent category. I do not say this lightly: there is no scheme that can ever exist without community input, in one way or another. At the very least, communities will populate the scheme and make it their own sooner or later. In that sense, I would go as far as to say that communities need to be considered as a type of client. Take the example of Case Study 1.1 in Chapter 2 and see how powerful community input can be in raising the quality of design.

To facilitate the visualisation of this system of influences, I have come up with a tool to map the design agents involved, a table that can be very useful to communicate to everyone taking part what their role is and how other agencies are also influential in the process. Sharing a table like this can help other parties identify gaps and suggest the inclusion of other relevant agents they might not have considered to begin with. In the end, early collaboration can help speed up the process and avoid preventable costs and delays.

Based on the topics we explored in this chapter, I would like to ask urban designers to reflect on how often they adopt methods to map the design agents of a project as I have done in Table 3.7. Now, I would ask

Chapter 3: **Design agents**

Table 3.7 Tool 3: Design agents' map.

Design Agent's Map Stage: Concept/Developed Design/Detailed Design

Industry Professionals

Name	Represents	Field	Email
Tony Carpenter	Carpenter Renovations	Builder/Joiner	CRLtd@...
Simon Beatty	Beatty Designs	Architects	BeDesigns@...
Owen Armstrong	Armstrong Ltd	Contractor	OwenA@arms...

Authorities/Service Providers

Name	Represents	Field	Email
Robbie Jackson	Walford Council	Market Manager	RJackson@Walford...
Audrey Roberts	Weatherfield Borough Council	Councillor	RJackson@Walford...
Eric Pollard	Hotten District Council	Councillor	Eric.Poll@hott..

Clients/Landowners

Name	Represents	Field	Email
Ian Beale	Beale Builds	Developer	IB.Dev@..
Michael Boldwin	Boldwin Property Ltd	HMO owner	mikebold@....
Tom King	King & Sons Ltd	Landowner	TomKing@K&S...

Communities/Residents

Name	Represents	Field	Email
Phil Mitchell	Phil Mitchell	Pub landlord	mitchelp@...
Kim Tate	Tate Haulage	Business owner	tateadmin@...
Emily Bishop	Community	Resident	Emily29@...

Chapter 3: **Design agents**

them to consider whether at times, they could have done more to include design agents they had not thought about until reading this chapter.

Notes

1 Greek mythology entity that was punished by Zeus, who instructed him to roll back a giant ball up a hill in the depths of Hades.
2 Designing a building resolving the layout first and the external shape and appearance later. With this approach, the design solutions for the building envelope (façades, roof, and so on) is subordinate to the layout.
3 Designing a building resolving the external shape and appearance first and the layout later. With this approach, the design solutions for the building envelope (façades, roof, and so on) are more likely to be in context, looking like the new building belongs in its place.

Chapter 4
Influencing design

In Chapter 3, we began to understand the agents involved in the design process and how lack of collaboration can jeopardise the quality and sustainable credentials of buildings and places. A very important point was the consequence of poor skills and lack of understanding amongst some agents, and how this tends to make design processes long, painful, and expensive.

In this chapter, we will look at the opportunities different agents might have to contribute to design solutions throughout the process and how they can exercise their powers within the limits of their scope of influence.

To begin the debate, I will go back to the tool presented in Chapter 3: the Design Agents' Map. It is clear that each project will have its own map, and that this as well as every other tool in the book is likely to change and evolve as the project develops. The relevance of this map is that it will become the basis to visualise the influence these agents might or might not have at different stages in the design process and beyond. Establishing this is a fundamental step to help urban designers set the basis of meaningful participation and just empowerment. But influencing design implies more complex dynamics than simply handing over or attaining power. Influencing design can happen when there is an ability to effect change, and this involves three components: will, power, and financial means (money). Sometimes agents who do not have much power can effect change by contributing to a cause. Other times, it is those with money that can make things happen, even when they are not in a position of power to start with. People who know how to balance these three components, how to trade them and make

Chapter 4: **Influencing design** 133

Figure 4.1 The diagram shows the change trilogy: how power, will, and money are all necessary to effect change.

them count, are those who find it easiest to achieve and implement change.

The route towards designing and delivering quality, sustainable places is incredibly complex, far more than most people imagine. Through the process, everyone involved, no matter their role, will have limited power to impose their opinion and have things their way. The idea that an architect or urban designer can be the sole master creator of a scheme and the custodian of a vision is frankly an urban myth; it is the result of the inflated ego of some narcissistic characters, some from history and some I had the misfortune to encounter in practice myself. I am sure that whatever line of work you are in, you can probably identify a similar character or two. I am equally sure that you do not fall into this bracket yourself, as otherwise why would you be reading this book when you already know everything?

Architecture students often leave university to realise the world of practice is nothing like the studio. Many become disheartened or morbidly bored when their creative power is so dramatically restricted. Making places is nothing like producing stylised, glossy images one could hang on the wall of a cocktail bar in a high-end hotel. In fact, I found I had far more influence on the design of buildings and places as a local authority officer than I ever had as an architectural designer; it was a good career move. The same could be said for so many of my dear friends and colleagues, local authority officers who also bemoan over a morning coffee: "After re-designing endless planning submissions to help applicants achieve consent, shaping most of British cities, my name is never on a plan; somebody else takes credit."

Perhaps we should face facts and accept that in a rapidly changing world, the role of place designers in the new millennium is increasingly departing from the image of a modernist 'master architect'. Place professions are becoming far more invested in delivery strategies, modelling operation systems, and adaptation tactics than in the futile, obsolete idea of achieving a finished design in the comfort of a drawing board. Those like me, who still own an old oak drafting table, do it merely for the romanticism associated with it or from fear of losing an antiquated, yet useful, skill.

Sustainable places never cease to evolve; our interventions are only a small moment in the much longer lifespan of a place. In order to secure better quality outcomes and higher sustainable credentials, designers need to think about whole systems rather than buildings; collaborative teams rather than personalities; level playing fields rather than hierarchies. So, it is time to begin to contemplate how designers can acquire the new necessary skills and develop the ability to shape better places.

Transparency and trust

If we are aiming to create a more resilient society, the first urgency in urban practice is to rebuild trust within communities and also between them and other agents like developers, designers, and authorities. According to Halpern,[1] social resilience is strengthened when communities can build up social capital and manage the aspects of social life that enable people to act more efficiently as a group in order to meet their objectives, connect socially, and develop norms and trust. Zautra, Hall, and Murray[2] showed that neighbourhood resilience is achieved when people trust each other, interact regularly, have a sense of community and cohesion, work together towards a common goal, and have public places to meet formally and informally.

Unfortunately, although trust is a key determinant of social capital, it is not rare to see local people, communities, and organisations in many parts of the world disbelieving their local authorities when it comes to regeneration and development. We all know large-scale development and significant investment opens opportunities for abuse of power and

Chapter 4: **Influencing design**　　　　　　　　　　　　　　　　　135

corruption. On the other hand, authorities can exert their power, organising people, their activities, and their lives through strategic placemaking. As if that were not enough, the realm of design and town planning comes with a wealth of jargon and technical vocabulary that is often foreign not only to locals, but also to other fields of expertise. After a lifetime of let-downs and poor communication, people start feeling left out, disenfranchised, and used.

To begin to establish an open and constructive dialogue, professionals need to start by adapting their language, just as the medical profession has managed to do so. This takes practice. Despite writing and giving talks and presentations about how to be more approachable and how to make oneself understood as a professional working with the public, I found myself more than once surrounded by confused looks and having to go a step back to explain jargon before I could move forward. Talking to people about very technical areas of expertise might be unfamiliar to us in industry, but it is not impossible. In my attempts to democratise placemaking as far as I can, I have been working closely with

Figure 4.2 Photograph shows primary school children working on a city centre masterplan.

Figure 4.3 Photograph shows members of the community working on design guidance for a city in the UK.

nursery and school pupils of different ages, as young as three years old. I was always interested in giving young people a voice and I wondered how much they would be able to influence design at their early age. To my delight, I found that it is possible to discuss place in a meaningful way with any human being, of any background, culture, or age. This is not surprising if we think people have been making places for millennia before anyone was called an architect.

Using the right communication tools as well as plain language is very important. I remember attending a consultation event back in 2017, one of the typical pin-ups: glossy plans up on the wall in the fashion of an art gallery. All very stylish and glamorous, black satin background, stunning shapes in excellent colour pallets. As I was looking at the masterplan myself, a member of the community approached me and asked me: "Do you know where they are building this park?" He was looking at the section of a building with an extensive green roof on a pitch. He thought the blue sky was a lake and that the main hall space, illustrated in grey,

Chapter 4: **Influencing design** 137

was a car park. This was not my only experience where people found it difficult to orientate themselves in a plan without clear, well-known landmarks and notes.

Another time, working for the local authority, my team was doing a review of a scheme and was presented with a 3D image, the view from the perspective of a pedestrian crossing the road. It looked lovely until we noticed that the door in the ground floor shops was circa 1.2 metres height.[3] The architects had made the 3D volume disproportionately shorter, reducing the height of every element in the façade to make it look less imposing near the adjacent historic buildings. Of course, the trick was skilfully done and the untrained eye could have been easily fooled.

At another local consultation event, the designers put up five posters: one with the existing map, another one with a list of the jobs the scheme would create and other wordy information, and three further posters containing one option each. People were very confused: they thought they were meant to vote which option they wanted to have but they could not find the ballot boxes. Talking in confidence with the designers, I found out that the developer had already chosen the third option but they were worried that people were not going to accept such a large building in their area, so they also produced other two options: one with a lot of greenery and one with a large public square with cafés and shops. They admitted that in doing this, they thought they would be able to please everyone and reduce the potential likelihood of complaints. The stakes are so high in this industry that deceit is not uncommon, and it comes in many forms.

As I write, I realise I have seen a lot of 'consultations'. What remains very rare, indeed, is the engagement process that is transparent, truthful, and productive. I can honestly say I could count those cases on one hand. What I still find fascinating is the fact that it is actually easier and far more productive to work in collaboration than to retain the power and the false perception of being fully in control.

Transparent, direct, frank conversations can save developers huge amounts of time and money and it can lower the risk of gaining a bad reputation. However, the problem is threefold: (a) the vast majority of professionals do not have the skills, training, or confidence to take empowerment schemes forward; (b) there are many design firms that would prefer to extend their working contracts as much as they can with numerous design iterations, prolonging their business beyond the ethically necessary; and (c) various parties, especially developers, are in fear of losing control and having to disclose critical information too early.

I was commissioned to work on a masterplan for 1,400 homes in a village extension in the UK. The Parish had developed and adopted a Neighbourhood Plan that showed the land that they designated for housing as agreed with the community. The village extension I was working on was not within the Neighbourhood Plan allocated plots. I recommended to the client that it would be wise to talk to the community very early before even thinking about developing a masterplan. As they wanted to approach the authority with an idea of development scale and discuss what that would entail in terms of new infrastructure, we did a feasibility study. There were two potential routes for me as a practitioner after that first commission: (1) to continue designing and preparing a planning application for the development, therefore securing a decent income stream for a few months, perhaps years; or (2) to stop all work until we had approached the authority and the community to ensure there would not be strong barriers later on. I recommended option two, as this seemed the safest way forward to me. The response we had from the Parish Council was robust: there would be no engagement at all. They felt that the community had expressed their voice through the Neighbourhood Plan process and that this should suffice to determine a refusal for development on that land. Disappointing perhaps, but also honest and effective. Secretly, I am still hoping for a change of heart from the locals because we had an incredibly green, inclusive, and people-focused design for their area that could have set a strong national precedent of design excellence, albeit not in the location of their preference. But the community had been given an absolute power to establish long-term legislation that leaves no room for further conversations.

If we believe that the issues of reduced trust, low participation, and poor collaboration are exclusive to relationships between different agencies, we would be making a huge error of judgement. An international trend is that different teams, departments, or directorates within large organisations often have different modus operandi, different goals and targets, and most importantly, different budgets. A very good example of this institutional dysfunction is the office building case I described in Chapter 3. Now, I feel I cannot move to the next section of the chapter

Chapter 4: **Influencing design** 139

without mentioning the time when my colleagues and I, all working for the same authority, did not even know we were in full agreement and had a developer playing one department against another to try to achieve some savings.

With climate change as a major priority, the health agenda at the forefront, and the idea of bringing beauty back to British towns, central government has recently revised the National Planning Policy Framework to make the delivery of tree-lined avenues in residential developments a key priority. Nobody in this world thinks this is a bad idea; at least, I have not come across anyone yet. Assuming every department in the local authority I was working for would adhere to this request, I included the notion of tree-lined avenues as a place quality criterion for a residential development of around 500 homes. The draft design code I produced went to other departments and came back with minor amendments. In my mind, large trees, expected to achieve a decent canopy cover, need soil to grow, so I specified a verge of 5–6 metres wide to plant a total of 22 large avenue specimens. The project went through a tender process; a large housing developer won the bid and a few months later, they submitted an adaptation of the plan with their specific house types to achieve planning approval. When I came across the plans, I looked at different versions of the layout in horror – the trees were nowhere to be seen. You could say they had ben axed. A local community group keen on protecting trees contacted their local Councillor, questioning why the local authority had removed those lovely trees in the original plan. It took some time to get to the bottom of the reasons behind the loss of those 22 large trees. What happened was that developers had reduced the size of the verge and the Green Spaces department had told them they were not happy with adopting trees planted in a space where they would not grow. Also, they had located the verge between the road and the footpath, so the Highways Officer rightly advised them that the authority would not be keen to adopt strips of land that are split because maintenance becomes an issue in the future. The developers probably felt the tree issue was giving them headaches – perhaps they wanted to save some money; somehow, they decided to remove them.

Of course, no one was in the wrong; yet, the designers were not able to reach a solution that met all standards. Logically, they had time

Chapter 4: **Influencing design**

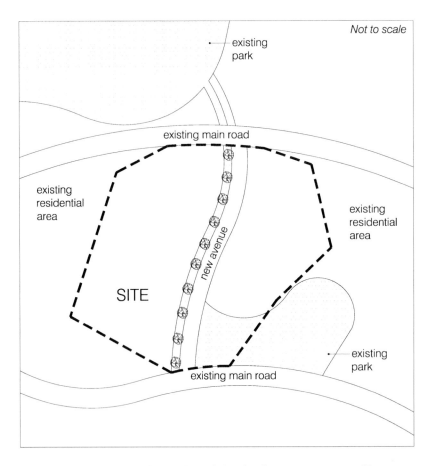

Figure 4.4 Diagram showing a plan of the development concept, with a tree-lined avenue connecting the site to main roads in the north and the south.

constraints and wanted to move on with the process fast. The local authority had a very good planning officer assigned to this case; he arranged a workshop with everyone involved and we came up with a solution that would work for all: a small private footpath to access the properties; adjacent, a 5-metre verge with the specimen trees and a 2-metre footway adjacent to the road. We now use that formula to create tree-lined avenues in other developments, but without the perseverance of the officers involved, working on this case over months to get to the

Chapter 4: **Influencing design**

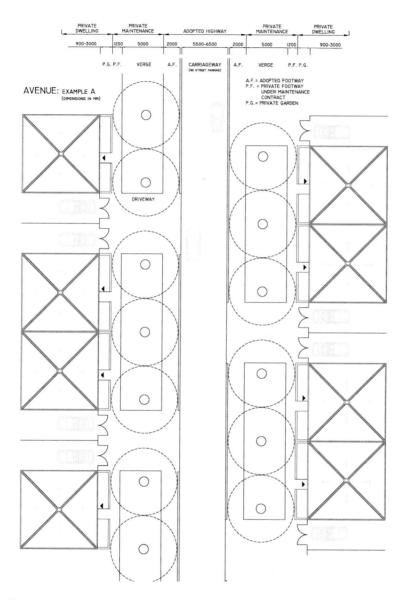

Figure 4.5 Plan showing a detail of the tree-lined avenue design as described in the text: a small private footpath to access the properties; adjacent, a 5-metre verge with the specimen trees and a 2-metre footway adjacent to the road.

bottom of the design issues, the tree-lined idea could have been easily lost. Avoiding delays, discrepancies, and contradictory information across local authority departments is only a matter of communication, collaboration, and mutual understanding. Without a good design quality assurance process, this issue would not have been picked up and probably those involved would have negatively influenced the final result without realising they were doing so.

Inevitably, whenever humans are involved in a process, there is a fight for power. Winning a battle seems inherent to the human condition; working against a win situation could be perceived by some as 'preparing to lose'. Power battles tend to be stronger amongst those already in power. In South America, it is not rare to see sudden changes of direction every time a different political party is in charge. Streets and squares can change names as often as there is an election.

In Britain, where local politicians make the most relevant planning decisions, one can guess who the most imposing figure is at planning committees by looking at the shape, colour, and detail of new buildings. It is not rare in the UK that planning committees, who make decisions to grant permission to build, exert an excessive amount of power. I sometimes fear the new British pursuit for beauty will validate the personal taste of strong characters even more. These politicians often claim that because they are elected members of government who represent local people, they must therefore have a huge influence on the aesthetics of design. The style of new buildings then becomes very dependent upon personal tastes, which is deeply associated with the age group and cultural background of these individuals. Designers complain that innovation and contemporary design are more difficult to achieve due to the likes and dislikes of committee members who prefer features they are already familiar with.

One word of advice I have for those influencing design would be to avoid the use of phrases like: "I find this ugly", "I like this", "I am not a fan of render". These comments mean very little outside the context of a valid technical explanation; they only represent the commentators' desire to surpass the power they are entitled to. However, a politician may not possess this sort of technical knowledge. A much better choice would be: "I would prefer not to see so much render because this tends to decay and stain in the English humid weather".

Chapter 5 brings up some useful tools, concepts, and language to evaluate design objectively. But the issue of personal taste is a very relevant one when multiple agents exercise their right to influence design.

Why do we like the familiar?

I often hear people from different backgrounds telling me they do not like a building because it feels strange or because it is not what they are used to. Mass house builders in the UK tell me their traditional products reflect their customer's choice and that they base their products on market research. I have no reason to disbelieve them; I am sure they know exactly what they need to produce to sell more and I do not believe they would opt to do otherwise.

In countries where the tendency is to self-build, people tend to mimic local vernacular styles and trends. Some time ago, I thought this was due to a response to the local climate or the technical building abilities and low cost materials in the area, but I have one clear example that is contrary to that hypothesis. I will go back to my roots a little bit to prove my point. I come from a town near La Plata, a beautiful city in Argentina that was founded in 1882. As was typical in South America at that time, buildings were designed to follow European models. The most popular in the area were the Spanish and Italian town house layouts, but one could also find large, imposing houses adopting French or English town house styles. In La Plata, plots are still sold individually for people to self-build. A design code establishes some design parameters like heights, building position, how much of the site can be built upon, and so on. However, if you drive 20 minutes South, towards Buenos Aires, you will find that places like City Bell or Villa Elisa are dominated by American and Swiss style chalets. Why? This was not totally due to building trends of that period because very recently built houses in La Plata still follow Mediterranean models. Building contractors on both areas were the same, the landscape does not change too much either, plot sizes are slightly wider in the South but not enough to make that much difference in style. There are some examples that stand out from the rest, where homeowners wanted a statement modern building, but these are a minority. A similar phenomenon took place in other parts of Argentina.

On the Atlantic coast, the use of timber is more prominent and details resemble the Gaucho culture.[4] It seems that, generally speaking, people can make an image of a place and its character and that they are more comfortable following that norm. This has, in time, given towns and cities in the Pampas region an individual character and identity despite streets always following the same pattern and dimensions. Why would the public choose to stick to what they see around?

There are many socio-psychological reasons why, on average, people tend to like more the things they are familiar with: historic or traditional building forms, a good old-fashioned fireplace in Britain, a pergola in Argentina. Scannell and Guifford[5] explained that some authors believe it is a matter of survival instinct. They argue that there is a cognitive bond with well-known things because when people become familiar with their locality, subconsciously they know how to make resources become available for use and consumption. Similarly, other scholars believe that our attachment comes from the psychological sense of security and comfort in relation to the services and resources we know we can find in that place. This sense of security in the familiar can also help individuals develop self-confidence and freedom of exploration. Places that can offer the services, activities, and support to enable people to achieve their goals and assess their progress with confidence soon become a safe haven for them. Other academics in the field added that cognitively, people try to link past and future behaviours together to make sense of their own self as a coherent continuous existence. When a place reminds someone of their past, it helps them identify with elements of their identity as a person, causing feelings of place attachment. This might be why immigrants tend to re-create their home environment when they settle in a foreign land, and probably why some Brits insist on a full fried English breakfast in sunny Spain!

The most successful contemporary designs in the UK have been those that extract core design premises from traditional buildings, giving people that familiarity, but then recreating them and adapting them for present lifestyles. It is possible to convey that sense of safety and comfort residents look for without exactly recreating the past. I have heard rural and semi-rural planners asking developers to add false chimney stacks to their house models to recreate the feel of the local place as it was

Chapter 4: **Influencing design** 145

traditionally. Sadly, I have seen these fake chimney stacks placed randomly in positions and sizes that do not correspond to traditional building methods. Aesthetically pleasing objects they might be to some, but they are otherwise irrelevant and therefore not suitable. The thought was genuine: it aimed to provide that sense of the familiar that people look for, something to evoke some comfort. The truth is that the same effect can be achieved with alternative design solutions, offering a reminder of the old chimney stacks but meeting modern needs. Nottingham City Homes has a brilliant example of sustainable social housing in The Meadows area, a leading green neighbourhood. Contemporary terrace houses incorporated chimney stack-like light wells above the stairwells and corridors, which make homes much brighter, also saving some energy. If we remember the good quality definition by Vitruvius (Chapter 1), we are looking for designs that are functional, durable, and delightful; we must aim to deliver all three.

So, going back to the issue of who holds the most power to influence design, we will soon note that who the figure in charge is can

Figure 4.6 Photograph shows a contemporary Nottingham City Homes dwelling where chimney stack-like light wells above the stairwells and corridors were introduced.

largely depend on the participation approach designers, developers, and authorities adopt; let us explore this a little more.

From coercing to empowering

Long-term engagement is preferable to ad-hoc consultation, but it is not always appropriate as a method; in fact, it should not be used in isolation. Instead, it should be a component part of a larger design influence programme. Most complex projects would require a range of participatory methods, tailored in accordance with the type and size of development, the nature of the agencies involved, the local politics, and the planning and legal systems in place.

The degree of participation is expected to range greatly and to differ from agency to agency, but what really matters is that no agent is denied the right to express their voice and exercise their already limited power. Prohibiting any agent from influencing a design that will have an impact on their lives is simply undemocratic, disenfranchising, and unjust.

The most basic form of participation is establishing a unilateral relation: doing something 'to' participants. This could be achieved by simply coercing or educating. In the coercing form of participation, the designer expects the user to act in a specific way or use a certain service in the place without telling them the reasons why they should do so. For instance, in Chapter 5 we will discuss how shopping centre designers sometimes create spaces that keep people circulating with the purpose of increasing sales; this is coercive design. The second form of unilateral participation happens when the designer shares with the users decisions already made or pre-processed information about the design. For example, when an architect states that a large oak tree will be planted in the middle of a scheme to represent the forest, the designer is not giving a choice to participants, it is simply reinterpreting people's choices and then telling them what their thoughts were. People are used to these two types of participation methods in place design. Authorities have been using these strategies for decades across the globe. I also used it to persuade my son to eat his vegetables.

The next form of participation happens in a two-way type of relationship and it involves a certain exchange: doing something 'for' participants. There are three key methods to achieve this participatory

Chapter 4: **Influencing design** 147

level: information, consultation, and engagement. Information refers to sharing data with people; this can include consultation results, historic data about a place, how a proposal works, and what the considerations behind the decisions made were, for example. The information shared in this case is not processed and it allows the reader to make their own judgement about the decision process taken. The consultation method refers to the designer asking questions to participants to gauge their opinion on specific topics. The most usual tools to gather this type of data are surveys or choice selection (e.g. whether they like the design or if they would visit the area). Designers then can use that data to inform or support their design choices. Engagement refers to opening a channel for participants to express anything they would like to say about the design, giving them regular opportunities to voice their views over time as the design evolves. In an engagement process, people might begin to find direct ways to influence the design.

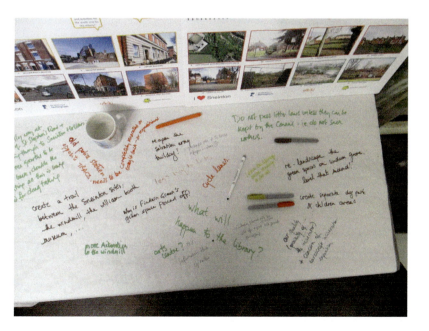

Figure 4.7 Photograph shows data collected during a community event. There is a poster and blank paper where people could make notes, add drawings, and leave messages for designers.

The next level of participation also happens in a two-way form of relationship, but it involves collaboration, placing participants at the designer's level: doing something 'with' participants. This can be achieved through co-design or co-production. The first form of participation implies inviting participants literally to sit down alongside the designer and to collaborate with the creation of the scheme. Later on, expert designers and builders would strive to make this design happen. I have exercised this type of participatory method many times with great success and fantastic rewards. However, co-production is the pinnacle of placemaking democracy and it happens when people produce the place together; in other words, people join the team and, with a hammer in hand, they build. So far, it has been much easier for me to achieve this level of co-placemaking in South America than it has been in the UK. Developers in Britain remain rather controlling, reluctant to let go for fear of malpractice; yet, it is not rare to see professional builders

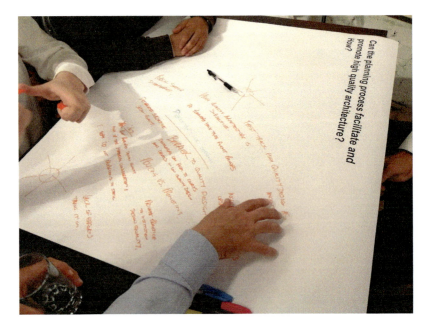

Figure 4.8 Photograph shows participants contributing towards improving the planning process during a community event. There is a poster and a large blank paper on the table where a group of people are making notes about how they visualise the future of the site.

Chapter 4: **Influencing design** 149

Figure 4.9 Photograph shows school pupils contributing towards the design of a new façade during a community event; they are looking at old photographs on a mobile phone, trying to understand place character in order to make design decisions.

delivering the most disastrous or sometimes amusing results. The truth is that with the right design quality systems in place and with adequate professional support, there is no need to fear poor quality in co-design and co-production approaches if interventions are within the capacity of those involved. Good examples of this hands-on approach would be constructing of raised planters for a community garden, planning and delivering a community mural, or designing and mounting a pergola in a public space.

Placemaking offers vast opportunities for designers to exercise all types of participation without onerous investment. A simple example of this would be to dedicate part of a park or public place to community planting. Some scholars commented on the advantages of allowing for a communal plot of land to suit the neighbours' demands, whether this is for allotments, communal agriculture, or recreation, as a vehicle to make new communities more engaged and attached to their places.[6]

Figure 4.10 Photograph shows a school pupil contributing by making a physical 3D model of a co-designed façade during an engagement event; he has tools and protective equipment and he is working on a piece of wood.

In terms of social sustainability, how 'public' neighbourhood places are perceived to be is as important as how 'public' they are. This perception factor is important because it is the community that will make the place work in the long term. When people feel they belong, they care for their places more and place care becomes far easier. Let us look at some of the research into this. For this topic, I felt the need to make a robust argument simply because this topic remains largely in the academic realm, but I believe it is fundamental to social sustainability and deserves due consideration. If academic reading is a little dry for your taste, feel free to skip to my summary at the end of the research text.

Research shows that land ownership and stewardship (also called place care) are deeply related to how much residents feel they belong to the place,[7] how much they love the place,[8] and how their place emotions lead them to happiness and wellbeing. When people cannot find the right level of place bonding through ownership or land management, urban

Chapter 4: Influencing design

appropriation takes place; in other words, people take over public places to make them their own (e.g. they place pots and plants in the public footway).[9] Experts in the field explained that stewardship, as opposed to illegal appropriation, refers to the group of actions people take to maintain, repair, and improve their community and these actions are motivated by a sense of responsibility.[10] These instinctive feelings sometimes translate into voluntary community actions or acts of a more global environmental activism. Design approaches must maximise the benefits of place emotion. Also, placemaking should be carefully tailored to enable long-term stewardship, which can lead to more resilient lifestyles. For example, places for community stewardship can become an instrument for hands-on learning where the community bonds by sharing physical labour whilst restoring their ecosystems. An example of this would be Arkwright Meadows Community Gardens in The Meadows, Nottingham, UK. Local people took over a derelict piece of land and turned it into a community garden and allotment where people can connect with nature and with each other, support the most vulnerable in their locality, and share urban agriculture skills and produce.

Researchers studied resilience in North Queensland, Australia, and they explained how emotional connection to place was found to be a fundamental element of environmental stewardship and land management and how it related to a huge sense of community responsibility towards their place.[11] This connection, the authors added, helps people build their adaptive capacity for change through a good level of understanding and responsibility on how to use their resources and how to manage their land. Another scholar looked at three case studies in New York. She discovered that stewardship can have a social as well as a physical dimension, in that bringing people together to restore natural environments can also strengthen networks and build bridges amongst different communities.[12] But the issue of perceived ownership and that of responsibility over place goes even further and does not limit to physical spaces with clear boundaries. Others discussed the relevance of communal areas in communities in developing democracy and social solidarity with a view that a physical common space can become a catalyst for new ways of governance, reclamation, and self-management.[13] This means that community structures can be formed or altered through emotional investment in place and its material or virtual assets, such as shared electric power, for example. Self-management of shared assets can lead to the creation of new relationships, a sense of ownership, and, therefore, a sense of responsibility towards the place and its people. Other researchers added that transferring assets – such as community centres – to public hands in the form of public trusts where local people have legal ownership of the communal assets could be a good way to increase capacity within communities by promoting bonding and bridging of social networks.[14] Some even call these types of self-management assets 'relational', because one of their main outcomes is the creation of new social connections, encouraging political and civic responsibility at local levels, making the design of social agencies more relevant than the physical design of common places.[15] The study of five cases of community energy ventures in Europe led researchers to conclude that community stakeholder in energy supply systems could be one of the resources designers have in order to bring together Passett's Spheres of Sustainable Development: Environmental, Social, and Economic. However, scholars also think that although place-based assets such as low-carbon infrastructure provide a way to create new social structures, they are not very flexible for future adaptation as they are slow, difficult, and expensive to change.[16] This is why every aspect of the design needs to be assessed through life-long evaluations, as discussed in Chapter 1. Designers must consider whether the communities they are working with have the capacity and skills to take on complex forms of place management and whether levelling up or balancing communities is a feasible option for the project in question.

Although it all sounds very intricate, the influence of community agents does not need to be too costly or complicated; soft approaches can go a very long way.

Research summary

The emotions we establish with our places are associated with how much we feel we belong to a place. These emotions can have a huge impact on how much we are prepared to care for them and maintain places in the long term. If a place gives us something we need (e.g. food, refuge, beauty), we would have an instinct to protect it more and to care for it.

Chapter 4: **Influencing design** 153

> People can become extremely attached to places and their people when they have invested efforts or when they have withdrawn emotions from it. A well-designed place will serve as a hub that triggers those emotions, brings people together, and sustains community relationships and collective action in the long term. This is why it is so crucial that designers think about place emotions and the social dynamics of end users. Providing communal spaces and assets, designers can help forming and strengthening communities. It is this type of social cohesion that forms the foundations to sustain resilient societies.

Closing the influence loop

In order to achieve quality, sustainable development, designers need all the influencing agents to work alongside them in the long term, reinforcing collective values in favour of individualism and redistributing opportunities, an approach that often results in increased participation levels and a build-up of social resilience. Placemaking as a process has a huge amount of capacity to offer participation opportunities to all without significant investment. According to Ferragina,[3] this is important because in societies with more participation and higher levels of civic or institutional trust, opportunistic behaviours are lower and people are more likely to make longer-term investments. The question is how the placemaking industry can contribute to achieving these goals.

As we mentioned before, establishing and maintaining certain levels of trust requires good, clear, transparent communication. All agents with influence in a project should feel valued and respected at all times during the process. This is why it is so important to establish open, continuous, and updated communication platforms where participants feel at ease and free to browse, and they can become fully informed and express their voices through appropriate channels and in their own time. Crucially, all agents must always have the same level of information simultaneously, to ensure everyone is able to read from the source and make their own conclusions rather than reading from informal media or journalism, which tends to be charged with a particular view, incorporating a risk of bias. In other words, using journalism to publish local authority or developer plans means that any information given to the public is already digested and evaluated by someone else, which removes the opportunity for the audience to make up their own minds, potentially leaving them unable to understand the decision-makers' thought process. It also avoids the risk of disclosing contentious information accidentally and there will be those authorities and developers that use public media as a means to validate their word. In a time of heavy social media activity with the potential of gaining immediate public response, the old-fashioned unidirectional type of press release that some local authorities and developers engage with does not only seem incredibly patronising but can also be very dangerous. This traditional press strategy can put the reputation of the organisation at risk by suggesting information control and lack of transparency. Additionally, as people are not always fully aware of the complex processes involved in placemaking and how schemes can change through the process, they may interpret artists' impressions as the final product; they may become too familiar with an image, believing that is the place they will have when the project comes to an end. Communities grow increasingly frustrated and mistrusting when their authorities do not deliver what they presented to be the final design. In summary, decision-makers, developers, and project owners need to consider the power of social media in this time and age as well as the huge risks associated with both its use and its omission during engagement processes.

A new form of communication that facilitates more sustainable, democratic, and inclusive forms of development needs to become the norm. A minor degree of control should be exercised purely through the selection of data released and the timing for this to happen. Data should be shared broadly to all agents simultaneously through dedicated platforms that can gather and automatically analyse responses to give an on-time result, also visible by all. Decisions made should be clearly and openly justified by evidence and participants should have a choice to agree or disagree with the path taken rather than second-guessing why things happen to their places the way they do. A good example of this type of participation when it comes to data and decision-making information sharing was the British Prime Minister's Covid-19 updates. On regular television appearances, experts explained their research

# Chapter 4: **Influencing design**

findings in simple slides in a way that the public could understand; then, politicians described how they made their decisions, what they prioritised, and what course of action they would take. The public had the democratic right to agree or disagree with the decisions made, but they were fully aware of the data that informed those decisions. The control the government had was not in hiding the process of decision-making, but in deciding what data to show and making sure the time was right to debate those particular points. This model is what we are likely to see emerging in the world of placemaking. Of course, a sound information sharing protocol and modernised on-time communication system will need to be adopted by planning departments and developers to progress to this level of place democracy. So, I guess it could be some time before this happens.

Case studies

Case Study 4.1 Neighbourhood plan engagement

I have had consultation events where nobody turned up, I have seen strong disruptions at both face to face and online events, and I have been at events delayed by more than five hours due to disagreements amongst participants and organisers. But I have never witnessed anything like this. I actually felt scared at the time…

This was a community event I organised on behalf of the practice I worked for at the time, which was based in the Midlands of the UK. The purpose of the gathering was to work together to define some of the criteria for a Neighbourhood Plan. Aware of some local conflict over the location of a proposed housing development in an area of local recreation and pasture, my naïve intention was to inform the community of their limited powers to begin with, setting people to work in groups to come up with alternative solutions together.

What I was not aware of, however, was that there were some long-term local politics standing at play and a series of historic decisions that had caused a sense of disempowerment and that had fuelled anger amongst some local people, who felt targeted over the years. Had I known all that history of mistrust and personal vendettas, I would have done individual workshops for those two sectors before joining them in the same room. As soon as the event started, one could cut the atmosphere with a knife. Such was the level of anger amongst some participants that I could not even introduce the exercise. I felt terrible for the few people that attended with the intention to participate in a positive way. Soon enough, some community members began arguing and in no time, these escalated to personal insults, physical aggression, and chaos. The police had to be called in. That night, a local Councillor's home and car were vandalised, and local rumours had it that their children were threatened.

Looking back, I realise that the main issue here was a historic lack of trust in relation to place management and development. The authority had over-promised regeneration just before the economic recession of 2008. Of course, proposals presented to the community as imminent had not been delivered due to the rapidly changing economic climate. To make matters worse, there were large plots of land that were much better located and more suitable for the delivery of new homes than the pretty recreation grounds local people wanted to preserve. The issue was that the more suitable land was in the hands of private ownership. Developers were sitting on it to see the commercial value of their land rise (also known as land banking) whilst the recreation grounds belonged to the regional authority. Perhaps people did not realise that local authorities have restricted powers to force landowners to release their assets for house building. Instead, they saw the whole situation as a betrayal from their authority. In their eyes, the local government was taking the easy route to meet the housing growth targets in the area. Of course, with new housing built on local land would come improved infrastructure, which would push the land value for private landowners, increasing their gains, therefore potentially

Chapter 4: **Influencing design**

triggering further land release and economic growth for the area. Had the authority been clear and transparent from the outset about opportunities, constraints, gains, and risks instead of showing a nice looking image of what the future could be, local people would have been better informed and perhaps they would have been able to have a different, more mature type of dialogue, and it would not have ended like a wedding in the Queen Vic.[17]

After this awful experience, I thought I had learnt enough to be able to prevent it from happening again, but a couple of years later, I had a very similar case elsewhere in the country. This time, I managed to keep angry delegates at bay by applying some newly acquired conflict management techniques, but I was disappointed I could not see it coming to prevent it fully from the outset. Understanding local politics in depth is crucial to engage in any type of dialogue. I am happy to say that since I began to apply the tool shown later in this chapter, I felt better prepared for events and I have not witnessed a similar situation again, yet.

Case Study 4.2 Social housing engagement

Working for an architectural firm in the Central England, I was commissioned by a housing association to produce a masterplan for a very complex site in an urban location. There were serious ground level and access issues that made the job very tricky, but the client's intentions were good: they wanted to include green areas for community planting, all forms of co-design projects, and energy-saving, family homes.

My team began by putting together a feasibility study to assess how many houses could realistically be accommodated on the site; we managed to achieve 75 homes. The brownfield site, in the centre of a social housing residential area, had been abandoned for some time, and although it was gated to avoid people climbing onto dangerous derelict buildings, it had festered into a state of disrepair and a fly-tipping zone.

The clients knew that the development would affect nearby neighbours and that it would bring more traffic to the area, especially if it were to include allotments, so they agreed to begin community engagement very early into the process. What I found strange was that they had their own modus operandi for consulting and engaging and they were completely inflexible, unwilling to listen to any recommendations or ideas from the design team. They requested that I attended the consultation on a weekday at 5 pm to help them collect data, so I did just that.

It took me half an hour to find the event room they had hired. Signage was poor and the building was hidden between some vegetation and the primary school rear fence. I thought to myself that this might be tricky to find because I was not local; perhaps neighbours knew where to go. We set up a table, and I had brought some chocolates for participants and some activities for children. It was 5 pm, then 5:30 pm. The place was quiet. The clock showed 6:00 pm, then 6:45 pm. Nothing, not a soul walked in. At 7:30 pm, we packed our equipment and left. Not one participant had turned up.

During the event, I went outside to see if I could invite anyone in, but parents were collecting their children from the school next door. They were busy, tired, and in need to get home to make dinner for their hungry children. The area was so packed with parents collecting their children that no other sector of the population wanted to be anywhere near the consultation room, as they were trying to avoid the chaos. I asked the clients' representative how the event was advertised. They said they had published it on their newsletter to tenants. I then realised that probably most people bin the leaflets without even looking at them. Also, the choice of event location, time, and date was not exactly inviting. My team produced a post-event report with some advice on how to improve participant attendance to events. I am not sure how they received this, given that they had been so strong to remind us they knew what they were doing in the past. To my surprise, they agreed to re-consult once more.

Following our advice, they hired a stall at the local Christmas fair where they gathered a huge amount of survey answers, which, in my opinion, were not exactly constructive because the questions they asked did not lead to answers that could influence the design or its process in any way. The box was ticked: they had 'engaged' with the local community.

I refer to this case study many times because it is a very common recurrence in the UK. Communities are frankly tired of spending time and effort offering their views when probably nothing will come of it. Speaking to people, I found out that many felt used, working to tick the developers' box, and never hearing any more about it. People like to know what happens with their input; they want to have some form of influence, even if it is minimal. Contrary to common belief, community influence can result in very positive design changes and, normally, the type of design change that will not cost much but that will make a real difference to people's lives. Examples I can think of where this was the case relate to topics like connecting a pedestrian link in a different location, planting a specific type of shrub, or installing an electric socket and a post for a Christmas tree. My advice to developers would be: there is no need to panic – bringing people on board with honesty and transparency can actually translate to very good public relations and better design.

Case Study 4.3 Two towns engagement

This is the case of a commission to produce a development framework for a couple of towns in the north of England. In a nutshell, my team had to create a brief for public viewing, showing how the towns could be improved if monies were made available in the future. Local authorities in Britain use this type of document to secure financial contributions from developers for public place improvements. The briefs normally contain graphics, an idea of priority for the works, and an illustration of how improvements could enhance the area economically, socially, and environmentally.

At the time, I was employed by a former design council alongside a delightful team under the direction of the inspirational Sue McGlyn, co-author of *Responsive Environments*.[18] We were working for a leading county authority with a strong design edge and a very talented young planner. Team members and clients were adamant to achieve a truly participatory outcome, so we decided to adopt the engagement route. As this was a good opportunity for innovation and to test new tools, everyone kindly agreed to let me include this work as a case study for my doctoral thesis. I am glad they did because by applying my research, we managed to think on the spot and adapt our strategy very fast when things were not going so well; true innovation at the time.

One of the highlights of the project was Sue's suggestion to include Walkabouts, a technique to capture perceptual, cognitive, and emotional interpretations of place from both professional and residents' perspectives at the same time. It is simple: residents and professionals' take a walk, map in hand, and have discussions, making notes about the highlights and problems in their neighbourhood. This brought to light a huge amount of data, charged with a level of emotion visible on the notes participants took themselves.

Additionally, we programmed pop-in sessions with flexible workshops where, using large maps, pens, stickers, and photographs, local people could tell us what they loved and disliked about the place. Sue preferred to call these 'happy' and 'gloomy' places. They also commented on what they thought was missing and what they would have liked to happen in the future. We hired the best-located venue at the best possible time and date, decorating it with banners and balloons, and with a free buffet with gorgeous cakes made by a local caterer and games for children to play with. Time passed; more time passed. People were not walking in. The same happened in both towns. At the first place, only one person came in, an elderly lady. At the second town, five people walked in. At least they could have had plenty of cake…

Chapter 4: **Influencing design** 161

Figure 4.11 Photograph shows a completely empty community hall prepared with chairs to receive 50 people.

We were at risk of leaving our engagement window without being able to collect much data at all. Here, in times of crisis, is where innovation can give surprising results. My thesis research on social sustainability was very concerned with social cohesion, trust, and social resilience. In order to understand those concepts, I had to dig deep into the field of sociology, looking in detail at the latest research on social network analysis. In order to test its relevance in the field of urbanism, I had introduced a pre-engagement task: to map social networks in both towns, looking at levels of activity and types of interaction by place, by date, by time of day. This was incredibly useful information because not only did we gain good knowledge about the geography of these places, which meant we could relate to people's comments, but we also knew exactly where to find people from different backgrounds at different times of the day. So, instead of waiting for people to come to us, the team was divided in two: half of us stayed to deliver the workshop in case people turned up, and the other half took the workshop to people where we knew they would be at the time. We went to the park, the local schools, the knitting group, the Women's Institute, the shopping precinct, the betting shops, a few hairdresser salons, and so on. Through the process, we discovered that people were not keen to attend the workshop because they did not trust the authority, claiming they had been promised a lot in the past but very little was ever delivered. A helpful entry point for us was the fact that we were an independent charity acting as advisors to their authority. The beauty of this method, which I called 'We come to you', was that after establishing a conversation with people and showing honesty and transparency as well as some empathy, people began to engage by email, by letter, and so on. A month later, we had a second event where we showed participants how their voices had influenced the proposals we were going to put forward to the authorities. The rooms were now full in both towns; we had to ask for extra seating and we ran out of cakes.

I had never seen so much data about a place in my life. The team hired a room at a beautiful hotel; we spent three days nonstop to analyse it all before our departure whilst it was still fresh in our heads. I have to admit there is something else I learnt from this experience: staying in a pleasant, quiet place is a great way to boost productivity. Another star goes to lovely Sue for the suggestion.

I felt participants really appreciated our honesty when we explained the limitations the authority had to make things happen. They were also grateful to see many of the points they had raised making their way through to a legally binding document. I would dare to bet these were the first pair of development frameworks in the UK that included 'social network analysis' as a placemaking methodology and which had a full session on how to strengthen local community networks. It did that by prioritising social investment needs and suggesting action points to move forward. Now the social dimension was an integral part of the development framework.

Lessons learnt

Perhaps this was a chapter of mixed emotions, or as we say in Spanish: 'one of sand and one of limestone'. In the first case, lack of trust and years of disempowerment had left part of a community engrained with anger, unable to think in a constructive way. My error in the management of that project was to be unaware of such history and not doing more to get to the bottom of the story before arranging the programme. Even after receiving specialist training on community conflict management, I repeated the same error again; but this time I was able to manage the situation and rapidly revert it by applying some of those learnings. In retrospect, what I should have done instead was to take the time to understand local politics and dynamics. With a larger budget and more flexible time frames, I could have probably approached different groups individually and simply talked to them before gathering everyone under one roof to discuss such hot topics. Nowadays, I plan for this preparation period as a crucial part of my work schedule. Sadly, designers do not receive community engagement training to the degree that is necessary. Moving forward, this should be a fundamental change for all university courses invested in placemaking.

Table 4.1 Case study analysis summary.

Case Study	Topic	What Was Different?	Outcome
4.1 Neighbourhood Plan engagement	Lack of local politics understanding	Insufficient contact with local people individually prior to gathering different groups	Negative: dangerous situation
4.2 Social housing engagement	Ineffective outreach and surveying strategies	Clients' inflexibility, reluctance to accept advice and change their modus operandi	Negative: poor participation outcomes
4.3 Two towns engagement	Innovative methods of engagement	Good understanding of place and people allowed the team to be creative to achieve better results	Positive: innovation increased participation

If all these experiences have something in common, it is the passion people have for the places where they live. The levels of attachment are such that people are prepared not only to spend time and efforts in having a say, but also emotional investment to the point of becoming agitated and aggressive towards fellow residents and the authorities. From my experience, I could guess that given the need to, people would be prepared to fight for their place just as they have done many times in centuries past.

Tool 4: Influence programme

Over the years, I found that a good way to include the relevant agents in my design engagement programmes is to use the Design Agent's Map introduced in Chapter 3 as a basis to create an Influence Programme. This is a document that helps me summarise the area of influence different agents might have, the new opportunities the process could create for them, the limits of their power, and the optimum timings for their input. This Influence Programme needs to be made available to all, so that different agents know when design changes might occur and the potential reasons for those changes. They will also understand, at a glance, when it will be appropriate for them to participate, what limitations they will face, and how exactly they can have their voices heard. Making this information public opens an opportunity for others to suggest key institutions, organisations, or groups that might need to be included in the map and that have been accidentally omitted. This way, everyone becomes a guardian of place democracy, rather than leaving that huge responsibility to those closely involved with the scheme.

Now, based on the subjects we discussed in this chapter, I would like to ask urban designers to think about how much effort they have made so far to empower other design agents to influence their designs. I would also ask them to reflect on whether they think there might have been missed opportunities to help end users to make the most of the process to create a stronger bond with the place.

In the next chapters, we will look at how designs can be evaluated objectively through the use of easy to apply appraisal tools with clear design criteria that both design professionals and lay people can understand.

Chapter 4: **Influencing design**

Table 4.2 Tool 4: Influence programme (refer to Table 3.7: Design Agents' Map for more information about the agents involved).

Influence Programme Stage: Concept (Developed Design/Detailed Design)

Industry Professionals

Name	Time Frame	Opportunity	Level of Influence	Type of Input
Patrick Phelan	Design: July 22–June 23 Building: July 23–October 23	Expertise in the use of wood and historic buildings restoration	Opinion sharing Problem solving	Specialist professional views and suggestions for delivery
Ian Beale	Vision/concept: March 22–June 22 Design: July 22–June 23	Project management and business network knowledge	Investment	Decision-Maker
Nicholas Cotton	Vision/concept: March 22–June 22 Building: July 23–October 23	Locksmith, home security, and rights of way expertise	Informant Problem solving	Specialist professional views and suggestions for delivery

(Continued)

(Continued)

Authorities/Service Providers

Name	Time Frame	Opportunity	Level of Influence	Type of Input
Robbie Jackson	Vision/concept: March 22–June 22	Social network knowledge	Informant	Outreach to community groups, businesses, and residents
Audrey Roberts	Vision/concept: March 22–June 22	Community rapport, understanding the authorities' point of view and priorities	Informant Ambassador	Attending public events, communicating with constituents
Eric Pollard	Design: July 22–June 23		Decision-making	Steering the design towards a compliant proposal

Clients/Landowners

Name	Time Frame	Opportunity	Level of Influence	Type of Input
Frederick Elliot	Vision/concept: March 22–June 22 Building: July 23–October 23	Business network and investors' knowledge	Networking collaboration	Outreach to potential investors and businesses; case study knowledge

(Continued)

(Continued)

| Michael Baldwin | Vision/concept: March 22–June 22 Design: July 22–June 23 | Potential investor | Informant | Customers' preferences, marketing, and business models |
| Kim Tate | Vision/concept: March 22–June 22 Design: July 22–June 23 | Understanding the landlord or landowner ambitions and vision | Decision-making | Anything from opinion sharing to co-design, depending on the level of involvement they wish to exercise |

Communities/Residents

Name	Time Frame	Opportunity	Level of Influence	Type of Input
Phil Mitchell	Vision/concept: March 22–June 22	Project delivery and business network knowledge	Informant Ambassador	Personal and public opinion sharing, potential use of the pub to advertise and host events

(*Continued*)

(Continued)

Name	Time Frame	Communities/Residents Opportunity	Level of Influence	Type of Input
Norris Cole	Vision/concept: March 22–June 22 Building: July 23–October 23	Understanding of community and their views, motivations, and concerns	Networking collaboration	Advise on different local opinions, knowledge of local customs and traditions; community network knowledge
Dorothy Cotton	July 23–October 23	Local food bank provision; fundraiser	Informant Co-design	Ideas, contacts, community event organisation experience

Notes

1 David Halpern, *Social Capital* (Cambridge: Polity Press, 2005) 4.
2 Alex Zautra, John Hall, and Kate Murray. 2008. "Community Development and Community Resilience: An Integrative Approach." *Community Development* 39 (3): 143.
3 The standard door opening height is 2.2 metres in the UK.
4 Gaucho: a cowboy from the South American pampas.
5 Leila Scannell and Robert Gifford. 2010. "Defining Place Attachment: A Tripartite Organizing Framework." *Journal of Environmental Psychology* 30 (1): 1–10. https://doi.org/10.1016/j.jenvp.2009.09.006.
6 Peter Hall and Colin Ward, *Sociable Cities: Legacy of Ebenezer Howard* (Chichester: John Wiley & Sons, 1998) 206.
7 Emanuele Ferragina, *Social Capital in Europe [Electronic Resource]: A Comparative Regional Analysis* (Cheltenham: Edward Elgar, 2012) 142.
8 Tonya Davidson, Ondine Park, and Rob Shields, *Ecologies of Affect: Placing Nostalgia, Desire, and Hope* (Waterloo, Canada: Wilfrid Laurier University Press, 2011) 4–8.
9 Nishat Awan, Tatjana Schneider, and Jeremy Till, *Spatial Agency: Other Ways of doing Architecture* (Oxford: Routledge, 2011).
10 Randy Hester, *Design for Ecological Democracy* (Cambridge, MA; London: MIT Press, 2006) 364–385.
11 Kirsten Maclean, Michael Cuthill, and Helen Ross. 2013. "Six Attributes of Social Resilience." *Journal of Environmental Planning and Management* 57 (1): 144–156.
12 Keith G. Tidball, Marianne E. Krasny, Erika Svendsen, Lindsay Campbell, and Kenneth Helphand. 2010. "Stewardship, Learning, and Memory in Disaster Resilience." *Environmental Education Research* 16 (5-6): 591–609.
13 Doina Petrescu. In: Pew Rawes, *Relational Architectural Ecologies: Architecture, Nature and Subjectivity* (London: Routledge, 2013) 261–262.
14 David Halpern, *Social Capital* (Cambridge: Polity Press, 2005) 304.
15 Doina Petrescu. In: Pew Rawes, *Relational Architectural Ecologies: Architecture, Nature and Subjectivity* (London: Routledge, 2013) 264.
16 Eva Heiskanena, Mikael Johnsona, Simon Robinsonb, Edina Vadovicsc, and Mika Saastamoinena. 2010. "Low-Carbon Communities as a Context for Individual Behavioural Change." *Energy Policy* 38 (12): 7586–7595.
17 The Queen Vic is a local pub in a British drama, a soap opera called *Eastenders*.
18 Sue McGlynn, Graham Smith, Alan Alcock, Paul Murrain, and Ian Bentley, *Responsive Environments: A Manual for Designers*, 1st ed. (London: Routledge, 1985).

Chapter 5
Design form

In Chapter 4, we looked at the influence different agents involved in the design process can have. Through the case studies, we saw how a lack of collaboration can jeopardise the quality and sustainable credentials of buildings and places by making the process more complicated and lengthy or by missing out key information.

This chapter will illustrate how some of the core principles of good design can remove a layer of uncertainty about the aesthetic quality and the appropriateness of development for its given context. It also begins to set core design criteria that can become determinants of design quality in appraisal tools.

An issue of skills

Local authorities in the UK have grown a reputation for lacking design skills and talent; possibly because of reduced staffing due to cost savings, but also because public service wages are no competition for private practice salaries, which means talent often leaks towards the private sector. However, whilst in practice, I have seen some exceptionally skilled officers, for example, in Nottingham and Leicester City Councils, and Northampton, North Leicestershire, and North Derbyshire County Councils. I have seen officers relentlessly trying to convey the principles of good design to professional, accredited designers (who, by the way, probably earn significantly more). These officers can spot a design error with their eyes closed, they can explain what exactly looks wrong, and they can come up with solutions

DOI: 10.4324/9781003244059-6

Chapter 5: **Design form**

to improve the design. However, sometimes they cannot direct applicants to the root of the issues, as they find difficulties in grasping that theoretical architectural explanation that will give designers a path to follow, a clue that will lead them to finding a new design solution of their own. Of course, planners are not trained in the theory of design and, therefore, often lack the background knowledge that would help them convey a design principle in that way. I believe this chapter will be very useful for officers as a communication tool, especially in the UK, where the Government is pushing for beauty in design as a criterion to fast forward planning consent to build.

Too many times, architects consider buildings in isolation. They worry about the merit of their designs as if they were creating a piece of art. Any good art curator reading this will understand exactly what I mean, as they know how difficult it is to organise a display in a meaningful way. Urban designers are like the curators of the built environment. Of course, there is nothing wrong with taking pride in the aesthetics and technical properties of buildings, but we must not forget that when we intervene in a complex structure, whether that is an urban or natural system, we have an inevitable impact on that environment: we change the place balance; that space will never be the same and the ecosystem will have to readjust. This privilege to alter the habitat of many species as well as our own comes with a huge degree of responsibility. You will have seen Sir David Attenborough documenting while he and his crew try their hardest to avoid interfering with the cycles of nature when filming. Well, built environment professionals do it all the time without a second thought. Something makes us believe that because humans created cities, we own them and can do as we please with them. The truth is that every time we make a change in an urban environment, we are disrupting an ecosystem humans share with other species. Of course, change also disturbs the social structures that support our communities, therefore affecting us, humans, directly as well. This is not to say that we should stop building, of course; but we should do it conscientiously. Why? Because we can; we have the faculties to do so.

Any new structure in a space will have some impact on its context. This is why buildings and places must never be conceived or understood purely on their own; they are an integral part of the ecological, social, and economic context. Adding, changing, or eliminating them will alter the balance of that environment and the whole system will need time to adjust and adapt. When a new scheme becomes well established, the human ecosystem flourishes around it. People gathering and performing different activities, users looking through windows, people arriving and glancing at a façade, they all reinforce the relationship between that structure and the space where it sits; those relationships transform a space to a place, as we already discussed in Chapter 1.

Over the centuries, designers around the globe have managed to understand some of the parameters they can use to measure the impact of new schemes on existing contexts. It should be clear to any urban design professionals that some environments are more delicate than others, mainly due to their historic, cultural, environmental, or symbolic significance. However, there is no space in this planet that is not worthy of respect and consideration. It is not rare to hear developers, and sometimes even planners or designers, claiming that since a place is of poor quality to begin with, they have no pressure as professionals to go the extra mile to deliver good quality. If we only build good quality in top-class places, there would be no room for positive change. Poor design is dangerous: it triggers negative behaviours, it affects our mental and physical health, and above all, it damages our planet and diminishes the legacy we can leave for future generations. No built environment agent with some degree of professional ethics should settle for lower levels of quality than the best that could be achieved.

Case studies

Case Study 5.1 Housing in context

This is the story of a small housing development in Sherwood, Nottingham, fairly local to me. Sherwood is a Victorian neighbourhood where typical English red brick, bay window houses with chimneys and pitched roofs dominate the streetscape. There are some terrace houses, some semi-detached and some detached, ranging from two to three storeys height. Gentle hills and mature street trees give the place a slight forestry feel. Of course, once upon a time, it was part of Sherwood Forest, home to the legendary Robin Hood and his merry gang.

Chapter 5: **Design form** 173

Figure 5.1 Photograph shows typical homes built in the Victorian and Edwardian eras in Sherwood, Nottingham, UK.

Figure 5.2 Photograph shows typical homes built after the Victorian era in Sherwood, Nottingham, UK.

Figure 5.3 Photograph shows typical semi-detached homes built in the Victorian and Edwardian eras in Sherwood, Nottingham, UK.

Figure 5.4 Photograph shows typical terrace homes built in the Victorian era in Sherwood, Nottingham, UK.

A colleague from planning (a witty, likeable character) and I worked together on this project to reshape a pre-application submission that did not sit comfortably within the urban context. The site was a small and rather intricate plot of land in an 'L' shape, with neighbouring homes in close proximity and facing two streets. The wider frontage was onto a major road where vehicular access was not permitted; the narrow frontage was facing a quiet residential street.

The proposal submitted for pre-application was for a few houses onto the quiet road and some flats onto the main road. The design principles were in general correct, but the scheme somehow felt out of place. The proximity to neighbouring properties was well thought through and dealt with conscientiously. I remember the planner saying: "I know – in fact, I am convinced – that there is something wrong with this design, but I cannot put my finger on what that is. It just doesn't feel right."

My colleague was concerned that the applicants wanted to achieve a contemporary design, but they were worried that planners would push them to adopt a more traditional aesthetic. The main issue with the submitted scheme was not the building style, but that the scheme had been designed *inside-out*. Once the footprint of the buildings and the access points had been established,

Chapter 5: **Design form** 175

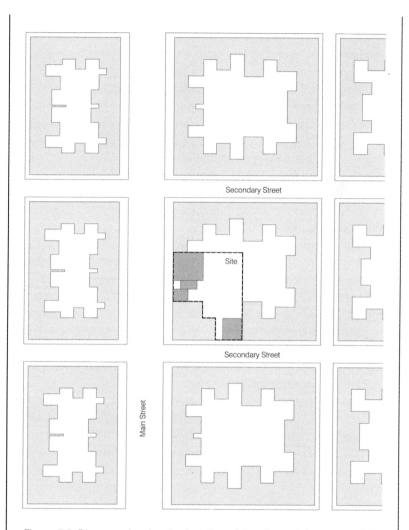

Figure 5.5 Diagram showing the location of the site and the proposals in the context of the neighbourhood.

which was done correctly, the architects began to design the layout of the flats, piling up four storeys and ending up with a cuboid building that did not respond to the setting. To begin with, the proportions were not corresponding with the Victorian neighbouring: because modern flats are designed in a metric grid, whilst the 1800s buildings used imperial dimensions (you know: 12 inches to the foot, 3 feet to the yard, 1,760 yard to the mile – all that easy stuff…). Another problem was that the flats were clustered to form a large volume that resulted in a heavy mass, contrary to the more elongated Victorian homes, which are narrow, deep, and tall, a strategy that was used to maximise land efficiency at a time of rapid urban growth.

The building for the flats was not the only problem. Houses were modern, also designed with the metric system, with wide frontages and low floor-to-ceiling heights. The roof ridge was parallel to the front, so the slope fell towards the street. Neighbouring properties had the pitch in the opposite orientation, forming a gable or triangular façade at the front of these houses. The development was completely different in proportions to the neighbouring properties; it was stumpy and looked robust when their neighbours were elegant and sleek.

The solution for the houses was simple: redesign them with the imperial system, in the same proportions as the neighbours and following their geometric pattern, especially for the roof. That was all that had to happen. As the core principles of the design were now correct, it was not necessary to add any detail that mimicked the Victorian style. These contemporary buildings, minimal but of high quality, would fit in with the context and reflect their own age rather than trying to imitate old styles.

The solution for the flats was also simple: we had to begin with a form that was carved from the *outside-in*. The geometry of neighbouring buildings was not appropriate for this large block of flats, but we could look for references in the many former industrial buildings in the area. Victorian neighbourhoods typically had residential and manufacturing buildings coexisting side by side, and

Chapter 5: **Design form**

there were numerous examples that we could use as a source of reference. Once again, this was not about recreating the old mills, but it was about de-codifying the mathematics behind their design and reapplying them to a contemporary building with a different use. So we pitched the roof at a specific angle and tall windows replaced the proposed square ones to achieve a more industrial, slender feel, also making the flats feel brighter and more spacious inside. The ground, middle, and top floors had different openings that replicated the proportions of windows typical in local industrial buildings. The volume was split in two parts, with a recessed access point in between to manage the impact of the building mass; this also made the frontage more legible, as the access lobby was easily identifiable (see Figure 5.6).

With those changes, a contemporary aesthetic could co-exist with the historic environment around it. To put the icing on the cake, the changes achieved more parking, larger private gardens, and improved bin storage and collection points. As it turns out, the Victorians were right: their proportions resulted in a more efficient use of land. Soon after, my colleague received a letter from the applicant thanking the team for making their scheme so much better. Sadly, this type of work has to take place at local authorities

Figure 5.6 Sketch of the development approximately as submitted by the applicant.

Figure 5.7 Sketch of the development as amended by the local authority. Illustrated by the author.

in the UK on a daily basis to compensate for the industry's lack of skills, pushing the resources of planning departments to the limit. I will celebrate the day when architecture and urban design courses teach these essential design strategies once again. It appears that the glamorous effect of illustration technology seems more attractive in university prospectuses than essential knowledge. Why can we not have both?

Case Study 5.2 Village extension in context

The scheme I will describe next is very close to my heart. I was working at a UK practice as both an architectural and urban designer. We received a commission to prepare a concept masterplan for a large number of houses in an historic village in the English Midlands. The place was what you expect to see on the cover of a chocolate box: stone farmhouses, some thatched roofs, outbuildings and barns, and charming small town houses with thick wooden doorframes and rugged brick walls faced a cosy public square, with a medieval fountain, of course. Sheep, hedgehogs, ducks, and swans wandered around the village, and as I walked on my way to the site, the scent of roses of all colours of the rainbow filled the air, already rich with lavender aromas. A beautiful stream ran from the medieval church site down to the area of study, meandering its way across farms and gardens. It was a dream, a true rural idyll, and we were potentially going to build 700 new homes right in the middle of that place. I have never felt such sense of responsibility in my life. Where to begin?

I arrived at the site early in the morning. Muddy wellies, angler hat, and a soaking wet map of the area; England is beautiful, but what they say about the weather is true. I stood at the site gate and looked around. I could not believe my eyes: it was like being on holiday at an idyllic setting; only that I knew I had a huge, challenging job to do. As you might expect, the site was big, and it took me a couple of hours to walk around the edges and across to check the soil, the levels, the microclimate, and the views. At that point, I was still taking it all in. Before I knew it, it was time for lunch, so I walked to the local pub and sat by the crackling fire with a warming bowl of soup and a cob.[1] I did a lot of thinking before I could decide how to tackle this job. I knew the time allocated at the office would not suffice for a scheme like this, so I went back to the village almost every weekend for a few weeks, trying to understand what the place was all about. I spent most of the time observing, capturing images, and sketching the urban patterns: the typical geometries, the urban grain and texture, the colour pallets, the composition of the village, the population's customs and behaviours, the role of animals in making it all feel so country-like, the mental mapping and wayfinding cues, the different rhythms that made the place feel the way it did, and so on.

The development we were about to propose was large enough to be considered an urban extension. The client, who was a landowner from a gentrified background, knew this was a highly sensitive case, and decided not to engage with the local community until we were certain the scheme was feasible. Sensibly, they did not want to cause alarm and stress unnecessarily amongst the locals at such an early stage in the process, even before a viability study was done to ensure the project was possible.

The design team worked really hard on this, trying to achieve a proposal that would make the village proud. I decided to try a new urban design method: a placemaking first approach, which was rare to see back then. I formed an initial vision for the place, piecing together data gathered whilst talking to local people week after week, finding out what they liked about their village and what they were concerned about. For the design, I decided to treat the new development as if it had grown organically over centuries. I recreated the urban patterns I found in the area, introducing the core design parameters according to the existing patterns, but using modern methods of construction, incorporating smart technologies, and catering for young children and an ageing population by adopting a dementia-friendly design. Years before, I had worked loosely with the regional Public Health authority in developing ten tips for legible places; an effort to draft a dementia-friendly design guide. I later adopted these tips for Nottingham Design Quality Framework to help designers achieve places that work for people of all ages and with different abilities.

1. Using a variety of urban landmark tools can help people identify routes:
   - SYMBOLISM: historic buildings, war memorials, churches, gateway.
   - DISTINCTIVENESS: clock towers, public art, phone boxes, seating, shelters.
   - ACTIVITY: mixed-use squares, parks, playgrounds.
   - COLLECTIVE MEMORY: doctor's surgery, schools, pubs.
2. Designing with a variety of carefully combined, different materials, colours, and textures can help distinctiveness.

Chapter 5: **Design form**

> 3. Using small design features to add distinctiveness in specific locations, such as chimney pots, different front doors, or bay windows.
> 4. Creating landscape landmarks, such as larger front gardens or unique trees, can help navigation.
> 5. Designing simple, well-connected, straight, or gently winding street layouts with uncomplicated road junctions and squares, as these are the easiest to use and understand.
> 6. Providing clear signposting by creating memorable 'end-views' to short streets.
> 7. Taking care to position design features in meaningful locations, avoiding clutter. Too much visual stimuli can have a negative effect, causing confusion and a lack of concentration.
> 8. Designing plain signs with large, dark lettering on a light background, as these are the easiest to read and understand. Many older people experience colour agnosia, a condition that makes it difficult to distinguish colours.
> 9. Avoiding changes in levels and designing flat, wide footways with gentle ramps, allowing people with walking aids to pass oncoming pedestrians.
> 10. Planning the design of landscape, streets, and architecture as one coherent system rather than separate elements.

What gave the place its structure was a series of interconnected public places that recreated the feel of the old village, but which were to be built with contemporary materials integrated closely with nature. The shape and hierarchy of streets, the position of buildings, the relationship between the landscape and the built form, all resembled the place I had already got to love. I had to incorporate a proportion of homes by developers and a proportion of custom-made homes, and I thought very carefully about the integration of these two prototypes to avoid any negative impact on the character of the place.

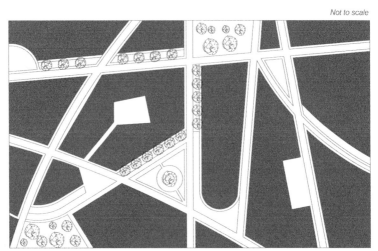
CONNECTED GREEN INFRASTRUCTURE LAYOUT

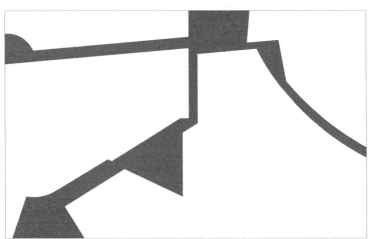
CONNECTED GREEN INFRASTRUCTURE DIAGRAM

Figure 5.8 Image shows a diagram plan of an urban zone where parks are all linked with tree-lined streets. Below is a figure-ground image of the connected green spaces.

Chapter 5: **Design form**

> The time came when the design team (landscape architect, highways engineer, planning consultant, clients and me; as usual, the only woman in the team) had to stand in front of a crowd of very concerned local people and talk about what we have been doing and how we thought the development had to be approached. Instead of talking about what we were going to build and where or what it would look like, I described the project as if I were talking about a day spent in the village. I told a story that could make people understand the place vision. I walked around these imaginary places with them and explained why would I go there, what could I do in the different zones, how I would feel walking around, how my children would play, who I would meet along the way, and so on. As I spoke, I could see the crowd becoming more and more interested, smiles began to shape, whispers could now be heard. When the whole team had finished the presentation, the locals clapped. A minute later, they were standing up. I felt like a member of the 1980s pop band; I could not believe their reaction.
>
> We stayed for a while absorbing the atmosphere, and once our nerves had settled, we ate the cake I had brought along. People said all sorts of things to us, like: "I didn't know this type of design could happen" and "we would take two thousand of your houses if that means we can stop bad, profit-seeking house builders". The comment I will never forget still brings a tear to my eye: "You understood our village". So, that is what I call a good job well done!
>
> A few months later, the community was putting pressure on the local authority to approve the scheme. I recently heard there were land transfer deals delaying the process significantly. I remain anxiously keeping tabs on this project, waiting to see how the place is developed and if the landowners proceed with the concept masterplan. I sincerely hope so.

Lessons learnt

This chapter has been tricky to write because so much has been said and done already when it comes to urban form, so I was in fear of omitting the obvious or repeating too much. I have tried to keep the balance right for those readers who are just entering the world of urbanism or those who did not receive much design training during their studies. I guess, naturally, designers find form very easy to convey on the ground. The intangible dimensions of place are far more difficult to grasp or represent graphically, and therefore tend to be dealt with by other fields, remaining on paper and rarely being transferred into design; but form is relevant and deserves a good discussion.

The case studies I have shown might seem different to each other, but both showed the importance of understanding the context in depth. In the first example, the quality of design from a morphological perspective was poor to begin with, but this was identified early through the use of a sound quality assurance system. The design and appraisal process itself dealt with the local authority's concerns without much trouble. Nevertheless, the problem with the design itself came from the lack of context understanding and the failure to apply some core design principles. Conversely, the second case study looked at an example where the design principles were established from an in-depth understanding of context. The study went to such a degree of local scrutiny that residents could not help but feel exhilarated to know someone cared enough for their village to invest such efforts in producing a considerate and considered scheme. I think there is a lot to be said by the way we presented the information, a way that resonated with the residents' lifestyles. We seem to have taken the time to understand the physical place, its natural assets, and its people: the complete settlement ecology. I feel this should be standard practice.

I have deduced from these experiences, and from almost every project I have worked on, that the most important stage in any design is the contextual analysis, considering people as much as space; in other words, understanding the urban ecology. This, combined with good technical site investigations and sound design skills, is a recipe that should not fail. Sadly, far too often in practice, I come across design teams that are in such a rush that they look at an aerial image of the site and jump

Table 5.1 Case study analysis summary.

Case Study	Topic	What Was Different?	Outcome
5.1 Housing in context	Lack of contextual analysis	Clients and designers willing to collaborate with the authority	Positive: overall design improvement
5.2 Village extension in context	Designing with a contextual placemaking approach	In-depth understanding of local place character, urban patterns, and community perception of their place	Positive: community support for the scheme

directly into design mode, often forgetting the level changes and assuming the land is flat.

This is, of course, a more affordable approach in the early stages of the scheme, but it also is – at the very least – hit and miss; anything built with this method is very likely to be of questionable design quality and low sustainability credentials; as a minimum it would suffer numerous iterations during the process (which can be costly anyway). Good design is one that can demonstrate how the key findings of a comprehensive contextual evaluation were transferred or re-imagined and applied to the proposed scheme. The true skill of place design lies in the understanding of the context to such extent that from it, one can draw the design parameters that give that place its essence, its own place character.

Next, let us look at the core form parameters I found to be critical when designing in context.

Tool 5: Critical form parameters

Composition

Like paintings or music, buildings and places need to be organised into component parts that will form a whole. The location of the parts in a space is fundamental to how the whole design works, but more importantly, to how we understand it, as how we understand places will dictate our behaviours.

Humans are equipped with a brain that can process face recognition, which means that we tend to perceive the wholeness before we see the individual parts. Sensing this capacity, philosophers have debated the transference of human properties to buildings for centuries. The work of Roman architect Vitruvius showed the correlation of classical architectural orders (Doric, Ionic, and Corinthian) with the human body, as does the Vitruvian Man of Leonardo da Vinci.[2] Symmetry might be easier to understand in buildings because, subconsciously, we refer everything we see to ourselves and our human forms. In the 1940s, Gestalt psychologists looked at how we interpret images not by simply focusing on every small part, but by perceiving objects as components of a greater whole and as parts of more complex systems. It seems that the easier the composition of a building or place is to read, the more we tend to like it; in fact, the more complex the physical environment, the more difficulty people found it to establish social codes and norms in the community.[3] Here is a good way to address the Social Sustainability Sphere through the form of the design: by making design composition easy to read. In other words: easily understandable. Following, I have summarised some essential rules of composition that apply to any type of design. I would like to encourage the reader to look at Figures 5.9–5.12 and observe how these rules might have been applied to the designs in each image.

Hierarchy

Within any composition, some parts have more emphasis than others. The natural way in which the parts of a place have a degree or rating of importance is called hierarchy. For example, in the case of a typical British Victorian house, a bay window will stand out more than other windows at first sight; in a city, a tree-lined avenue leading to the main park will be higher in the hierarchy than a narrow residential street serving only a few houses. In fact, scientists have found that we use semantic memory to create something called a *hierarchical spatial network* of a place or building, which means that we identify objects of different importance and we mentally link them to make sense of the whole; in other words, we *read the space*.[4] The more we can identify the main

Chapter 5: **Design form**

Table 5.2 Basic rules of composition.

	Basic Rules of Composition
Create a focal point	Every design must have a core message, something that stands out. The viewer needs to know where to look first. In a building, this is normally the front door.
Create visual hierarchy	Viewers' eyes need to follow visual hierarchy arrangements that communicate the relative importance of each part of the place or building. For example, by using different materials.
Use leading lines or grids	A grid layout helps place elements in a harmonious and visually appealing manner, making the work of composing the design a lot simpler.
Scale the elements	Another way to indicate the relative importance of elements is to adjust their scale. The most important elements are usually larger or more prominent.
Balance the elements	Each element carries a visual weight determined by its size, colour, and shape, though these need to be balanced to achieve visual harmony; too much of everything creates clutter.
Repeat some elements	We recognise elements that are arranged with a rhythm as a pattern. A small variation in the pattern can add interest and help manage scales.
Apply the rule of thirds	When symmetry is not the right solution, divide the space into thirds and place the focal objects in the intersection of the lines.
Create contrast	We tend to group similar objects together and differentiate between those that are dissimilar. Contrast can help make some elements stand out.
Use negative space	The shape and size of negative spaces (such as structures like walls in a building) are just as important as the positive elements (windows or details).
Create a cohesive whole	In a well-composed building, elements tie together to form a whole. All the parts play a role in achieving a sense of unity and cohesion.
Align design and functionality	A building becomes more welcoming and the space around it feels safer when we can understand what is happening behind its walls.

188 Chapter 5: **Design form**

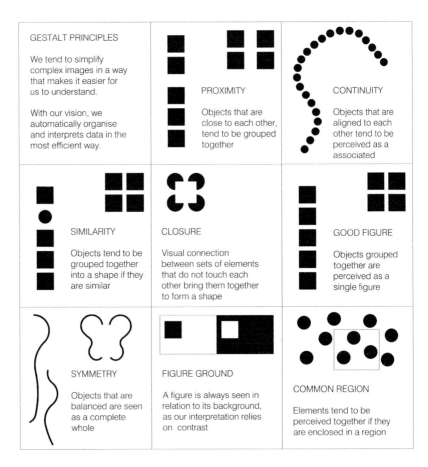

Figure 5.9 Sketch of some of the Gestalt principles.

parts from the less important parts of a building, the more we will appreciate it, and probably, the more we will like it.

Humans understand the hierarchy of building and city components without even noticing; this is part of their neurological capacities, cultural learning, and genetic memory. The obvious way to think about this would be that traditionally, a bathroom has a smaller window than a living room, so when we see a building from the outside, we can guess what might be happening inside without even realising. At times, architects use this strategy to push the boundaries and challenge the observer. For example, they might decide to put the larger window in a

Chapter 5: **Design form** 189

Figure 5.10 Photograph shows an internal courtyard in the Palace of Alhambra, Granada, Spain, where the Palace façade forms a geometrical pattern that makes each one of the three floors distinctive by applying different heights and details surrounding the arches. The central arch is elevated in relation to the side arches, demarcating the entrance.

190　　　　　　　　　　　　　　　　　　　　Chapter 5: **Design form**

Figure 5.11 Photograph shows the façade of the church of St. Domenico in Ancona, Italy, with a very clear composition: an element of symmetry only broken by a bell tower on the right.

Chapter 5: **Design form** 191

Figure 5.12 Photograph shows the façade of the Alte Oper building in Frankfurt, Germany, with a very clear composition: a threshold, a middle floor, and a top floor, with components that express a sense of hierarchy.

Figure 5.13 Photograph shows typical homes built in the British Victorian era, where different windows have different levels of importance or hierarchy.

Figure 5.14 Photograph shows a façade of a building in Alhambra, Granada, Spain, where the middle arch is the higher of five, indicating the presence of a path or entrance.

bathroom and a very small glass panel in the corridor to give the wrong impression of what happens inside. They design a building intentionally confusing by breaking the norm and they provoke us with unexpected design solutions.

The human capacity to read a place means that exceptionally talented designers can create a language for their buildings using architectural grammar tools. They mix the design components as if these were the letters they use to form words. Then, they look for rhythm patterns to create poetry. Untrained or lay people might not know this consciously, but I am sure they can perceive it. This is why there are buildings that are almost universally liked, or, at least, appreciated, as we saw in Chapter 1 with the case of the Roman Pantheon. Similarly, it is why some buildings are universally loathed!

Buildings and places can actually tell a story through design; when students begin to master this art, a whole new world opens before their

Chapter 5: **Design form**

Figure 5.15 Photograph shows a neoclassical building in Nottingham, UK. Although the façade has two doors, there is a sense of hierarchy given to one of the doors by the use of side columns, steps, façade reveal, and central position. The side door was designed as a window in the hierarchy, and therefore, it is clear this is not the main entrance.

Figure 5.16 Photograph shows a three-storey modern building in Nottingham, UK, with a façade where all windows are exactly the same and are equally distributed across the front. There is no sense of hierarchy in this design and it is not possible to determine whether one part of the building is more important than other parts or not.

Figure 5.17 Photograph shows the World Maritime University in Malmö, Sweden, where an exotic geometry and a contrasting colour were used to make the architecture stand out from the context.

Chapter 5: **Design form**

eyes, and once they reach that point, they can never go back. I hear colleague architects telling me they spent their holidays reading architecture whilst walking on the streets, trying to interpret those places and their languages. For dedicated architects (I personally do not know any other type), there is no such thing as 'switching off'.

Now, let us think a little bit more about the urban design equivalent. In research, there is a social take on how the morphology of place relates to how people interact in different environments. Studies of the relationship between layouts and people's contacts in the work environment showed that accessibility and visibility were directly related to the number of contact instances amongst staff. When people had more access to each other, they came into contact more often. Similar results have been found in the urban environment.[5]

Roads and streets give structure to urban neighbourhoods, forming plots of various types, shapes, and sizes in between them where buildings are placed. The characteristics, function, and importance of streets, referred to as road hierarchy, can influence the overall level of social contact or fragmentation in urban areas. Appleyard and Lintell looked at how traffic in residential streets became a deterrent to neighbouring contact, increasing the social separation between neighbours living in front of each other.[6] Busy roads can become barriers, as, by instinct, people prefer to walk through safe, clear, and open paths that offer least resistance to their movement. Therefore, the shape, character, and relative importance of roads is a hugely significant component of our public place network: amongst other things, it can directly influence how we connect in a community, as discussed in Chapter 1.

Legibility

Scientists have also found that another primary function of an animals' brain is the ability to navigate to their home or place of safety.[7] Finding the way round is a key ability for human survival, and it concerned the field of urban design for many decades.[8] Not being able to find our way can cause us stress and anxiety, as those of us who are old enough to remember driving without a SatNav know only too well! For this particular function, identifying the prominent parts in a place and the link that connects them is crucial. Back in 1960, a renowned architect who was apprentice to Frank Lloyd Wright, called Kevin Lynch, studied the form of cities, identifying five main components based on how residents interpreted the place (see Figure 5.18):[8]

- Paths: channels that allow movement.
- Edges: boundaries between two areas.
- Districts: areas with specific characteristics.
- Nodes: junctions and crossings or points of shift in structure.
- Landmarks: elements that differ from the norm and which are used as signals.

This theory of how people understand their places is also known as *mental mapping* and it has proven to be highly applicable in urban design practice and studies. For example, in urban terms, one would expect to see the market square in an English village not far from the church and the town hall, and this is also true for many European settlements. So, finding the church spire, one can almost find anything else. Urban designers use this place theory to create walkable neighbourhoods that are easy to understand and

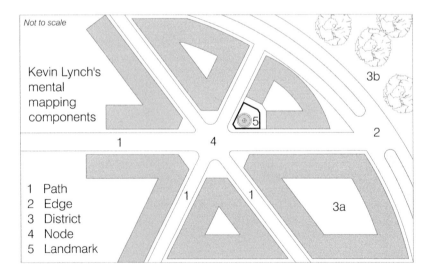

Figure 5.18 Diagram representing Kevin Lynch's five principles of mental mapping.

Chapter 5: **Design form** 197

Figure 5.19 Photograph shows the Chinese Bell Tower monument in the Arboretum, Nottingham, which is often used as a landmark for wayfinding and mental mapping due to its unique geometry and height.

where people can navigate whilst feeling safe. The more we can identify the prominent parts of a building or place and link them mentally, the more we will feel at ease with the design; we will find it more pleasant and we would probably want to stay there longer. This is often an issue with large housing estates that have no other uses – they are monotonous and lack hierarchical definition.

Some shopping malls and retail complexes are designed by applying mental mapping exactly in the reverse way. Every node and link looks the same and there are no landmarks or districts which makes people disorientated and confused, especially when they are trying to come back the way they came in to find the exit. This is a strategy retailers use to retain customers on the site for longer, but it is not the healthiest place design approach, as it can lead to anxiety and stress.

Figure 5.20 Photograph shows a church spire in Riga, Latvia, which can help navigation and mental mapping due to its original design.

After Lynch, a multitude of authors have recognised the importance of public spaces being defined by the buildings and other elements around them.[9] Places with a sense of enclosure help humans identify their surroundings and establish their position in space. When a place is easily understood, navigating it becomes a more relaxing experience.[10] There is a link between form and social factors: neighbourhoods without

Chapter 5: **Design form** 199

clear wayfinding cues are not child-friendly and the elderly can find them difficult to navigate.

Rhythm

In music, we add a temporal measure to a sound in order to create a certain pattern or repetition. Place designers can also create rhythm. The concept is very simple: let us imagine a person walking at leisure along a large façade, always maintaining the same speed. Every time this person walks by a window, the church bell chimes. If the windows are equal in size and equally spaced, this will create a constant rhythm. Now imagine that a large bell chimes when the window is large and a very small bell chimes when the window is small (see Figure 5.26). Add enough window sizes, use a different instrument for each floor level (ground floor, first floor, and so on), and you can end up playing a tune. This is called architectural rhythm, and it can also be recreated on an urban scale. For example, the large bell can chime when a bus reaches

Figure 5.21 Photograph shows the front façade of the Adams building in Nottingham, UK, where the location of entrance door is easily identifiable through the design emphasis on the façade above the door, and is therefore very legible.

the avenue and the small bell can chime when that bus crosses a lane. Design and music are very compatible in principle, both ruled by mathematical codes. Many people could not compose a tune but most people can understand music: we tap along, we sing, we dance. With the same criteria, most of us subconsciously understand architecture and urbanism, and we can appreciate exceptionally good spatial design, beautiful cities, and handsome buildings, although we might not be able to design them. Built environment design is a form of communication with a language and a sound. Just as we read words, we can read buildings; as we feel music, we can also feel the rhythm of space. Just as music, harmonic environments can have a positive effect on our mood and can reduce the levels of stress and perhaps even bring us more happiness. Similarly, the reverse is true.

Proportions

When working with communities, students, and some built environment colleagues, I used to struggle to explain the concept of proportions in

Figure 5.22 Photograph shows a cityscape image of the city of Oxford, UK, where several spires are visible rising above the city's roofline.

Chapter 5: **Design form** 201

Figure 5.23 Photograph shows a white church in Riga, Latvia. The colour is contrasting with the urban street scene, which makes the building a landmark that can aid navigation and mental mapping.

202 Chapter 5: **Design form**

Figure 5.24 Photograph shows an urban pocket square in Stockholm, Sweden, where the tree makes the place identifiable from other similar squares.

Figure 5.25 Photograph shows an inexpensive way to create a landmark by painting a strategically located building. In this case, a house in a residential area of Nottingham, UK, was painted in a distinctive light blue colour whilst the rest of the homes in the area are built in brick or stone.

Chapter 5: **Design form** 203

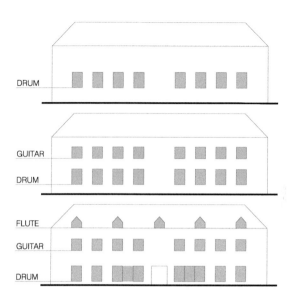

Figure 5.26 Diagram demonstrating an example of architectural rhythm.

Figure 5.27 Photograph shows a Hanseatic building on Bremen Market Square, Germany: the rhythmic complexity of the façade is immediately apparent in both the composition and in the details.

Figure 5.28 Photograph of a corner building in London, UK, with different size windows that create a complex rhythm across six storeys.

design and I found it even harder to explain how to apply it. I am not sure why this happened, because in my mind, I could only conceive thinking in a 'proportional way'. As such, I developed an analogy that seemed to get the message across:

> If one wants to bake a lemon drizzle cake and the recipe asks for four eggs and 400 grams of flour, what do you do if you only have three eggs left in the pantry? Would you still use 400 grams of flour? Probably not. The wisest move would be to use a proportional ratio: fewer eggs, less flour. If you are short of eggs by one quarter, you would probably use one quarter less of flour. So, for three eggs, 300 grams of flour. It is simple: every ingredient is in proportion with each other, so if you change the quantity of one, you need to change the amount of all the rest.

Chapter 5: **Design form** 205

Figure 5.29 Building with intense rhythm in King's Cross, London, UK, where there are many windows in different locations.

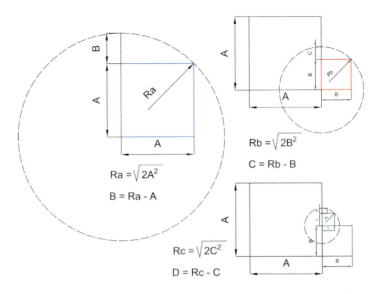

Figure 5.30 Diagram demonstrating how geometrical mathematical ratios work in practice, if A plus B add up to the radius of a circle and the radius equals the square root of two times A square, then A and B are dimensions in proportion to each other.

Figure 5.31 Photograph shows buildings of slender proportions, distinctively narrow and tall, in Stortorget, Stockholm, Sweden. The overall orientation of this composition is vertical.

Chapter 5: **Design form**

Figure 5.32 Photograph shows the façade of San Ciriaco Cathedral in Ancona, Italy. This composition is rather wide, with an overall horizontal orientation.

The same criteria also apply to buildings: the components need to be in proportion to one another. Normally, the proportions of a building relate to the proportions of the human body: the door is tall enough for us to walk through, the windows are high enough for us to see the outside world. When the size of a component is changed to create a design statement, it is a better design choice to change the rest of the components as well, so that the design is in proportion, for example, in classical architecture. If you made the front door wider and you had a triangular roof often placed above the porch (called tympanum), you would need to increase the door height and the height of the tympanum, as well as the width.

Very mathematically versed architects and urban designers can establish exotic relationships between the different elements of a design, skilfully altering the size and scale without losing sight of mathematical ratios. For example, sometimes they exaggerate the dimensions of some parts whilst keeping the others of standard size. The problem begins when designers without the dexterity to create new arithmetical relations randomly alter objects or their positions, moving far away from a clear mathematical pattern. For example, in music, it would equate to huge distortions and different instruments playing in different keys or at different rhythms. As with music, every piece of good design is mathematically sound.

Mass

Although scale and mass are two different concepts, even trained designers often confuse them. A building mass refers to how voluminous it is and how heavy and dense it looks. Like mass in scientific terms, a cubic metre of steel has a larger mass than a cubic metre of candyfloss, although the volume is the same. It is very much a matter of perception. Imagine a garden shed made of timber with a door and a couple of windows. Now imagine you place a solid rock of exactly the same shape and dimensions next to the shed. The rock will seem heavier even if that wooden structure had been filled with lead. Urban designers would say the mass of that structure is higher than the mass of the garden shed because it is perceived to be lighter. Now imagine two garden sheds: the first one you thought about and a replica of that one but twice its size. Although the door and windows are exactly the same size in both, urban designers would say the larger shed has a higher building mass; it appears more imposing. When a planning officer tells an applicant that the massing of the proposal does not work, they probably refer to how it compares in perceived weight with the adjacent or nearby structures. Large developments often have to be built in areas of historic interest, where existing buildings are small in mass. In that situation, designers need to do their best to create the impression of splitting the volume of their proposals into smaller fractions or using lighter materials. For example, joining various segments together with a different element that is set back and contrasting in colour, to make that division more apparent (see Figure 5.33). Urban designers and architects call this an *articulation*, something that links two parts of a building like an elbow joins the two parts of an arm. This design strategy makes the volume look smaller than it is. This is a good way to respond to contexts where local buildings have a smaller volume than the proposed one.

Chapter 5: **Design form** 209

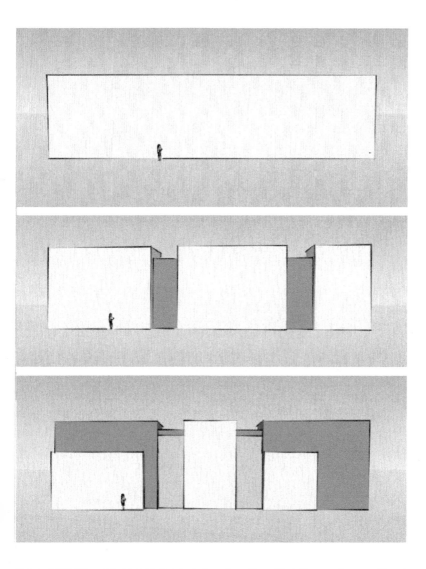

Figure 5.33 Diagram comparing one façade with articulation and one without it, as a way to illustrate the visual impact of breaking the massing of buildings.

210   Chapter 5: **Design form**

Figure 5.34 Photograph shows narrow three-storey buildings in Nottingham separated by a very narrow gap. This was a traditional way to build to prevent fires spreading from one building to another and to provide a rear access to the deep properties.

Figure 5.35 Photograph shows a contemporary three-storey building in Nottingham that is built over three original plots of land. The designer used a narrow curtain wall glazing to create the effect of a gap to replicate the traditional building separation shown in Figure 5.34. This is a good design resource to reduce the scale and impact of a new building in the historic context.

Chapter 5: **Design form**

The built form of an urban area defines spaces in between; these spaces form the public realm network. Building size, in particular height and density, has an indirect correlation with the use of public spaces, the levels of social interaction within neighbours, and the sense of control over neighbourhood public spaces.[11] This stresses the importance building massing as a design parameter might have in neighbourhoods, particularly in public spaces designed to function as social hubs, where people need to feel comfortable to interact and develop their networks. Perhaps here lies another way to address the Social Sustainability Sphere through design.

Scale

The scale of a building refers to its relative size or the dimensions of the building and its parts in comparison with something nearby. A good way to manage the scale of a design is to put its key components into a grid: the closer together the lines of that grid are, the smaller the scale of that design is in comparison with a template pattern (see Figure 5.36). Imagine you discover a beautiful island where all the streets in every town and village are in the shape of a grid forming blocks that are 100 metres × 100 metres in size. Then you visit the capital of the island and you realise the blocks there are 200 metres × 200 metres in size: urban designers would say that the capital is larger in scale than the average city on that island. Paris is larger in scale than York, as demonstrated by my own error of judgement, which I described in Chapter 1 when I explained how I miscalculated Notre Dame's size by ignoring the scale of its urban context.

When a planning officer tells an applicant that the scale of the proposal does not work, what they probably mean is that the grid designers used to produce the proposal does not match the average or significant grids in the local area. It is always a good idea to begin by doing an analysis of contextual scale as part of the site investigations to ensure the local character is well understood before venturing to resolve façade designs.

Urban environments of larger scales are less people-friendly than smaller-scale places. This is evidenced by the fact that people tend to

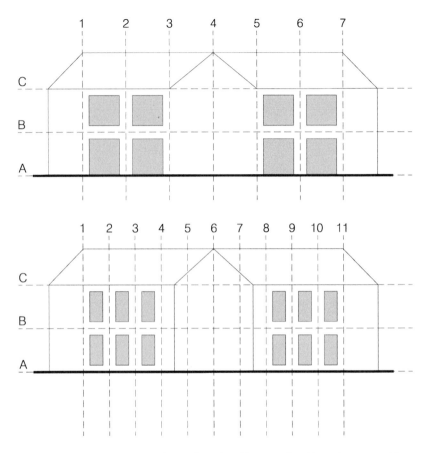

Figure 5.36 Diagram comparing a façade with a small grid against one with a large grid. Illustrated by the author.

walk more in small-scale settlements and they tend to depend more on cars in larger-scale places.[12]

Geometry

This is one of the most intuitive design parameters: it simply means what it says on the tin – shape. A building of simple geometry might be a cube or a cylinder. A complex geometry would be one that mixes a variety of three-dimensional shapes. The only caveat with this parameter is that in

Chapter 5: **Design form**　　　　　　　　　　　　　213

Figure 5.37 Photograph of a child next to a plant with giant leaves in Cornwall, UK. The size of the specimen would not be apparent if the child had not been in the photograph. Comparing the size of the vegetation with the size of humans, we can establish the plant is of large scale.

Figure 5.38 Photograph shows a man walking towards the Doll's Palace at La República de los Niños theme park in La Plata, Argentina; it is the human figure that puts the size of the building into perspective. Without the man, the palace might have appeared to be much bigger.

214 Chapter 5: **Design form**

Figure 5.39 Photograph shows a public square in Birmingham, UK, where the typical colonnade surrounding the space was recreated in a smaller scale for a feature building.

combination with others, it can become very powerful as a design tool. The best architects know exactly how to shape buildings so that these feel part of the context. It is like carving a block of marble to create a sculpture: the building form reveals itself. Although it is hard to believe, some designers really struggle with this parameter in practice, and that is often because they begin the building design from the *inside-out*, so they end up with a geometry that might respond to the building function; but that does not feel like a component part of the city, as happened with Case Study 5.1.

Skilled architects can visualise three-dimensional forms in a way that allows them to conceive both function and geometry in context at the same time. Throughout my career, I have delivered many workshops with schoolchildren on this, and I was surprised to find out how perceptive and open-minded they are. If only industry professionals were all so open-minded!

Chapter 5: **Design form** 215

Figure 5.40 Photograph of industrial buildings with angular roofs that accommodate a series of triangular windows, which bring natural light to the working space. This creates a distinctive form in this area near Sheffield, UK.

Figure 5.41 Photograph of roofs with distinctive form in Riga, Latvia. A series of shallow domes of different sizes on top of turrets mark a distinctive geometry and make the building stand out in the area.

216　　　　　　　　　　　　　　　　　　　　Chapter 5: **Design form**

Figure 5.42 Photograph of buildings with distinctive form in Bergen, Norway. A series of historic wooden buildings flank both sides of an alleyway. The roof lines and projecting volumes on the first floor are angular and sharp. Some buildings are white, others dark, which strengthens the geometrical effect.

Chapter 5: **Design form**

Figure 5.43 Photograph shows the Bullring Shopping Centre in Birmingham, UK, with its distinctive organic form. The building looks like a curved mass, all covered in metallic circles.

Colour palette

Managing colour well requires high level of skills. Colour theory is not something that is taught at length in architectural or planning courses, and yet it is so relevant today, when mechanised material manufacturing has evolved so much. Traditionally, architects were less concerned with colour and were more dedicated to understanding the ability and capacity of materials (called tectonics); in simple terms, they designed following the logic of the substance itself. For example, using timber, one would cut the log in lengths to form posts so that the fibres of the wood provide some strength. Flaky stones were traditionally used for flat items such as tiled roofing whilst more robust stones were used in blocks to form foundations. This was necessary because most of the building work was locally crafted by hand, using readily available resources. This way of working resulted in villages, towns, and cities that have a very distinctive look, which architects and urban designers call *character*.

Figure 5.44 Photograph shows how buildings in Flåm, Norway, are painted with colours picked from the landscape, appearing contextual in colour palette.

Chapter 5: **Design form** 219

Figure 5.45 Photograph shows the use of different brick colours to create variation and to break up the mass of the housing block in Trent Basin, Nottingham, UK.

Figure 5.46 Photograph shows how service installations in Trent Basin, Nottingham, UK, were specified in different colours according to the façade they are in. This detailed thinking elevates the quality of the design, which appears stylish without adding excessive costs.

When clients wanted an iconic building, they sponsored a landmark. Then, architects could resource foreign materials that stood out when placed amongst the local vernacular. Of course, not many people could afford a landmark building so there you have it, an organically developed urban form with clear, distinctive structures that provided cues for mental mapping.

Figure 5.47 The Library of Birmingham, UK, uses bright yellow and blue colours to enhance the building, a design solution that strengthens the value of the structure as a landmark.

Chapter 5: **Design form**

With the advances in industrialisation and the pre-fabrication of globally available materials, new buildings located in historic urban areas need to work extra hard to fit in with and respond to the place character. This type of attention to detail involves a very careful consideration of colours and their combinations. To make things harder, new materials do not age the same way as crafted local resources or the intricately detailed components of old buildings. For example, carved stone or moulded masonry cannot compare with the modern equivalents. These details project shadows, they age, they gather dust, and they become darker in places, all of which adds to the place feel and character. This creates richness in colour palettes; it is no longer the colour of the stone but all the shades that the material itself has produced over the years that matter, along with the variation in tonalities over seasonal changes in light and shadow.

A good way to prevent poor use of colour is to create a site-specific colour palette before the design phase begins. I use a colour match app on my phone to capture the specific shades of neighbouring buildings and vegetation, and I include various alternative palette in my site investigation briefs. With that information in hand, material specification becomes a lot easier and far more accurate. If I cannot match the historic materials or if that is not appropriate for the design, at least I know that façade product manufacturers can recreate almost any colour you can ask for, as mentioned before. In the UK, planners tend to approve schemes but imposing some conditions, for example, on material choices. This is their way to allow construction to begin without delay, but keeping some a degree of flexibility and further scrutiny on quality. If all applicants supplied some colour palette they could commit to early on in the process, the job of the planner would be much easier. It might also prevent delays for applicants.

Texture

The texture parameter is often confusing because it can mean different things, depending on the scale and nature of the project. There is a texture in the building materials which refers to the porosity of the surface (spongy appearance or roughness), for example, how rough a brick is to the touch in comparison with a glazed ceramic tile. There is

Figure 5.48 Photograph shows the texture of a stone wall in Rimini, Italy, given by the porous rocks that were used to build it.

Chapter 5: **Design form**

Figure 5.49 Photograph shows the texture of a typical gothic window frame, created by the depths and sculptures surrounding the opening.

Figure 5.50 Photograph shows a typical street façade in Amsterdam, the Netherlands, where houses are deep, narrow, and between five and seven storeys in height, with many windows at the front to make the most of daylight into the deep layouts.

also a texture in the building façades, which refers to the level of detail, the amount of three-dimensional objects, and the shadows created by them. If I had to describe a highly textured façade, I would probably refer to a gothic building with lots of intricate gargoyles, ribbed vaults, and rosettes.

Texture at a larger scale would involve the porosity of an urban streetscape, for example, a façade with buildings close to each other and full of windows, like the street façades of Amsterdam. Contemporary design can address the historic texture whilst applying modern

Chapter 5: **Design form**

Figure 5.51 Photograph shows a modern street façade in the Java Island development in Amsterdam, Netherlands. Modern forms and materials were used, but the façades replicate historic patterns in their size, composition, rhythm and scale.

techniques. If a developer were to knock one of the buildings down or re-clad a building frontage with a plain material and no windows, the proposal would not be in keeping with the texture of the streetscape. There are times, though, when this is desirable, for example, if the design approach is not to mimic the historic setting but to make clearly identifiable to the human eye what is old and what is new.

The next scale level would be the texture of a neighbourhood or an urban area in a village, town, or city. A clear example of this would

226 Chapter 5: **Design form**

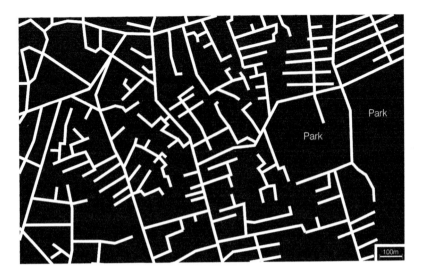

Figure 5.52 Diagram showing a sketch plan of a fragment of Marrakesh, Morocco; an urban grain that seems easy to walk, but one that is confusing and difficult to navigate.

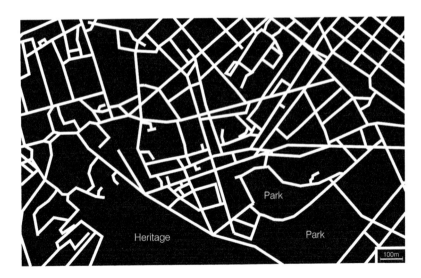

Figure 5.53 Diagram showing a sketch plan of a fragment of Rome, Italy; an easy to navigate permeable urban layout, with clear paths, nodes, landmarks, edges, and districts.

Chapter 5: **Design form** 227

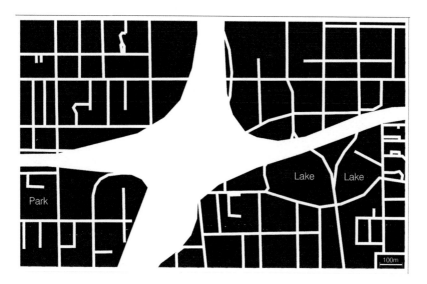

Figure 5.54 Diagram showing a sketch plan of a fragment of Orlando, USA; this is rather impermeable as pedestrians have to walk long distances before they find cues or landmarks that might help them orientate themselves.

be looking at urbanisations from a bird's-eye view. Take Hong Kong for example: thin, tall towers in close proximity of each other project upwards to touch the sky. This is a city with intense texture. Now think of a bird's-eye view of El Paso in Texas, USA: large blocks with low buildings, wide roads spreading across the desert. This is a city with a wide, open texture. The curious reader might want to explore these examples by using an aerial view application in an online search engine.

There is a specific type of texture urban designers call *urban grain*. This refers to the granularity that the built form gives to a city. I explain this to my students and co-designers by referring to throwing a handful of dry grains or seeds on a table and observing how these disperse. A large urban grain would probably resemble broad beans or cashew nuts; a small urban grain might look like couscous or polenta. Understanding the urban grain is necessary from an urban activity and movement perspective: the more porous the grain, the more permeable the city is and the easier people find it to walk through it, like water filtering through sand. But be careful not to confuse permeability with navigation: the

Table 5.3 Tool 5: Critical form parameters.

Principle		Definition
1	Composition	The general arrangements of the parts that make the design and the relationship of this arrangement with the context.
2	Hierarchy	The relative importance of some parts of the design in relation to the others.
3	Legibility	How easy it is to understand a building or place, or to find the way to navigate it.
4	Rhythm	The frequency in which certain elements of the design repeat, forming a pattern.
5	Proportions	The mathematical relation between the dimensions of the design parts and the whole.
6	Mass	The relative perceived weight/impact of the design in relation to its context.
7	Scale	The relative perceived size of the design in relation to its context.
8	Geometry	The form of buildings and place components (in two and three dimensions).
9	Colour palette	The group of principal colours in the design.
10	Texture	The porosity of the surfaces (materials, façades, rooftops, etc.).

former refers to how easy it is to circulate through an urban area; the latter refers to how easy it is to find the way round to reach a destination. Another very important reason to understand urban grain is microclimate: porosity and texture combined can have huge implications on air movement, ventilation, and overheating.

Although these are some of the form parameters I personally find fundamental during work in practice, I would encourage designers to have a good think about the key design criteria they would classify as a top priority to control design quality. These types of exercises and the kind of critical thinking they involve are not as common as they should be in the built environment world, and embracing them could be a way towards higher quality place designs.

Notes

1. Having lived in Britain for a few decades now, I have found that most people are relaxed, easy-going, and have a great sense of humour. However, if you are ever in need of starting an argument, simply ask a group of people from different regions what they call a bread roll and watch the sparks fly: cob, bun, bap, stottie, barm cake, and so on.
2. Marcus Vitruvious Pollio, *The Ten Books on Architecture*, 2nd ed. (Morris Hicky, Morgan trans.; Ipswich: Deez Books, 2004).
3. Oscar Newman, *Creating Defensible Space* (Washington, DC: US Department of Housing and Urban Development, 1996) 28–29.
4. Paul Bell et al., *Environmental Psychology* (Cengage Learning, Inc., 1990).
5. John Zeisel, *Inquiry by Design* (New York: W.W. Norton & Co., 2006) 346.
6. Matthew Carmona et al., *Public Places, Urban Spaces. The Dimensions of Urban Design* (London: Routledge, 2010) 103.
7. Martin Chadwick et al. 2015. "A Goal Direction Signal in the Human Entorhinal/Subicular Region." *Current Biology* 25 (1): 87–92. https://doi.org/10.1016/j.cub.2014.11.001.
8. Lynch, Kevin. *The Image of the City* (Cambridge, MA: MIT Press Harvard-MIT Joint Center for Urban Studies Series, 1960).
9. Reid Ewing R. and Otto Clemente, *Measuring Urban Design: Metrics for Livable Places* (Washington, DC: Island Press, 2013) 7.
10. Reid Ewing R. and Otto Clemente, *Measuring Urban Design: Metrics for Livable Places* (Washington, DC: Island Press, 2013) 18.
11. Oscar Newman, *Creating Defensible Space* (Washington, DC: US Department of Housing and Urban Development, 1996) 28–29.
12. Pedestrians First measures walkability for babies, toddlers, their caregivers, and everyone in cities, available at: https://pedestriansfirst.itdp.org.

Chapter 6
Evaluating design

In Chapter 5, we had a look at some of the critical design criteria that set the basis for design quality from a morphological point of view; in other words, form or aesthetics. But we must never forget that morphological design qualities only touch the surface of one of the many dimensions of much more complex place systems. As we saw in other chapters, design criteria can address far more than just form.

In this chapter, we shall look at setting up efficient and effective ways to evaluate proposals against project-specific criteria, with a view to implementing appraisal systems that can secure design quality and more sustainable outcomes.

It is common to assume that the existence of design criteria, whether in the form of a design code or a process guide, would be sufficient to secure design quality, but my experience in the field has told me otherwise. As well as defining those criteria, finding a good way to check compliance at different stages in the process is crucial to ensure the design is evolving along the right track and that it does not depart too much from the original vision and concept initially established.

Morphological design criteria like the type referred to in Chapter 5 are what practitioners tend to focus on, and therefore, what we tend to see in contemporary design codes. However, this approach, highly associated with the 'bring delight' facet of good design (see Table 1.1), fails to address the real complexities of place, and could not possibly address all three Spheres of sustainable development regulated in isolation. Far more would be achieved by aiming to capture the other critical parameters of good sustainable design as well, many of which are normally dealt with by other fields of expertise. In basic terms, designers

DOI: 10.4324/9781003244059-7

Chapter 6: **Evaluating design**

alone are not currently qualified to achieve sustainable design in the broader sense. It is when different fields of expertise work in collaboration with designers that place begins to take a whole new meaning, and then quality, sustainable design becomes a far more achievable goal. For example, in the field of sociology, scholars referred to the notion of designing public space networks to facilitate the creation of new community rituals such as going grocery shopping, taking part in local sport events, attending festivals, walking the dog, or making a weekly trip to the farmer's market.[1] Some of these activities, remain for centuries, others change, but providing space for them to happen could be a powerful tool in the hands of designers. Researchers also found it important that the community discovers its essence, because the landscapes will transform to reflect this.[2] Public space networks acquire status through the treatment the community gives to them, whether they are places of ritual or they have special values or virtues. Humans connect deeply with their landscapes, individually and as part of their communities, enhancing their sense of belonging. I am sure most of us would agree with this from our own experiences.

It would be fair to say that place quality can have an impact on society, as it is directly associated with wellbeing: people tend to be happier in better places. In higher quality places, people also tend to behave with greater consideration towards other people and the environment. Well-designed places strengthen the economy in the long term because they tend to be looked after more and they generate more human activity. Better quality places are more attractive and therefore people stay there longer. This is the cornerstone of the tourism industry.

Researchers also found that a sense of ownership over place was one of the motifs associated with strong territorial behaviours.[3] Some claimed that neighbourhoods in socio-economic disadvantage show stronger incidence of territoriality that correlate strongly with social fragmentation.[4] A fragmentation that allows individuals to find their own social identity. Territoriality, although often contested as a term in academia, is a key aspect of people's psychology and happens when boundaries that are not visible in maps become present in the residents' mental map of their neighbourhood. A good representation of this could be observed at the sunbeds by the pool on a holiday resort, or at the beach, where people tend to mark their territory, often becoming defensive and even returning

232 Chapter 6: **Evaluating design**

to the same spot day after day. On a recent trip to the Canary Islands, I found it quite chucklesome to see patrons queuing an hour before opening, towels in hand, ready for the sprint upon opening.In the UK, there has been consistent resistance to new housing nearby existing residential areas; which some refer to as the 'not in my back garden' attitude.

Other research explained that when political structures and community agencies find public places where they operate, and that the form and detail design of these public spaces can influence the way individuals perceive ownership and how the effect change over the space.[5] Now we might begin to grasp the complexity of social and psychological dimensions of place and how these might relate to place morphology. The literature in the field is vast and topics of this nature have attracted researchers from many fields for decades; yet, designers tend to keep a strong focus on form because, tragically, it is the only place dimension they master through their formal education.

People regularly ask me how can we possibly begin to think about evaluating design quality with all this complexity. The answer is simple:

Figure 6.1 Photograph shows children demarcating their play zone in a public beach in Cornwall, UK.

Chapter 6: **Evaluating design** 233

Figure 6.2 Photograph shows demarcation of territorial occupation in a public beach in Cornwall, UK, during the Coronavirus pandemic. There is a mark made in the sand surrounding a tent and matt, with a '2m' sign also marked in the sand.

we will never be in a position to evaluate every single aspect of design in practice – we must, instead, focus on what matters the most for the project, as long as we always consider the broader meaning of place and all three Spheres of Sustainability in equal measure, not merely the morphological dimension. This is why place evaluations must be project-specific. This is not to say that generic principles cannot be adopted to evaluate schemes; what this means is that each scheme will require a different prioritisation of criteria for all three Spheres and probably additional site-specific criteria as well. In practice, I found that citywide design codes always work better when they are accompanied by site-specific codes, as both scales are difficult to cover in one single document. A citywide code might regulate character zones, whilst a site-specific code could resolve access and connectivity issues and refer to microclimatic adaptation strategies.

Objectivity of design appraisals

A point of real concern, and one that keeps coming up at conference question times, is the objectivity of design evaluation tools. I already mentioned the current 'hot potato' in the UK: there is a motion by the Government to make beauty a reason to fast-track planning permission to build, and this is causing great concern in the field. My answer is always the same: design quality is objective because it is measurable. A design can be compared against an agreed set of design criteria. Beauty is subjective for the reasons discussed in Chapter 1. Therefore, it will be impossible to create a tool that measures beauty consistently, whether this is operated by a human or a machine. It might be possible to gauge an idea of beauty standards amongst a certain group of participants, for example, by conducting surveys on aesthetic choices. But that approach does not measure beauty in itself; it only measures stylistic preferences amongst a set population, which is what housing developers often do to create their housing prototypes.

I would dare to suggest that the idea of adopting beauty as a design compliance criterion, expecting that arguments over the beauty status of proposals could withstand trial in a court of law, is simply ludicrous. Design quality, however, is a plausible measure, as long as clear design quality standards have been defined and adopted in the form of policy, creating a legal threshold to be met by proposals. This, of course, does not mean that beauty is not relevant; in fact, it is extremely important, but something that cannot be objectively measured probably should not become a material consideration in a court of law.

Another recurring question topic at conferences relates to concerns over the validity of design quality appraisal tools, and how to ensure that different people would not arrive at different results. I am always pleased to explain this was one of the major topics I have explored through research, simply because I also held that concern. Here is my response: Ewing and Clemente developed a rating scale and measuring system to appraise urban design principles.[6] The grading went from 0 to 5: none, poor, average, good, very good, and excellent, respectively. With this tool, they demonstrated that, provided the principles were well explained, the rating method gave consistent results independently of the assessors' skills. They used a standardised assessment form containing a list with the name and description of each measurable factor. With this technique, they achieved a systematic collection of quantitative data in relation to public place qualities, which was a good way to correlate urban form principles with social data. I adapted this method for my own work with great success.[7] Part of my analysis involved asking a range of people to identify, map, and rate the urban qualities of public places where neighbours could potentially meet and interact, both indoors (e.g. community centres, churches, clubs) and outdoors (e.g. parks, commercial areas, playgrounds). I found consistency in the evaluation results and a minimal level of discrepancy that did not affect the study. Later on, working on the development of the Nottingham Design Quality Framework for the city, I made sure the tool testing stage was as sound as possible. Participants from different backgrounds, including communities, industry, academia, and the local authority as well as school children, were asked to apply the evaluation tools for each design guide on real-life planning applications, looking only at the documentation submitted by applicants. To my enormous surprise, the consistency in the appraisal results across participants was remarkable, for both small and large developments. The average discrepancy across results was a negligible margin that in no way affected the planning decision output.

Regardless of my own research, regulating design quality is nothing new – many countries across the globe have been doing this for centuries. The Laws of the Indies, for example, is a well-known design code produced by Spanish experts for the Conquest territories in the 17th century. Given that design parameters were present throughout history, I often wonder why the UK debate surrounding their usage is still rampant and why industry remains so averse to design quality assurance systems. I have to conclude that the concerns practitioners and developers have are more to do with the idea of appraising beauty rather than quality, and with the prospect that in a reformed planning system that fast-tracks beauty, they will have to adhere to different sets of rules in different places across the country. The reality is that once designers know how the model operates, they will probably be able to work similarly across the UK. Although the design criteria might differ from place to place, the process will be similar across the nation; at least, this is how design codes work in many other countries, and so there is no obvious reason why this should not be the case in the UK also. Despite the misgivings of many in industry, there are many optional design quality appraisal tools already being broadly used in practice with great success. Building for a Healthy Life, for example, is a simple but effective design appraisal system that deals with the main principles of good design in residential developments. After a period of resistance from industry, the tool became incredibly successful in the UK, with many local authorities and housing developers adopting it as a stamp of design quality, similar to the 'Red Tractor' stamp in food production. Despite a few issues with some ad hoc appraisals done by unqualified assessors, overall, the tool not only works but also sets a good basis for residential developers to explore how they can create customised quality assurance systems, as demonstrated in the following case study.

Case studies

Case Study 6.1 Edification code

My first encounter with an urban design code was as a student in the History of Architecture module (led by my prodigious tutor Fernando Aliata) at La Plata University, Argentina. Back then, I learnt about the aforementioned Laws of the Indies, the fascinating design and regulation code first published in the 1600s for Spanish Conquistadors who were tasked with creating new settlements overseas. I developed a fascination with design policies and guidance since I first read about this groundbreaking compendium.

The city of La Plata is a prime example of how 19th-century urban designers combined Garden City principles with the critical criteria of the Laws of the Indies to plan a new urbanisation.[8] So, inevitably, I came across the Edification Code for La Plata in its full extent: a city-wide regulatory framework in the form of a design code. The code itself is very useful for designers, as it establishes permitted development criteria and sets boundaries, with a brief explanation of the reasons why certain constraints are in place. For example, it determines maximum footprint coverage, edification lines, and protection of urban block centres that maintain a good level of ventilation and light for all homes, crucial in a warm, humid climate.

Chapter 6: Evaluating design

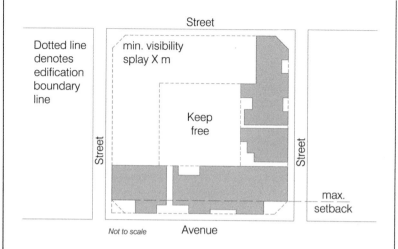

Figure 6.3 Diagram showing an example of a building block in La Plata with a restriction to build in the centre (rear gardens) and a set back restriction to create a continuous façade along the building line.

The document goes into issues of party wall arrangements that can prevent conflict between neighbours and it sets maximum heights and some aspects of façade treatments. Those requesting permission to build will need, as a bare minimum, to find a registered architect that will check their designs against the code and sign the drawing before submitting them to the authority. Planning officials will then conduct their own checks, and if they find areas of discrepancy, they will contact the architect to resolve any issues. Of course, there are also legal and statutory checks like fire safety requirements and so on. The process seems simple and effective. A downside to this method is that when the codes are adopted, they are in place long term. Amending an edification code is incredibly difficult, because professionals developing these regulations understand that changing one criterion could have huge implications on another; domino effect, if you will. In other words, the whole coding system might be affected if one component is changed in isolation, jeopardising the aspired vision

Figure 6.4 Photograph shows the major square, Plaza Moreno, in La Plata, Argentina, where the edification code permitted high buildings to be built in close proximity to key heritage buildings.

 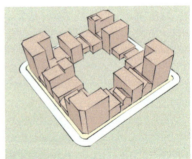

Figure 6.5 The illustration shows a 3D image of a building block where each plot has a building of different form and height but always built to the front line, forming a continuous street façade with great variation of heights.

Chapter 6: **Evaluating design**

 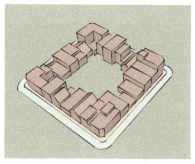

Figure 6.6 The illustration shows a 3D image of a building block where each plot has a building of different form and height but within certain height limitations, and always built to the front line, forming a continuous street façade that is moderately uniform in height.

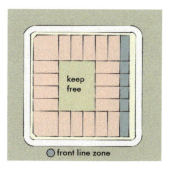 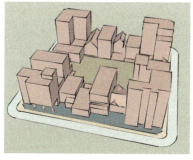

Figure 6.7 The illustration shows a 3D image of a building block where each plot has a building of different form and height, always built to the front line, except for one street where front gardens are allowed within a certain depth range; this results in a porous façade with great texture.

for the city in the long term. Another reason for lack of flexibility is that, due to high levels of corruption in some countries and governments, professionals feel ethically compelled to secure a threshold of design quality through a legally binding code.

What we see over time with long-term edification codes like the one in La Plata is a clear place character emerging from adherence to a few simple rules. Of course, as applicants only need to comply with limited criteria but anything else is permitted, the city has evolved in a very eclectic style that might not be so palatable in other contexts, such as areas with existing historic character or where the public has a more traditionalist taste, like many British do.

Case Study 6.2 Code compliance appraisals

Some time ago, my colleagues and I were commissioned by a county authority to conduct a series of design code compliance appraisals for a sizeable new town in England. The design code for the whole development was prepared for the landowners by a well-known architectural firm based in a different region. It was hundreds of pages long and it comprised several volumes. It had cost a five-figure sum to the landowners to commission this document.

We arranged a couple of workshops at the office to become familiar with the lengthy document before we began the appraisal process. As we were doing this, we found a multitude of discrepancies within it, and we began to wonder if appraising against it would be feasible at all. We soon found out that applying the code in practice was an impossible task. House builders from different firms had interpreted the criteria in different ways depending to which section of the document they had looked at, which led to huge inconsistencies and recurrent non-compliance. The code had no appraisal tool associated with it; in fact, not even a suggestion of appraisal process assessors could adopt. The focus was entirely on the urban form, but with a clear lack of substantiated evidence that could associate morphological choices with place quality outcomes. The criteria included were very concerned with morphology, but with just one simple objective: to deliver the urban form the architect had envisioned for the town (which was not a particularly inspiring one in any case!). Clients, authorities, designers, and auditors all came up with different interpretations, and consensus seemed impossible to achieve.

After serious delays and in order to deliver a housing layout that was compliant with both highways and planning requirements, we had to deliver workshops involving the clients, the authority, and us, the auditors. These were very effective, though inevitably, they resulted in design and appraisal costs that were higher than expected. Nevertheless, working together, all design agents managed to agree which parts of the code they could adhere to and which parts were undeliverable, negotiating along the way to achieve a solution that worked for all. This happened for each parcel of Phase 1. For example, the building blocks were either too deep or too narrow, making it difficult to achieve a land-efficient layout.

After three painful years trying to battle with this document on Phase 1, the landowners finally agreed to ditch the large, extortionately expensive, useless code and commission a far simpler one, which was far more affordable and which made compliance far easier to appraise and could actually achieve design improvements on the ground for the forthcoming construction phases.

Trying to protect a form-first design as a way to secure the delivery of a vision or concept is not the right approach to coding and can do more damage than good. With this take on coding, those designing to criteria compliance are forced to deliver morphological outputs at the expense of other critical aspects of place. Design codes should be loose enough to allow a certain degree of design flexibility whilst securing critical aspects of quality and sustainability.

Something I learnt from this experience is that every design code or guide must be subjected to a testing or piloting phase, and this should be done with real-life case scenarios. For example, inviting housebuilders, local practices, and other agencies involved to test drive the code in order to find any gaps or incongruences.

Case Study 6.3 Design quality system

Back in the early 2010s, a friend of mine, also a doctor in urban design, was commissioned by a large housing developer in the UK to help them produce their internal design quality system. They had been using Building for Life,[9] but they felt they could go a step further and create a more detailed tool that reflected their corporate ethos. Knowing of my background in social sustainability, my friend asked me to work with him on the project. At the time, it was very rare coming across anyone in urban practice in the UK with a doctorate in the subject, let alone that we were both the type of urban designers that prefer being hands-on, yet still with a foot in practice and a foot in academia. It was not difficult to find theorists that claimed industry was falling short in their quest for profits or sceptics that felt academics lived inside a utopian bubble or, as we would say in Argentina, in a mayonnaise flask. However, we knew theory and had pragmatism, and we were willing to face the barriers of the industry as long as we could influence place quality somehow.

Of course, we agreed the first task would be to understand the culture within the firm and to audit design performance carefully, so that we could target the criteria in the tool. Fortunately, we had incredible support from determined, visionary staff at the housing developers who wanted to create something that had never been done before, and so, together, we did just that.

Chapter 6: **Evaluating design**

The tool worked with a wheel of eight key principles that designers had to aim to address. Each principle had two compulsory criteria: design targets that were non-negotiable. For example, one of those was treating corner buildings by designing the two façades that faced public spaces as if these were a frontage, one with more hierarchy than the other, and so where the main door would be located. Of course, explained in that way, this criterion seems common sense, but I could not count the number of developments where I found completely blank façades facing the street (keep your eyes peeled on new building estates and you will soon stumble upon this). Each principle also had a 'star' criterion with examples of how a certain level of excellence could be achieved. If designers managed to deliver one or more stars, the tool would highlight that example as best practice for that principle, and the data would be directed to a compendium where designers could find examples of achievable ideas and sound delivery processes in the future.

Figure 6.8 Photograph shows a corner home with a blank side elevation facing a street in Nottingham, UK.

Figure 6.9 Photograph shows a corner building with windows on both elevations.

The tool was designed to complete the appraisal of schemes in just five minutes over a cup of tea. No specialist software was required – we simply used the standard office package. The score for the scheme was calculated automatically and immediately. If a principle did not reach the minimum threshold, a warning sign would instantly indicate the designers had to address the particular issue. When designers were unable to resolve an issue due to technical, political, social, heritage-related, or regulatory constraints, then the problem would be logged and automatically entered onto a design barriers database. These would become lessons learnt for designers working on future schemes and, potentially, evidence to share with government agencies.

A few years later, the same house builders got back in touch with us to confirm that the tool was working very well as they had clear evidence of design quality improvement. Furthermore, raises in design quality levels corresponded with the level of use of the tool: the more the tool was used, the higher the quality attained. As per the original intention, they were able

Chapter 6: **Evaluating design**

to collect very valuable data regarding barriers to achieving design quality in each region.

The wheel of design principles, along with its iconography and the simplicity of the criteria included, was crucial to the applicability of the tool. Also important was the fact that conducting the appraisal was a simple and speedy process. Wheels of principles have been around for a long time and seem to be an effective illustration technique. In fact, a few years after we launched this tool, the British Government published the National Design Guide with a wheel charter containing ten broader design principles.[10] However, what we found with this graphic style was that the wheel format, although very effective, was not great for future adaptation, and therefore, I decided not to adopt it for tools that had to be more flexible and, capable of growing organically, like the Nottingham Design Quality Framework.

Case Study 6.4 Design code

Having learnt how design codes work in my years studying and working abroad, I was delighted to be charged with producing a simple design code with very core principles for an outline planning application concerning a village extension of 450 houses in a small historic settlement in the Midlands of England.

Being so early in the design process, the code could not include much detail because the landowner had not yet made all the necessary agreements; they did not even know who the developers would be at that stage. The real difficulty was to choose the type of design criteria that would make this extension feel like part of the existing place without restricting the product and detailed design that would come afterwards, at full planning stage and in the construction phase.

Having originated in the Anglo-Saxon period as a farmstead, the village already had a typical place character that was given by the shape of streets, the landscape that surrounded it, the presence of water, and the relationship between buildings of particular form and size. My job as the designer was to unveil the design criteria that house builders would be able to recreate with their own modern products and with the highway requirements of modern Britain. I spent a long time walking around, sketching, sitting on the front steps of little cottages, and trying to feel the place as part of the initial site analysis. I noticed there were certain trends, patterns in the form of the place: the angle between the buildings and the garden walls, the height and materiality of those edges, the way the light hit the cottage frontages, most of which were orientated facing east or west to get sun in both front and rear gardens. The placement of buildings and landscape also followed a pattern (housebuilders of the past knew what they were doing!) – I guessed in the old days people depended on sunlight to sustain their productive landscapes. I also looked carefully at cars; I felt it was critical to understand how it was possible that in such a small, compact traditional village, cars did not appear to have a strong presence at all. I looked carefully at how people managed to park their vehicles out of sight.

After serious deliberation, I had a formula: I could code the relation between the main components of the village in a way that would recreate the place feel rather than the visual characteristics of the built form. I worked out how often these key spatial patterns repeated and where in the village one could find more of some patterns and fewer of others. With that percentage calculation, I created new character zones on the basis of a mathematical proportional ratio, working out how much of each coding formula I had to apply to the whole place to achieve a similar balance and where to position each zone type. I tested this code myself on numerous occasions, pushing the boundaries as if I had a financial target margin to achieve; it worked successfully every time.

The scheme was never built, a common occurrence for an urban designer, but I am pleased to say that not only I did enjoy that job, but I also managed to learn a great deal from it.

Table 6.1 Example of a design code that addresses place character variables.

Zone	Built Form			
	Buildings	Floor/Paving	Rear Boundary	Front Wall
	50% or more		Total Height Maximum in metres	
Green Edge	White render	Beige blockwork	Brick wall with capped top 1.2–1.5	Wall/gated Clear edge: 0.9–1.2
Mews	Sandstone	Grey cobblers	Stone wall: 0–1.2 Vegetation: 0–1.5	Less formal Stone wall: 0–1.2
Waterside	Reclaimed brick	Grey blockwork	Brick wall: 0–1.2 Vegetation: 0–1.5	Vegetation Clear edge: 0.9–1.2
Centre	Red brick	Tarmac	Brick wall with capped top: 0.9–1.5	Formal: 0–0.6
Farm	Conservation area approach	Fence: 0–1.2 Vegetation: 0–1.5		Less formal Softer: 0–0.6

(*Continued*)

(Continued)

Zone	Buildings	Built Form Floor/Paving	Rear Boundary	Front Wall
	50% or more	Total Height Maximum in metres		
Parking Modalities Zone	On Street	Integral Garage	On plot (Permeable)	Curtilage
	Maximum Percentage			
Green Edge	0%	40%	43%–83%	10% (maximum)
Mews	20%	0%	35%–80%	45%
Waterside	0%	26%	35%–80%	0%
Centre	0%	83%	17%	0%
Farm	0%	30%	70%–100%	0%

Typologies for each character zone based on survey of dominant character trends in the different neighbourhoods in the existing village.

Lessons learnt

It is clear from the case studies in this chapter that there are many different types of design evaluation tools and that these can be put in place for many different reasons: from legislating to improving the quality of the places we build; from crating a clear and well-established place vision to gathering data for research. What these quality appraisal tools have in common is that they must establish clear, measurable criteria that directly or indirectly can be translated into either a design or a process. Effective quality tools tend to express clearly what must be considered, why that is important, and how adherence to those rules will be policed.

Based on my experience from practice, I put together a tool to create design evaluation systems.

Table 6.2 Case study analysis summary.

Case Study	Topic	What Was Different?	Outcome
6.1 Edification code	Historic design code for a new city	Combined historic and new knowledge	Positive: adopted 140 years ago and still valid
6.2 Code compliance appraisal	Defective design code for a new town	Code focused on morphological dimensions of place only	Negative: impossible to appraise compliance
6.3 Design quality system	Design quality system for a British organisation	Developed through engagement, simple to use, multipurpose	Positive: design quality improved and relevant data gathered
6.4 Design code	New design code for a village extension	Design criteria based on placemaking as opposed to place morphology	Positive: place character secured through coding

Tool 6: Design evaluation

The bottom line on the design quality evaluation debate is that having a quality threshold in the form of a code or set of principles for good design is pointless without a clear tool that enables the accurate appraisal of proposals and without an enforcement mechanism associated with the tool. I am sure that those of you who are parents think your children are incredibly well behaved. So, I have to ask you to imagine a child throwing a tantrum, maybe in a supermarket during a weekly shopping trip. If that child is given no consequences for their bad behaviour, they would probably do it again. Children need clear rules boundaries, but they also need someone to remind them of those rules every now and then. Likewise, any law and order designed to safeguard a standard needs a solid policing infrastructure behind in order to be effective.

A quality assurance system that does not work within the political frameworks, power structures, and decision-making processes already in place is set to fail. Those pursuing the implementation of design quality systems must secure leadership support first. Quality systems and their evaluation tools are often a strong weapon to negotiate the added value of design. This is why it is critical that evaluation tools must include evidence and a scientific theoretical framework that supports the criteria; in other words, explaining why it is important to achieve that particular standard rather than giving the impression that the standard is a matter of preference. Additionally, there needs to be a way to score how far proposals might be allowed to depart from the set criteria. This can be done in numerical terms or it can be done with more visual methods like a traffic light system: red for non-compliance, amber for partial compliance, and green for full compliance.

We can now begin to see how this section is closely related to the previous chapter and the critical design principles featured. Once a design code or guide is created with its specific design criteria setting the bar, an appraisal method needs to accompany it to enable policing agents to conduct sound appraisals. I am regularly asked how can we decide which criteria must be included in any tool. The answer is simple: design quality tools are there to resolve or prevent a design problem; so we need to begin by knowing what the problem might be in the first place.

Below, I go through some useful tips that can help design agents create their project-specific design tools, with the certainty, having tested this in practice for some time now, that specific, measurable design quality criteria can be reliably and consistently appraised.

Targeted

The starting point of any quality system is a good understanding of current conditions. In other words, how things are working at the moment, what the successes are, what the typical errors or reasons for poor quality are, if the power structures are affecting the outcomes, and so forth. The efficiency of any quality tool relies on a thorough audit, targeting the understanding of the current state of affairs.

A good way to make a start with this when there are no evaluation methods in place is to do an audit that covers a representative range of cases. For example, a house builder wanting to develop a quality tool will appraise a range of models: from small houses to large apartment buildings. Crucially, we must not forget that quality assurance always relies on not just an evaluation of the outcomes, but also of the processes involved. The sample audited needs to cover a good period of time; this way, comparisons between measures done in different instances have the potential to highlight any errors in measurement. Once the cases subjected to study have been selected, practitioners have to be careful to formulate the optimum lines of enquiry; asking the wrong question will lead to superfluous information.

Achievable

The production of a quality assurance tool itself can be a daunting task, one that is perceived to consume large amounts of time and resources, and that is thought to be costly to commission. But this does not need to be the case – there is no need to reinvent the wheel every time. To develop any new tool or quality system, one must remember to begin the delivery plan by mapping all the work already done by others, highlighting what can be of use and what needs amending. The tool can begin by targeting particular aspects of the audit, so quality officers can begin with very little: adopting, expanding, adapting, or referring to part of existing tools or using case studies to exemplify. Then, they can begin building up the compliance criteria and evaluation tools over time; in other words, turning the quality screw gradually.

For the process of implementing and adopting a quality tool to be successful, those doing the work must remember to have a good understanding of the roles and responsibilities in the organisations involved, timescales, resources, and goals. Furthermore, it is hugely important to know who exerts the power and how decision-making processes take place. Inevitably, there will be times when valuable information to support the production of the tool is difficult to achieve or when sceptic staff members need a nudge.

Practical

The quality tool itself has to be of high quality for evaluations to work smoothly. Those creating quality system methods need to have in mind who will be exerting leadership or power along the process and how this might affect the applicability of the tool. It is important to bring the final users on board early in the process to make sure that the method is practical for them and will not hinder, delay, or complicate their normal daily jobs.

Sometimes, various departments within an establishment, or several organisations working together, have to make use of the system. In this case, those developing the tool must remember that both the method and the results obtained have to work for everyone involved. For example, the type of software required and whether operators need special training to use the tool are critical considerations to the overall success.

A good way to ease the process of tool adoption and applicability is to identify natural leaders, officers that could become champions of the method, supporting colleagues and keeping updated with the tool revisions and adaptations in the long term.

A practical tool always has an instructions section that explains how to apply it, a clear guide for those who might have to use it in the future without formal training.

Simple

With simplicity comes quality. This is the case because in order to achieve something simple, creators have to leave all the noise – or

Chapter 6: **Evaluating design**

unwanted bits – behind; they need to condense the product to its bare bones, to what really matters. This process requires intelligent, reflective thinking, discipline, and precision. If an evaluation method looks simple but does the job it was designed to do, then it is a successful tool.

Crucially, everyone that will ever use the tool, either to appraise or to comment on a decision made through its application, needs to understand it fully. The world of development is packed with technical and legal jargon, so much so that I have witnessed planners and architects struggling to understand each other's design ideas. Whilst writing this book, I have tried my very best to write in everyday language, and yet I have found myself rapidly increasing the glossary list. It is not easy, but those in charge of developing quality appraisal tools must remain conscious of the language they use. Place democracy depends on this, and so does the success of the systems they are developing.

The wording length is another consideration when it comes to simplicity. In a time and age of virtual communication, people often do not read long paragraphs. I congratulate you for getting so far in this book! Graphics, photographs, diagrams, infographics, and videos work much better as a communication tool than wording, especially when the aim of those using the tool is to get on with the job as fast and easily as they possibly can. During the development of the Nottingham Design Quality Framework, participants of all backgrounds agreed that a good way to represent ideas is to show the expected outcome next to the unwanted outcome, with a footnote explaining only the point being made.[11]

Graphics are very important and must be clear in the message they send. There is always the risk of adding too many graphics to represent different points, and upon revisions, unwittingly making those points contradict each other. I have seen numerous design codes produced in a very messy way, extensive and confusing, with huge amounts of unnecessary information. It is not rare to come across practices that believe they can charge a higher fee if the document looks large or fancy, without much meat in the bones. Those commissioning design codes and quality evaluation tools must always be aware that simplicity is not only more effective, but also far more efficient. Simple tools require higher levels of skills to prepare but far fewer specialist skills and resources to run, and they facilitate for better placemaking democracy.

Effective

A design appraisal tool is effective when it does what it is meant to do. The effectiveness of a quality tool must always be assessed in practice prior to its adoption. No tool should be implemented as part of a quality system without having gone through a sound testing period first.

When testing the effectiveness of a tool, it is important to make sure that the test is conducted by a population of the same characteristics and demographics as those who will operate it. It is also pertinent to use realistic samples for the piloting stage, recreating the different scenarios in which the tool will be applied.

The learnings from this testing period should inform any changes or adjustments to the method, the software, or the criteria and should help create a clear scope for its application. If the testing shows the effective application is limited to specific uses, then this should be clearly noted. Once the tool has been revised, a smaller test can be conducted to ensure any errors have been amended. Only then is the tool ready to work.

Flexible

Quality appraisal tools must be flexible to adapt because goals, products, and processes change all the time. Those producing a quality tool must remember that once the criteria knowledge is absorbed and the process understood and internalised by those in the production line, the tool might begin to have little or no effect. However, new problems might emerge that compromise quality. For example, new trends might appear, new materials might become available in the market, or new commercial trends might emerge, which may mean that new criteria will be required. Then, it will be time to adapt or revise the tool.

Those developing the tool must remember that flexibility also needs to be present in the overall structure of when setting up numerical classifications or choosing section titles. Being able to add fragments and full sections to address topics that become important in the future is critical to the success of any quality tool. For example, new issues concerning climate change might appear or new research might throw light on aspects of design associated with public health and wellbeing.

Chapter 6: **Evaluating design**

Table 6.3 Tool 6: Qualities of a good design evaluation tool.

	Principle	Definition
1	Targeted	Regulating the critical design quality and sustainable development criteria for the specific project
2	Achievable	Feasible to deliver it with the skills, time frames, and resources available
3	Practical	Simple to implement in the geographical, political, and legislative context
4	Simple	Uncomplicated in a way that removes the possibility of interpretative variances
5	Effective	Able to work in practice, with demonstrable results
6	Flexible	Able to adapt to changes in circumstances and to absorb new knowledge and technological advances

The quality loop is a closed circuit infringed by external forces: events outside the system alter the balance of the components of the loop. The worst thing anyone can do when it comes to trying to secure design quality is to create an inflexible appraisal tool, one that, once adopted, will be difficult or costly to amend. Decision-makers must be aware of this when commissioning design quality systems.

In the next chapter, I join all the thinking of Chapters 1–6 into a simple, practical tool: The ABC of Quality, Sustainable Design.

Notes

1 Randolph T Hester, *Design for Ecological Democracy* (Cambridge, MA; London: MIT Press, 2006) 37–79.
2 Randolph T Hester, *Design for Ecological Democracy* (Cambridge, MA; London: MIT Press, 2006) 100–133.
3 In Peter Hopkins, *Young People, Place and Identity* (Oxon: Routledge, 2010) 125.
4 Peter Hopkins, *Young People, Place and Identity* (Oxon: Routledge, 2010) 125.
5 Paul Bell et al., *Environmental Psychology* (Boston, MA: Cengage Learning, Inc, 1996) 256–259; 71.

6 Reid Ewing and Otto Clemente, *Measuring Urban Design: Metrics for Livable Places* (Washington, DC: Island Press, 2013) 2–3.
7 Laura B. Alvarez, "Morphological, Social and Perceptual Dimensions of Public Places in British Neighbourhoods." PhD thesis (University of Nottingham, 2018).
8 Refers to the Garden City concept by Ebenezer Howard (1898)
   The Garden City Principles are an indivisible and interlocking framework for their delivery, and include: Land value capture for the benefit of the community; Strong vision, leadership and community engagement; Community ownership of land and long-term stewardship of assets; Mixed-tenure homes and housing types; A wide range of local jobs within easy commuting distance of homes; Beautifully and imaginatively designed homes with gardens, combining the best of town and country to create healthy communities, and including opportunities to grow food; Development that enhances the natural environment, providing a comprehensive green infrastructure network; Strong cultural, recreational and shopping facilities in walkable, vibrant, sociable neighbourhoods; Integrated and accessible transport systems.
   Town and Country Planning Association (2022).
9 Relaunched as Building for a healthy life (Birkbeck et al., 2020).
10 https://assets.publishing.service.gov.uk/government/uploads/system/uploads/attachment_data/file/962113/National_design_guide.pdf
11 The Design Quality Framework is a series of design guides produced for Nottingham City in 2018 (available at: www.dqfnottingham.org.uk).
   MHCLG (Ministry of Housing, Communities and Local Government), *Design: Process and Tools* (Wolverhampton, UK: MHCLG, 2019). See https://www.gov.uk/guidance/design#effective-communityengagement-on-design (accessed 14/05/2020).

Conclusions

The ABC of quality, sustainable design

Over the course of this book, we have seen how typical errors of judgement and outdated forms of practice can have huge implications on the quality and sustainable credentials of schemes. Combining classical design training with the analysis of the case studies I showed led me to summarise four critical considerations:

1. Good design is one that is durable, functional, and that brings delight (see Table 1.1).
2. Overall, in correlation with known quality assurance systems, consistent design quality depends on the quality of both the built product and the process applied to achieve it (see Table 1.2).
3. All stages of the lifespan of a building or place need to be considered throughout the design process: design, construction, use, and disposal (see Table 1.3).
4. Achieving higher sustainability credentials requires equal consideration of all three Passet's Spheres: Economy, Environment, and Society (see Figure 1.10).

Chapter 1 established the core concepts surrounding a new approach to urban design and suggested a working ethos that brought quality assurance and overall sustainability together. Following this philosophy and learning from experience, I examined the case studies I included in this book – and many others – in some depth and realised that a different way of working could potentially prevent recurrent critical errors, raising both the quality and sustainable credentials of design. In writing this book, I have been able to share some of the tools I regularly use

DOI: 10.4324/9781003244059-8

in urban practice, which are displayed at the end of each chapter and summarised in Table 7.1.

This package of tools steered me towards an attempt to formulate a proposal for an improved form of practice, one that recognises the urgent need to establish greater accountability, make design decisions that are more balanced, and increase collaboration amongst design agents. I have therefore summarised this thinking into a working ethos I call The ABC of Quality, Sustainable Design. Below is a step-by-step guide to its application in practice.

Accountability

What does not get measured has little weight.

> I. Situate the project in the zone labelled 'SD' in Passett's Spheres of Sustainable Development (see Figure 1.10). The main characteristic of that central zone is that it encompasses all three Spheres in equal measure: Economy, Environment, and Society.
> II. Now, start considering each stage of the Urban Design Plan of Work (Table 2.6), but do it by trying to apply the quality assurance ethos at all times by looking at both the product being designed and the design process adopted.
> III. With the Design Agents' Map (Table 3.7), ensure that all parties involved have adequate, proportionate, and just degree of influence and that they are all fully aware of what their rights and powers are.
> IV. With the Influence Programme (see Table 4.2), ensure that all parties involved know when and to what extent they can influence the design. Also ensure everyone involved has the means to make all three of Pasett's Spheres count, recording measures and assessing assets, gains, and commodities as much as they would normally consider financial budgets.

> V. Set up the critical design criteria for the project for all three Spheres of Sustainable Development (Economy, Environment, and Society), ensuring that compliance with these rules is not only measurable, but that it would result in the expected design outcomes. Test the tool in practice using a broad, representative sample and a mixed cohort of assessors that represents the design agents involved.

Balance

Equitable measures lead to more balanced judgements.

> VI. Ensure decision-makers and influencers clearly see the weight of all three Spheres, so they have a greater chance of making more informed design choices with more balanced results.

With this step, the overall value for money can be clearly expressed without the risk of over-compromising on any of the Spheres at the expense of the others. This approach evidences the importance of negotiation skills and how designers need to be trained in working with trade-offs during the design process. For instance, planning officers might want a low building but they might accept an extra storey if that means providing larger green spaces.

Collaboration

Innovation and improvement are normally prompted by fusing different worlds.

> VII. Instigate a culture of team work, good communication, information sharing, collaboration, and mutual support.

The caveat with this approach is that in order to negotiate trade-offs, agencies and experts from all three Spheres need to work closely together. Crucially, all parties need to make their goals very clear, debate each other's expectations, and create a shared vision from the outset. Along the process, everyone involved should refer back to that vision, evaluating the scheme against it to make sure cuts have not over-compromised any of the Spheres (Tables 7.1 and 7.2).

Table 7.1 Summary of tools for urban practice

Chapter	Theme	Tool
1	Sustainable development	Sustainable design priorities checklist
2	Design process	Urban design plan of work
3	Design agents	Design agents' map
4	Influencing design	Influence programme
5	Design form	Critical form parameters
6	Evaluating evaluation	Design evaluation
7	Bringing it all together	The ABC of Quality, Sustainable Design

Table 7.2 TOOL 7: The ABC of Quality, Sustainable Design

Design Stage: e.g. *concept*	Accountability	Balance	Collaboration
Economy Environment Society	Agree a method or tool to measure impact on each one of the three strands	With the results of the accountability appraisals, balance the compromises across the three Spheres	Co-ordinate the different fields of expertise that need to work together across spheres to achieve informed, balanced decisions

Conclusions

Over the course of this book, we have seen examples that demonstrate how a lack of accountability, balance, and collaboration have seriously compromised the quality and the sustainable credentials of schemes. We have also explored how poor working methods can lead to the need to cover some quality gaps through the difficult, intricate, and expensive application of ad hoc, inefficient practices, which no one benefits from.

In placemaking, the time spent in doing a good, thorough job is time saved along the line; a stitch in time saves nine, as they say. Urban designers, or anyone tasked with placemaking, can now use The ABC of Quality, Sustainable Design and apply it in practice, with the facility to tailor the tools to the individual needs of their projects and schemes. If design agents have done their best to avoid poor quality – by collaborating effectively with all parties and putting mechanisms in place to account for all three Spheres of Sustainability in a balanced way instead of continuing the common practice of overachieving in one Sphere at the expense of the others – they can be satisfied they have made strides towards quality, sustainable design.

My aim in writing this book has been threefold:

1. Help those with very limited or no knowledge of the built environment understand the industry, to thereby empower them to embrace their democratic rights to partake in placemaking with confidence, swaying design solutions within their areas of influence. Places are for all – most especially those who live and use them, and so placemaking must be for all.
2. Encourage those in industry and academia to reflect on their own work and how they can implement improved practices towards a more equitable, more sustainable future, challenging the status quo and traditional, antiquated methods.
3. Bring all design agents – communities, authorities, and industry – together to deliver greater accountability, more balanced design solutions, and collaborative processes that will result in higher quality, more sustainable design.

Glossary

Architect A graduate professional qualified to design and project manage building design and delivery processes.

Area of Outstanding Natural Beauty In UK, an area of notable environmental or natural interest or importance which is protected by law against undesirable changes.

BREEAM "The leading and most widely used environmental assessment method for buildings and communities." The Building Research Establishment (BRE), 1990. Also see Acronyms.

Building A structure that provides a shelter.

Bungalow A low house having only one storey in height or, in some cases, upper rooms set in the roof, typically with dormer windows.

Cognitive Relating to, being, or involving conscious intellectual activity such as thinking, reasoning, or remembering.

Conservation area In UK, an area of notable environmental or historical interest or importance which is protected by law against undesirable changes.

Coverage: the area a building occupies on the site; the ground floor footprint.

Design team All the professionals that have a direct input in shaping the design of a place or building.

Detached house A stand-alone residential structure that does not share walls with another house or building.

Environment agency An official agency or authority providing information on environmental issues such as rivers, flooding and pollution.

Gradient The measure of the steepness of a road, path or ramp. In other words, the magnitude of its incline or slope as compared to the horizontal.

Highways The authority responsibly to manage and maintain the road infrastructure.

Highways authority The authority responsibly to manage and maintain the road infrastructure, also often called simply Highways.

Legible (also legibility) A place, building or design that easy to read or understand.

Listed building In UK, a building or building feature of notable environmental or historical interest or importance which is protected by law against undesirable changes.

Main routes Larger transport arteries or roads that carry heavy traffic and public transport such as buses, trams and so on.

Morphology The form of a place or building.

Place A component part of a geographical space that is populated and which hosts some form of human activity, whether this is temporarily or permanently.

Place democracy System of organization or government where the people or residents decide strategies, planning laws and policies, either directly or through elected representatives.

Place hierarchy The relative importance of some parts of a place or design in relation to others. For example, a main square might be larger and have more infrastructure than a small square; a public building will look more important than a private residential dwelling.

Planner A graduate professional qualified to plan and write place growth and transformation strategies and policy regarding permission to build.

Planning committee In UK, the group of local elected members government who make decisions regarding granting permission to build.

Planning conditions (UK) A condition imposed on a grant of planning permission which means those in charge of delivering the place or building must demonstrate to the planning authority how they are intending to comply with the specific request prior to building. For example, demonstrating the type of brick or the colour of a cladding system.

Planning deferral (UK) Applications are deferred either for a site visit or if the planning authority feels that it needs more information in order to determine the application (grant or refuse permission to build). In some circumstances planning applications can be delegated to an officer for determination and would not be considered by the planning committee.

Primary routes The main - normally larger or wider - roads within a zone or development.

Secondary routes The roads that are narrower or smaller in category than primary routes within a zone or development. These normally connect to a main or primary route.

Semi-detached house A single family dwelling house that shares one common wall with the next house.

Site analysis A series of technical investigations regarding a particular space or place, which results in critical information that the designer can use to make decisions regarding their proposals.

Snagging The process of checking a new building for minor faults that need to be rectified.

Social capital The networks of relationships among people who live and work in a particular society, enabling that society to function effectively.

Space A component part of a geographical space that has not yet been transformed into a place (see Place).

Terrace house House built as part of a continuous row in a uniform style.

Tertiary routes The roads that are narrower or smaller in category than secondary routes within a zone or development. These normally connect to a secondary route.

Tympanum The triangular element normally installed above a doorway, porticus or window. In greek ancient architecture, a triangular part of the roof above the entrance columns.

Urban designer A graduate professional, often with a master's or post graduate degree, qualified to design and project manage the design and delivery processes of spaces between buildings.

Vernacular Architecture concerned with domestic and functional rather than public or monumental buildings, which applies traditional building methods typical of their setting.

Bibliography

Alvarez, Laura et al. *A Bifocal-Ecological Approach for Enhancing Social Resilience in Neighbourhoods*. AIARG 2015 Systems Thinking and the City: New practices and connections. Dublin: Fourth Annual Meeting University College Dublin, 2015.

Alvarez, Laura et al. The role of social networks on participation and placemaking. *Sustainable Cities and Society* 28 (2017): 118–126.

Alvarez, Laura et al. The social value of place: An appraisal method for sustainable neighbourhood development. In *AR 2015 Architecture and Resilience at the Human Scale*. Sheffield, UK: The School of Architecture University of Sheffield, 10–12 September 2015, 323–331.

Awan, Nishat, Tatjana Schneider, and Jeremy Till. *Spatial Agency: Other Ways of doing Architecture*. New York, NY: Routledge, 2011.

Baker, Susan. *Sustainable Development*, 2nd ed. New York: Timothy Doyle, Routledge, 2015.

Bell, Paul et al. *Environmental Psychology*. Boston, MA: Cengage Learning, Inc, 1990.

Birkbeck, David and Stefan Kruczkowski. *Building for a Healthy Life*. London: Design for Homes, 2020.

Carmona, Matthew et al. *Public Places, Urban Spaces: The Dimensions of Urban Design*. London: Routledge, 2010.

Chadwick, Martin et al. A goal direction signal in the human entorhinal/subicular region. *Current Biology* 25(1) (2015): 87–92. https://doi.org/10.1016/j.cub.2014.11.001.

Department for Transport. *Manual for Streets*. London: Thomas Telford Ltd, 2007.

Ewing, Reid and Otto Clemente. *Measuring Urban Design: Metrics for Livable Places*. Washington: Island Press, 2013.

Ferragina, Emanuele. *Social Capital in Europe [Electronic Resource]: A Comparative Regional Analysis*. Cheltenham: Edward Elgar, 2012.

Hall, Peter and Colin Ward. *Sociable Cities: Legacy of Ebenezer Howard*. Chichester: John Wiley & Sons, 1998.

Halpern, David. *Social Capital*. Cambridge: Polity Press, 2005.

Heiskanena, Eva, Mikael Johnsona, Simon Robinsonb, Edina Vadovicsc, and Mika Saastamoinena. Low-carbon communities as a context for individual behavioural change. *Energy Policy* 38(12) (2010): 7586–7595.

Hester, Randy. *Design for Ecological Democracy* Cambridge, MA: MIT Press, 2006.

Lynch, Kevin. *The Image of the City*. Cambridge, MA: MIT Press Harvard-MIT Joint Center for Urban Studies Series, 1960.

Maclean, Kirsten, Michael Cuthill, and Helen Ross. Six attributes of social resilience. *Journal of Environmental Planning and Management* 57(1) (2013): 144–156.

McGlynn, Sue, Graham Smith, Alan Alcock, Paul Murrain, and Ian Bentley. *Responsive Environments: A Manual for Designers*, 1st ed. London: Routledge, 1985.

Newman, Oscar. *Creating Defensible Space*. Washington, DC: US Department of Housing and Urban Development, 1996.

Petrescu, Doina. Gardeners of commons, for the most part, women. In *Relational Architectural Ecologies*, 261–276. Taylor & Francis eBooks. http://www.tandfebooks.com.libproxy.ucl.ac.uk/ISBN/9780203770283.

Raiden, Ani, Andrew King, and Sir John Peace et al. *Co-creating Social Value in Placemaking: The Grand Balancing Act*. Oxford: Routledge, 2021.

Tidball, Keith G., Marianne E. Krasny, Erika Svendsen, Lindsay Campbell, and Kenneth Helphand. Stewardship, learning, and memory in disaster resilience. *Environmental Education Research* 16(5-6) (2010): 591–609.

Vitruvious Pollio, Marcus. *The Ten Books on Architecture*, 2nd ed. Morris Hicky, Morgan trans.; Ipswich: Deez Books, 2004.

Zautra, Alex, John Hall, and Kate Murray. Community development and community resilience: An integrative approach. *Community Development* 39(3) (2008): 130–147.

Zeisel, John. *Inquiry by Design*. New York: W.W. Norton & Co., 2006.

Electronic Sources

British Ministry of Hosing Communities and Local Government. "National Design Guide (2019)." June 3, 2022. https://assets.publishing.service.gov.uk/government/uploads/system/uploads/attachment_data/file/962113/National_design_guide.pdf

British Ministry of Hosing Communities and Local Government. "National Planning Policy Framework (2012)." June 3, 2022. https://webarchive.nationalarchives.gov.uk/20180608095821/https://www.gov.uk/government/publications/national-planning-policy-framework--2

Bibliography

New York Institute for Transportation and Development Policy. "Pedestrians First Measures Walkability for Babies, Toddlers, Their Caregivers, and Everyone in Cities." August 28, 2022. https://pedestriansfirst.itdp.org

Nottingham City Council. "Carbon Neutral Plan 2028." June 3, 2022. https://www.nottinghamcity.gov.uk/cn2028#:~:text=The%20draft%20Carbon%20Neutral%20Action,carbon%2Dneutral%20Nottingham%20by%202028.&text=The%20document%20is%20broken%20down, Carbon%20Reduction%20Measures (Last accessed 03 June 2020)

Nottingham City Council. "Co-PLACE." June 3, 2022. https://www.co-place.org

Nottingham City Council. "Design Quality Framework (DQF)." June 3, 2022. https://www.dqfnottingham.org.uk

Report of The United Nations Conference on Environment and Development. "Rio Declaration on Environment and Development (1992)." August 28, 2022. https://www.un.org/en/development/desa/population/migration/generalassembly/docs/globalcompact/A_CONF.151_26_Vol.I_Declaration.pdf

Royal Institute of British Architects. "Plan of Work (2020)." August 9, 2021. https://www.ribaplanofwork.com

Royal Institute of British Architects. "Sustainable Outcomes Guide (2019)." August 28, 2022. https://www.architecture.com/knowledge-and-resources/resources-landing-page/sustainable-outcomes-guide#available-resources

Town and Country Planning Association (2022). "Garden City Principles (concept by Ebenezer Howard, 1898)." August 28, 2022. https://tcpa.org.uk/garden-city-principles/

Further reading

Academy for Sustainable Communities. *Mind the Skills Gap: The Skills We Need for Sustainable Communities*. Leeds: Academy for Sustainable Communities, 2007.

Adams, Davoid and Steve Tiesdel. *Shaping Places: Urban Planning, Design and Development*. London: Routledge, 2013.

Allmendinger, Philip. *Planning Theory*, 2nd ed. China: Palgrave MacMillan, 2009.

Bannon. In: Richard Coles, and Zoë Millman (Eds.). *Landscape, Well-Being and Environment*. Oxford: Routledge, 2013.

Barry, John, Brian Baxter, Richard Dunphy, and Brent Dawson. *Europe, Globalization and Sustainable Development*. London: Routledge, 2004.

Barton, Hugh, Marcus Grant, and Richard Guise. *Shaping Neighbourhoods: For Local Health and Global Sustainability*. Oxford: Routledge, 2010.

Barton, Hugh. *Sustainable Communities: The Potential for Eco-Neighbourhoods*. London: Earthscan Publications, 2000.

Beatley, Timothy. *Green Urbanism: Learning from European Cities*. Washington, DC: Island, 2000.

Bell, Simon and Stephen Morse. *Sustainability Indicators: Measuring the Immeasurable?* London: Earthscan, 2008.

Bizer, Kilian. *Regional Sustainability: Applied Ecological Economics Bridging the Gap between Natural and Social Sciences*. Heidelberg: Physica-Verlag, 1999, 217–226.

Bourdieu, Pierre. *The Social Structures of the Economy*. Cambridge: Polity Press, 2005.

British Department for the Environment. *Draft Planning Policy Statement 14: Sustainable Development in the Countryside*. London, October, 2007.

British Department for the Environment. *Green Claims Guidance: How to Make a Good Environmental Claim*. London, 2010.

British Department for the Environment. *Planning Policy Statement 15: Sustainable Development in the Countryside*. London, October, 2007.

British Department for the Environment, Transport and the Regions. *By Design: Urban Design in the Planning System: Towards Better Practice*. London, 2000.

Further reading

British Government, Communities and Local Government. *An Action Plan for Community Empowerment: Building on Success*. London, 2007.
Bunt, Laura and Michael Harris. *Mass Localism: A Way to Help Small Communities Solve Big Social Challenges*. NESTA, 2010.
Coaffee, Jon. Towards next-generation urban resilience in planning practice: From securitization to integrated place making. *Planning Practice & Research* 28(3) (2013): 323–339.
Creasy, Stella. *Everybody Needs Good Neighbours? A Study of the Link between Public Participation and Community Cohesion*. The Involve Foundation, 2008.
Davidson, Tonya, Ondine Park, and Rob Shields. *Ecologies of Affect: Placing Nostalgia, Desire, and Hope*. Waterloo, Canada: Wilfrid Laurier University Press, 2011.
Davoudi, Simin. On resilience. *The Planning Review* 49(1) (2013): 4–5.
Eagle, Nathan, Michael Macy, and Rob Claxton. Network diversity and economic development. *Science* 328(5981) (2010): 1029–1031. doi:10.1126/science.1186605.
Edwards, Gemma. *Mixed-Method Approaches to Social Network Analysis*. ESRC National Centre for Research Methods Review Paper, 2010.
Ellin, Nan. *Good Urbanism: Six Steps to Creating Prosperous Places*. Washington, DC: Island Press, 2013.
Elkington, John. In: Henriques, Richardson, and Myilibrary (Eds.) *The Triple Bottom Line: Does It All Add Up? Assessing the Sustainability of Business and CSR*. Electronic Book. Sterling, VA: Earthscan Publications Ltd, 2004.
Ferrão, Paulo and John Fernandez. *Sustainable Urban Metabolism*. Electronic Book. Cambridge, MA: The MIT Press, 2013.
Fraker, Harrison. *The Hidden Potential of Sustainable Neighborhoods [Electronic Resource]: Lessons from Low-Carbon Communities*. Electronic Book. Washington, DC: Island Press, 2013.
Fuad-Luke, Alistar. *Design Activism: Beautiful Strangeness for a Sustainable World*. London: Earthscan, 2009.
Fusco Girard, Luigi, Baycan Levent, and Peter Nijkamp. *Sustainable City and Creativity: Promoting Creative Urban Initiatives*. Electronic Book. Farnham: Ashgate, 2011.
Great Britain Department of Health and Facilities. *Environment and Sustainability: Health Technical Memorandum 07-07: Sustainable Health and Social Care Buildings: Planning, Design, Construction and Refurbishment*. London: The Stationery Office, 2013.
Habermas, Jürgen and Frederick Lawrence. *The Structural Transformation of the Public Sphere*. Cambridge: Polity Press, 1989.

Hamdi, Nabeel. *The Placemaker's Guide to Building Community*. Electronic Book. London: Earthscan, 2010.
Jacobs, Jane. *The Death and Life of Great American Cities*. New York: Modern Library, 2011.
Kopec, Dak. *Environmental Psychology for Design*. Quebec: Fairchild Publication, 2012.
Kusenbach, Margarethe. Street phenomenology: The go-along as ethnographic research tool. *JSTOR* 4(3) (2003): 455–485.
Luhmann, Niklas. *Social Systems*. Redwood City, CA: Stanford University Press, 1995.
Luhmann, Niklas. *Trust and Power*. Chichester: John Wiley & Sons, 1973.
Manzo, Lynne and Patrick Devine-Wright. *Place Attachment: Advances in Theory, Methods and Applications*. London: Routledge, 2014.
Marshall, Graham and Riannon Corcoran. *Pro-social Research Programme*. Liverpool: University of Liverpool, 2014.
McGlynn, Sue and Ivor Samuels. *The Funnel, the Sieve and the Template: Towards and Operational Urban Morphology*. Oxford: Joint Centre for Urban Design, 2000.
McGrath, Brian. *Urban Design Ecologies*. Chichester: Wiley, 2013.
Moloney, Susie and John Fien. Transitioning to low carbon communities – From behaviour change to systemic change: Lessons from australia. *Energy Policy* 38 (2010): 7614–7623.
Morrissey, Mike, Kat Healy, and Brendan McDonnell. *Social Assets: A New Approach to Understanding and Working with Communities*. Belfast: Community Evaluation Northern Ireland, 2008.Musterd, Sako and Zoltán Kovács. *Place-making and Policies for Competitive Cities*. Chichester: Wiley-Blackwell, 2013, 103–123.
Newman, Oscar. *Creating Defensible Space*. Washington, DC: US Department of Housing and Urban Development, 1996.
Oxford City Council. *An Introduction to the Oxford Character Assessment Toolkit*. Endorsed by English Heritage, Oxford Preservation Trust, 2015.
Pearson, Leonie, Peter Newton, Peter Roberts. *Resilient Sustainable Cities: A Future*. London: Routledge, 2013.
Pickett, Steward, Mary Cadenasso and Brian McGrath. *Resilience in Ecology and Urban Design: Linking Theory and Practice for Sustainable Cities*. Electronic Book. Dordrecht: Springer, 2013.
Scannell, Leila and Robert Guifford. Defining place attachment: A tripartite organizing framework. *Journal of Environmental Psychology* 30(1) (2010): 1–10.

Index

Note: **Bold** page numbers refer to tables; *Italic* page numbers refer to figures and page numbers followed by "n" denote endnotes.

accountability 108, 258–259
ad-hoc consultation 146
Alte Oper building *191*
Arkwright Meadows Community Gardens 151
artificial intelligence 4, 9
ARUDO social network 12, 41n4
Attenborough, David 171

balance 259
beauty, design quality 14; emotional response 20; national UK policy and guidance 19; Notre Dame, Paris, France *17, 18*; Roman Pantheon dome ceiling *15*; sound appraisal system 16; York Minster *17, 19*
building materials, construction industry 13–14
Building Modelling software 4

Carbon Neutral 41n9
Clemente, Otto 234
code compliance appraisals 240–242
collaboration 108, 259–260
communication tools *81*
context 10, 16, 46, 48, 78–79, **96**, *117,* 125, 171, 172, *173–175,* 174, 176–178, *177–178,* 184, **185,** 214, **228**

critical form parameters **228**; Alte Oper building *191*; colour palette 218, *218–220,* 220–221; composition 185–186, **187**; geometry 212, *213–217,* 214; Gestalt principles *188*; hierarchy 186, 188, *191,* 192, 195; legibility 195–199; mass 208, *209–210,* 211; Nottingham, neoclassical building *193*; Palace of Alhambra *189, 192*; proportions 200, *200–207,* 204, 207–208; rhythm 199–200; roads and streets 195; scale 211–212, *212*; St. Domenico *190*; texture 221, *222–227,* 224–225; three-storey modern building *194*; World Maritime University *194*

design agents **128,** 241, **260**; accountability 108; collaboration 108; continuous engagement strategy 110; design team 102–105, *106,* 107–108; ecosystem 104; engagement/consultation event 104; feasibility studies 100–101; map 129, **130,** 132, 164, **165–168**; market traders 111; modular system 111; office building 123–124, *125,* 126, **126**; place design 107; project layout *109–110*; roles of

112, **112**; social housing 118, *119*, 120, **121–122**; urban supermarket 112–116, *116*, **117**, *117*
design code 22, 94, 143, 230, 233, 235, 236, 240, 245–246, **247–249**, 250, 253
design evaluation **249**; achievable 251–252; code compliance appraisals 240–242; design code 245–246, **247–248**; design quality system 242–245, *243–244*; edification code 236–237, *237–239*, 240; effective 254; flexible 254; morphological design criteria 230; objectivity of, design appraisals 234–236; play zone, public beach 231, *232*; practical 252; project-specific criteria 230; public space networks 231; qualities **255**; quality assurance system 250; simple 252–253; site-specific codes 233; social identity 231; spiritualism 231; targeted 251; territorial occupation, public beach 231, *233*
design form **185**; critical form parameters (*see* critical form parameters); housing development 172, *173–175*, 176–178, *177–178*; human ecosystem 172; skills 170–172; village extension 178–181, *182*, 183
design influence **163**; ad-hoc consultation 146; Arkwright Meadows Community Gardens 151; change effect 132–133, *133*; community event 147, *147–149*; decision-making information 154; emotional investment 151; European models 143; Gaucho culture 144; global environmental activism 151; land ownership and stewardship 150; master architect 134; neighbourhood plan engagement 155–157; Nottingham City Homes 145, *145*; physical 3D model *150*; placemaking democracy 148, 149; self-management 151–152; social housing engagement 157–159; social resilience 153; transparency and trust 134–140, *135–136*, *140*, *141*, 142–143; two towns engagement 159–162, *161*
design process: Belfast Catholic area 77; Belfast Protestant area 77; city planners 44; climate emergency 46; co-design 48, 49; cultural references 78; land value (*see* land value); neighbourhood arrangement *52, 53*; The Plan of Work 45; RIBA 44, 45; site analysis 47; skill sets 43; social sciences, school design 49–51, 53–54, **76**; sustainable credentials 49
design quality: buildings and places, lifespan 38, **38–39**; natural cycles and ecosystems 37; sustainability 37
design quality debate. *see also* beauty, design quality: beauty judgement *21*; design codes/regulations 22; professional accreditations 21; quality appraisal 24; quality assurance **23**, 23–24; sustainability credentials 25
designing places, primary parameters 8, *8*

edification code 236–237, *237–239*, 240
engagement 80, 93, 110, 146, *150*; classification *81*; *vs.* consultation **34**, 104; groups 87, 88, 94; neighbourhood plan 155–157, **163**; placemaking 33, 34; social housing 157–159, **163**; two towns 159–162, *161*, **163**
Environmental Impact Assessment 36, 37
European models 143
Ewing, Reid 234

Index

feasibility **34**, 55, **65–66**, 100, 101, 113, 123, 138, 157
Ferragina, Emanuele 153

Garden City concept 256n8
Gaucho culture 144
Gestalt principles *188*
global legislative frameworks 4
Guifford, Robert 144

Hall, John 134
Halpern, David 134
Howard, Ebenezer 256n8
human place interpretation 12, *12*

'immoral' designers 7
inclusive capitalism 1
influence programme 164, **165–168**
innovative economic models 2

land value 54–57, *55,* 61, **76**; Houlton, Rugby *71*; land optimisation **72–75**; The Malings *70*; Nottingham residential area *71*; residential arrangements *60*; *Responsive Environments* 56, *57*; traditional vs. alternative approaches **61–69**; traditional vs. author's plotting process *59*; Trent Basin *70*; urban layout pattern 57, *58*
landmark 48, 137, 180, 181, 196, *197, 201, 202*, 220, *220, 226, 227*
Le Corbusier 10, 41n3, 46
legibility: Chinese Bell Tower monument *197*; church spire *198*; components 196; human survival 195; mental mapping 196
Lynch, Kevin 196, *196,* 198

McGlyn, Sue 160–162
mental mapping 196

Ministry of Housing Communities and Local Government 82, 99n4
morphology/morphological 2–3, 30, 31, 184, 195, 230, 232, 233, 241, **249**
multifactor systems 4
Murray, Kate 134

National Planning Policy 139
Neighbourhood Plan 138
Nottingham City Homes 145, *145*
Nottingham Design Quality Framework 180, 235

participation 33, 50, 80, **163**; continuous engagement 35; empowerment 132, 146, 148, 149; forms of **34**; social resilience 153, 154
Passet, René 25, 94, 152, 257
placemaking 10–11, **63**, **98**, 107–108, 153–154, 261; democracy 148, 253; engagement 33, 34; innovative 4; need for 7–9, *8*; participation types 149; social network analysis 162; urban design method 180
plan of work 45; accountability tools 83; agents and influencers 80–81, *81*; concept design 88–89, *89*; context 78–79; data gathering 86–87; detailed design 93–94; developed design 90–91, *92,* 93; development brief 90; development framework 87–88; networks 79–80; place vision 82–83; post-occupancy 94–95; site analysis 83–86, *85*; supplementary documents 88; SWOT/CO 87; urban design 78–95, **96–98**, 98, 100, **260**
public space networks 231

quality assurance system **23**, 23–24, 142, 184, 250, 257

Renaissance Era 7
Royal Institute of British Architects (RIBA) 44

Scannell, Leila 144
social capital 99n8
social housing 118, *119*, 120, **121–122**
social inequalities 1
social network analysis 79–80
social resilience 134, 153
sustainable design, ABC of Quality: accountability 258–259; balance 259; collaboration 259–260; design training 257; placemaking 261; quality assurance 257; urban practice, tools **260**
sustainable design checklist 39–41, **40**; critical thinking 40
sustainable design debate: climate adaptation 35; climate change 28; consultation *vs.* engagement 34, **34**; economic benefits 29; economic currency 28; Environmental Impact Assessment 36, 37; gentrification 30; lifetime embodied carbon 28; Loch Lomond, Trossachs 26–27, *27*; operational carbon 28; placemaking engagement 33–34; road morphology 31–32; social cohesion 32; social value 33, 35; Spheres of 25–26, *26*; sustainable development tools **36**; United Nations Sustainable Development Goals 29; urban morphology 30
sustainable development 1, 2, 4, 28, 29, 33, **36**, 95, 153, 230, **260**
Sustainable Development Goals (SDG) 1

The Ten Books on Architecture 7
transparency 134–140, *135–136, 140, 141,* 142–143
trust 134–140, *135–136, 140, 141,* 142–143
two towns engagement 159–162, *161*

UK National Planning Policy Framework 82
urban design 43, 48, **96–98**, 100, 102, **260**; accountability tools 83; agents and influencers 80–81, *81*; concept design 88–89, *89*; context 78–79; courses 178; data gathering 86–87; design agents role **117, 126**; detailed design 93–94; developed design 90–91, *92, 93*; development brief 90; development framework 87–88; layout efficiency **121–122**; mental mapping 196; networks 79–80; place vision 82–83; post-occupancy 94–95; site analysis 83–86, *85*; supplementary documents 88; SWOT/CO 87
urban designer 44, 47, 48, 56, 101–105, *106,* 196, 208, 211, 218, 227, 246. *see also* urban design
urban ecosystem 4, 6, 10, 37, 79, 90, 95, 104, 151, 171–172
urban supermarket 112–116, *116,* **117,** *117*

viability 55, 61, **63,** 89, 180
Vinci, Leonardo da 7, 10, 41n2, 186
Vitruvius 7, 9, **11**, 19, 145

Williams, Amanico 46
Wright, Frank Lloyd 195–196

Zautra, Alex 134